Development of Tourism and Travel Industry

An Indian Perspective

Development of Tourism and Travel Industry

An Indian Perspective

Prem Nath Dhar

KANISHKA PUBLISHERS, DISTRIBUTORS
NEW DELHI-110 002

KANISHKA PUBLISHERS, DISTRIBUTORS
4697/5-21A, Ansari Road, Daryaganj
New Delhi -110 002
Phones : 2327 0497, 2328 8285
Fax : 011-2328 8285
E-mail : kanishka_publishing@yahoo.co.in

First Published: 1997
Second Edition: 2006
Third Edition: 2011

ISBN : 978-81-7391-169-X

PRINTED IN INDIA

Published by Madan Sachdeva for Kanishka Publishers, Distributors, 4697/5-21A, Ansari Road, Daryaganj, New Delhi-110 002, Typeset by Sunshine Graphics, Delhi, and Printed at Rajdhani Printers, Delhi.

Preface

India with its fabulous monuments and unparalleled scenery of mountains, deserts and seascapes should not be missed by the footloose and fancyfree holiday makers of the world; but owing to a great number of negative aspects, poor PR and government apathy, at state and national level, less than one per cent of the world's tourists make their way to India. Even if there were a greater influx of visitors the infrastructure is so frail that the slightest overload would spell disaster.

This infrastructure which incorporates the means of getting into India in the first place, is travelling unhindered from destination to destination (non-Indian visitors tend to cram as much as possible into their trip), in good time, with good accommodation (clean and tidy) and not going down with the little stomach bugs that have made Delhi famous all over the world.

India, at present, cannot hope to draw more than a handful of these no-risk, middle-income holidaymakers, for there is just nowhere to put them. Although the Indian Central Government has paid up lip service to the burgeoning tourism industry, worth many billions of dollars worldwide, the present Ministry of Tourism is chronically short of ideas and charisma. As a consequence very little has been done to correct or remedy the negative characteristics that India, as a tourist destination, has been painted with. Even within the country there are enormous difficulties facing would be entrepreneurs who might wish to take advantage of the new liberalism. To build hotels, amusements leisure-sports facilities, etc.—all the things that go to make up an all, in holiday for the typical western tourist—requires sanction from several different quarters and related bodies. At present the Ministries of Sports, Environment and Culture operate independently, and all have a very distinct say in whether or not a certain project should or should not be promoted. All of which takes time. Hands have to be greased before action is taken. This, of course, just adds to the frustration time.

Outside India too, Indian embassies and High Commissions, have been found wanting in promoting not only Indian tourism but Indian industry as well. The information and statistics needed for both fields of activities are rarely at hand and have led potential customers to other embassies (like South Korea, for example) where the information is not only instantly available, at the touch of a computer key, but also in the form of glossy handouts and videos. Expecting them to talk gushingly about terracotta temples in West Bengal seems highly fanciful.

The Minister for Tourism has also proved to be less than effective in most directions, but, he was reportedly in favour of a merger of these three ministries to provide a better service, to 'would-be' investors and the legions of 'may-be' visitors. India would do well to emulate British tourism. The professional manner of British tourism is a glowing indication of what can be done with a little more thought and a lot more government backing. In 1993 they introduced the Ministry of National Heritage which has, under its auspices—tourism, sports, broadcasting, the arts, museums, galleries, public libraries, film and various art collections. As a result it is able to promote Britain and its many different facets, direct to the world as if they were the government's own private PR company. In Britain itself there are more than 800 tourist information centres, all of which give free advice and information regarding their own immediate area, and with access to all others.

Madhya Pradesh and West Bengal are prime examples of this new awareness crossed with naivete. Both states have recently introduced a separate budget for promoting tourism. MP has allocated Rs. 6 crores like Goa and Kerala that along with Rajasthan, take the bulk of foreign visitors. West Bengal was only allocated a snivelling one crore but at least it has seen the light. The need of the hour is not only to attract first-time visitors to these shores but also to build on the goodwill. Adequate road networks have to be laid down along with enough hotels to accommodate them. What is the point of having 50 five-star hotels in Delhi if the like of AP, Orissa, and MP have just a handful?

Many visitors to India tend to be students on a limited budget. They should be encouraged, for the goodwill effect lasts a long time, well into their professional lives. If, however, there are scenes enacted similar to the ones at Kovalam where, on New

Year's eve, all the locals were systematically cleared from the beach by a combing line of police, then tolerance will become prejudice before very long.

Word-of-mouth is the best form of advertising and if you can get enough people to come to give them a good time and send them off with a headful of happy memories, then the pass-on effect will help ensure that there is a steady flow of foreign exchange coming in. If, as at present, India is regarded as a case in survival, then most of the 'may be' types will continue to go elsewhere.

About Rs. 500 crores of foreign and private investment will be made in the next few years in the development of tourist infrastructure, according to a recent study, covering the impact of tourism on economy, culture, sports and ecology. Most of this investment will go to the building of hotels, development of recreational facilities and the augmentation of travel related services. In an interview, the then Minister for Civil Aviation and Tourism, said efforts were afoot to have five million foreign tourists annually by the turn of the century. The tourism industry has to be prepared for this massive influx; so has the nation. The materials presented in the following papers and articles provide a meaningful insight into the structure, infrastructure and working of the tourism concept in India. It is intended primarily for students of travel and tourism courses.

— Premnath Dhar

Contents

1

Tourism Industry in India : Problems and Prospects

Introduction

Though tourism is considered an important foreign exchange earning industry, the Indian government's decisions reflect the contrary. The tourism-related control goods imports attract customs duty of 100-150 per cent. Hotels and other hospitality services have to pay at least 40 per cent of their earnings to state exchequer as expenditure tax.

On repeated pleas to provide fiscal relief in order to boost tourism, the government has shown signs of leniency, while the tax has been promised to be slashed, a lot still needs to be done on the infrastructure front.

The ambitious Rs. 39,000 crores tourism development plan aims of raising tourist inflow from the present 1.8 million to five million by 1995-96 and an earning of Rs. 18,000 crores in foreign exchange. But for this, we must set our targets rights.

In 1990-91, 1677 lakhs tourists came to India. In 1991-92, the foreign tourists arrival rose to 1877 lakhs and the following year, 1992-93, it dropped to 17.16 lakhs. From this, the government generated Rs. 2918.11 crores in 1991 while the next year, the earnings were Rs. 3915.56 crores. In 1993, the amount rose to Rs. 4247.76 crores.

When plans are made to boost foreign tourists arrival, focus is on luxury five star hotels. This is probably without taking into consideration the aspirations of the foreign tourists. Obviously, they are not coming here to stay in luxury Indian culture and savour the beautiful sights. Luxury hotels may be good for conferences, tourism will do better with functional hotels. And in the process, one must never forget the domestic tourist who is equally important.

Another thing that must be clear before giving shape to our plans is, who are the tourists that come to India and what are their demands. The definition and categories of tourism must be worked out. All those people that register border-crossing for more than 24 hours are treated as foreign tourists, irrespective of the purpose of the visit. But not all travellers are tourists. The others may be visiting friends and relatives, non-resident Indians, visiting businessmen and government delegations; the profile of each of this category is as different as their needs. Those visiting their relatives may not need hotel accommodation or even travel advice. And NRIs who come here may have their own office, house or transport. Another growing section is that of visiting businessmen. All they need is luxurious accommodation and expensive shops and can do without conducted tours or sightseeing as a tourist does. Government delegations too bring only a high quantum of shopping money.

Needs of all these sections are different. Some may look forward to a loose weekend on the beach while other long for comfortable conference facilities.

Another idea is redefining tourists maps. Since ages, India has been offering only cliched destinations—the Golden Triangle, Goa, Kovalam beach and Kashmir, for example. There was no deviation from the set pattern. But tourists want to see more of India.

That gave rise to the search for greener pastures—to step onto the virgin soils or less-visited sites. This effort of the tour organisers paid and the results were encouraging.

Ups and Downs of Tourism Market : Economics of an Industry

The year 1993 had begun with a very bleak message for tourism in India. The riots following the Ayodhya dispute were still haunting the country. Then there were bomb blasts in Bombay and Calcutta, the Hazratbal turmoil, Assembly elections and the earthquake in Latur. As if all this was not enough, the Indian Airlines pilots went on strike.

The most hard hit by all these was obviously the foreign tourist industry. Predictably, the foreign tourist rush which was

16.77 lakhs in 1991-92 fell to 14.16 lakhs in 1992-93. This was this, in addition to the related fall in domestic tourism as well.

This dismal performance of foreign tourism in 1993 showed in the revenue collection, specially foreign exchange. This made the government sit up and review the situation again. An ambitious Rs. 39,000 crores tourism development plan was chalked out to help increase the tourist inflow to five million by 1995-96.

"Things have improved," said the then Union Minister for Tourism and Civil Aviation, "We are moving in the right direction and soon India will become a major tourist attraction," he added.

The Tourism Development Board had tightened its belt and is promoting India in the world, "Foreign publicity is our major thrust area," said the Minister. In the past six or seven months, officials of the Indian Tourism Development Corporation have toured as many as 32 countries which include 10 European countries, four African nations, the CIS and Gulf countries. "Apart from informing prospective tourists about the enticing destinations in India, our team convinced them that tourists in India were the safest as compared to other parts of the world," the Minister said.

Pointing out that terrorism and riots have affected most parts of the world, like New York, Bosnia and even England, it has been said "We succeeded in making the foreign tourists understand they are rather safe in India and unaffected by terrorism." In addition, Indian people's warmth and hospitality is known all over the world and most tourists know that foreign tourists are highly regarded here. The efforts paid and December 1993 witnessed a whopping increase of 24 per cent in foreign tourists arrival. In January 1994, this increase was 28.4 per cent while in February the figure fell a little to 15.3 per cent. March again showed an increase of 21.1 per cent and till April 1994, the increase retained the upward trend and reached 24.2 per cent. This rise is the largest in the last 45 years. The foreign exchange revenue also looked up and from Rs. 3990 crores in 1992-93 it went up 14 per cent to Rs. 4005.73 crores in 1993-94.

The Tourism Minister said that as far as foreign exchange earning for the country is concerned, tourism industry is in third position. Maximum foreign exchange is generated by export of gems and jewellery followed by garments exports. He is optimistic that within the next five years, tourism will be the highest foreign exchange earning industry. But there is still lot to be done. The authorities are ready with various plans. The industry is steering in the right direction. What it needs, is to achieve acceleration.

Today India offers 50,000 room accommodation in classified hotels apart from a large number of non-approved hotels. A plan for 3,000 more rooms in classified sector is in the pipeline. The government offers three per cent loan subsidy on the loan amount for construction and addition to hotels. Hotels or hill resorts, pilgrim centres and heritage hotels, or converted havelis get more discount from the government. The income from hotels gets a 50 per cent tax rebate and if the remaining 50 per cent is used in the renovation of the hotel, in some cases, it would in fact be a total rebate. Hotels in rural areas, hills and pilgrim centres get a 50 per cent rebate in expenditure tax for 10 years, provided they have become operational by March 31,1994. Attention has also been paid to the discount in custom and import duties. Some special items of the hotel industry get generous discount for the promotion of tourism and to provide better facilities to the tourists. Adventure tourism has also been taken special care of in importing equipment or special discounted duties. Government is encouraging heritage centres a lot because these offer the foreign tourists the splendour of past ages with modern-day facilities. Heritage centres are those havelis, bungalows or palaces which are more than 75 years old or have some historic importance. Government provides all help to develop these into modern-day luxurious hotels. Similar is the encouragement given to those people who have enlisted themselves for providing paying guest accommodation to foreign tourists. To ensure that everything is progressing well, the tourism department holds regular meetings with concerned states departments like PWD, forest etc. and it is seen that these meetings also enable them to develop newer destinations and provide more facilities.

In March the then Tourism Minister of India had gone to Germany with a team to promote India as a tourist centre. It was surprised to know that people from there wanted to visit the North-East. As soon as he returned, he held emergency meetings with Chief Ministers and concerned department heads of the north-eastern states. Together, they chalked out a plan and assured all help that the states needed for development and for providing more facilities to the tourists.

As development of new destinations is catching on fast, the tourism department has asked each state to spot two monuments each and develop them on the tourist map.

Global Tourism and India

More than 528 million tourist arrivals recorded all over the world during 1994, registering a three per cent increase over 1993. According to the estimate of Madrid-based World Tourism Organisation, tourism has now become the world's largest industry, ahead of automobile industry and petroleum products. The report says that international tourist receipts rose to $ 321 billion, registering a 5.1 per cent increase over 1993.

The pattern of world tourism flows indicate that South Asia recorded 7 per cent increase in tourist arrivals and 11.2 per cent in tourist receipts during 1994. India has accounted for the highest share of tourists arrivals in South Asian region during last year, with a little over 51 per cent. India has recorded a growth rate of 7.8 per cent in terms of tourist arrivals and 12.6 per cent in tourist receipts during 1994, well above the world average.

According to World Tourism Organisation's forecast, tourism growth prospects for India are very bright and tourist arrivals and receipts are likely to increase by 10-15 per cent during the coming years.

A Retrospective

While, at the same time, the country's share in world tourism continues to decline, managers of the industry remain unconcerned about the problem. They fight over the size of their share of the cake or respective areas of power instead of putting their heads together to tide over the crisis.

According to figures provided in the Rajya Sabha, the decline has been continuous with no bright spots around. The share of the country which stood at 0.72 per cent in 1988 declined to 0.46 per cent in 1993. During the same period regional tourism receipts also went down from 74.0 per cent to 70.0 per cent. The government gladly explained the reasons for the fall in 1993, like the law and order situation, but remained silent on the fact that the decline has been continuous and there is no hope that the trend will ever change. The reasons for this dismal prospect are not far to seek as India has repeatedly failed to put its act together as every sector, be it the tour operators of travel agents or hoteliers, have always worked at cross-purposes to serve their limited purpose, at the cost of other sectors. The captains of industry are not the only guilty party as the officials of the tourism department have done no better. As of today the reports are that number one and number two spend more time in sniping at each other than in working together to meet the situation. The fight between the permanent staff of the department and deputationists from the Indian Administrative Service has been a continuous story where more time has been spent on counting the scores in terms of foreign postings instead of putting as end to this fight. The biggest victim of it has been the recommendation to have a separate tourism cadre, suggested by the high-powered committee set up by the Ministry.

India also enjoys the unique distinction of wasting away major chunks of its budget for tourism on payment of salary and other fixed expenses instead of spending money on actual promotion. It is no secret that our publicity budget has been shrinking in terms of actual purchasing power or in terms of dollars due to the continuous decline in value of the Indian rupee. Whatever little is left is also spent on looking after the visits of VIPs who are always competing to establish new records of visiting large number of countries in the shortest possible time.

The year 1994 started well with improvement in arrivals particularly the increase in business travel following the opening up of the Indian economy as a result of the policy of liberalisation. This has resulted in boom-like conditions for hotels in cities like Bombay and Delhi. But instead of cashing in on it, the travel industry has revived the controversy relating to dual tariff. The dual tariff is not only charged by the hotels but also by our domestic airlines. The controversy started the day the Finance Minister announced concessions to the industry as a foreign exchange earner. Since then the tour operators and travel agents, on one side, and hotels on the other side have been fighting for a large share of this tax benefit. Even taxi operators and transporters have been claiming a part of it.

The Minister who was impressed by the representations received while travelling abroad directed the Ministry to end this system in July, 1993. The Ministry, however, was unable to implement it and set up a new panel to examine the issue a few months later. As a result of subsequent discussion, it was announced that the hotels have agreed to end the dual tariff system and a statement was also made in Parliament. The hoteliers however challenged this view and a leading chain owner promptly wrote to the Minister that they had only agreed to reduce the gap between dollar tariff and rupee rate as the same cannot be done away with.

From this point onwards there has been no meeting ground. The ministry itself does not seem to be serious as it has further perpetuated the dual tariff system by allowing revision of rupee fares for Indian Airlines while leaving the dollar fares unchanged. The result is that hotel owners rightly ask if the Government bodies like airlines and International Airport Authority are allowed to charge dual tariff, why should it be denied to the hotel industry.

Even on the issue of promoting India, there is no unanimity among official agencies. While one sector is promoting a tourism mart, now an annual feature, to be held in September, which will be attended by foreign buyers and Indian groups interested in selling in-bound tours, the other has set its eyes on a tourism fair with large public attendance. It speaks volumes about the initiative or the competence of our tourism department that both the events besides our air show are privately sponsored. The only contribution of the official agencies is that they instead of promoting both the events as two have different ends in view are working to sabotage them. It is becoming difficult to explain to the Ministry officials, whose understanding of the subject is obviously limited, having spent most of their lives in tackling administrative or law and order problems, that a travel mart which is essentially a gathering of buyers and sellers, has to be a closed affair with limited attendance. It does not in any way conflict with a fair which will be attended by public looking for bargains in terms of tours available within the country as well as to foreign destinations. The audience in one case will be buyers from abroad while in the second case they will be local consumers. This should have made the task of the Tourism Ministry easy, but these arguments obviously have not impressed them. They feel that a tourism mart also like a fair of an exhibition will involve import of exhibits as well as equipment. This however is not the case as in the mart displays have to be local and no exhibits or machinery has to be imported from abroad as the attempt will be to sell India.

One only hopes that the Minister and the Deputy Minister will take some time off from their other pre-occupations and try to sort out internal conflicts. This is required as India may not be on the verge of a tourism boom, but can certainly look forward to a sustained growth of six to nine per cent. This however will be possible only if we are able to put our act together and stop infighting. Besides, tourism can thrive only in a peaceful atmosphere, any rumour of riots and disturbances will scare away the tourists.

Events and Effects

The Union Tourism and Civil Aviation Ministry believes that had it not been for the demolition at Ayodhya in December 1992, the country's tourism map would have been different. As it is, tourism managers are convinced that foreign tourists who decided to stay away from the country after riots broke out in several towns and cities in the aftermath of Ayodhya, are coming back. The next 2-3 years are crucial. We have certain projections and we are hopeful they will succeed, according to a Minister, after returning from a trip of 30 countries where he and his team of hand-picked officials were hard-selling India as the perfect holiday destination. According to him, there is tremendous enthusiasm in West Asia and South Africa, apart from the regulars who come in droves from Europe and North America, about visiting India. "It is still undiscovered, and with the liberalisation that is being introduced, it will grow, " the minister pointed out.

India's contribution to the world's largest industry is minuscule—0.4 per cent of a total international tourist traffic of little over $ 300 billion. The major moves that have been initiated to boost tourist traffic include removing the limit on foreign investment; until about a year ago, there was a ceiling. There could be no foreign investment beyond 51 per cent. Now the sky is the limit. According to a senior official, this has given more options than ever before to the potential foreign inventory. In addition, there is expected foreign equity to the tune of over $ 250 million; all to make a foreigner feel at home. There has been a substantial growth in the number of small town hotels. But the services provided still fail short of requirements. According to India Tourism Development Corporation (ITDC) calculations, the country needs close to one lakh rooms in all kinds of hotels for foreign tourists. Against this, the supply is about 45,000 rooms—barely enough to accommodate half of them. The emphasis has to be two or three star hotels. Not everyone can afford the five-star tariff, which is in any case higher than what is charged in some of the neighbouring countries like Thailand and Singapore, both of which figure on the international tourist map, says a travel operator who was attending the Overseas Marketing Conference in the Capital, which brought together tourist mandarins from the directorate, operators who have to sell outside the country, officials of the Air India and regional tourist officers. In addition, officials point out, for the middle-class tourists, the "playing-guest option" is fast gaining popularity. All they want is a homely environment and clean surrounding.

In place like Rajasthan, heritage hotels are popular with a certain class of tourists. These are the type who are not interested in the traditional hotspots like Goa or the hills. But the single most important factor that is likely to boost tourism is the mushrooming of private airlines. And after the agreement that private taxi operators have had with the Civil Aviation Ministry on flying even non-conventional routes, more and more places which are not easily accessible can now be visited. To that end, the ministry is working towards furbishing airports in five small towns.

Problems and Prospects

India has miles of beaches, the world's highest mountains, varied wildlife, delicious cuisine, dazzling cultural variety, ancient monuments and some of the world's finest hotels. Yet it gets only 4 per cent of the global tourist traffic. So what's wrong? True the figures are less dismal than they sound, because visitors stay much longer in India—about 21 days—then they do in places like Singapore which got 5.98 million people last year, but who only stayed three or four nights each. Nonetheless, the 1.6 million tourists we welcomed last year was a low figure, even though it was the year we advertised ourselves with Ayodhya, the bomb blasts and the Indian Airlines strike. So what can be done? Though people in the travel trade may differ on the specifics, there is near-unanimity on the major problems. First, the lack of a clear, consistent, sustained policy. Because tourism appears to be a subject anyone can handle, every new Minister or Secretary experiments with his own notions. Since transfers and reshuffles are frequent, tourism is guided by a series of *ad hoc* adventures. Secondly, the infrastructure is patchy, so while we have some first-rate hotels, our roads are appalling, our inner city taxis often unfit for human use and the airports even at such critical points as Agra and Jaipur are a national disgrace. Thirdly, we need to develop other circuits than just the Golden Triangle, so that if there are problems one of the areas, traffic can quickly be transferred to the others. Lastly, create a National Tourist Authority that will combine people from the private sector as well as from the Government, which will function in a non-bureaucratic fashion and which will ruthlessly implement policies.

According to a former Tourism Secretary, currently a member of the UPSC and something of father-figure to the tourism business: "Take the Mohammed Yunus Committee Report as the Bible and just implement that." But even without that he suggests a dramatic improvement of airports, guides, customs and immigration. "Once you have the right product, word of mouth will get you people," he believes. He also urges the opening of Bhubaneshwar and Bangalore to international traffic since both have hinterlands that are rich in tourist potential. But while pushing for the development of adventure, golf, Buddhist, island and museum tourism, he warns against overloading an area. "The carrying capacity must be surveyed," he cautions, "tourism mustn't affect the social values, the environment, or the cultural values. For example Manali today is a shattering experience"

Another experienced hand, the Chairman of SITA Travels, believes that we're spreading overselves too thin. "Our resources are limited, so let's prioritise, " he counsels, "Our strong points are cultural and beach tourism. Let's find our niche in the tourism market and concentrate on that." He also recommends that we encourage tourists from among the nearby countries since the trend now is for people to take shorter holidays closer to home. India is still heavily dependent on the long-haul traffic, a market that has been in decline recently. Overall, however, he believes that tourism is so inextricably linked with the country's total image that tourism will rise when India does. The president of Welcomgroup agrees in part about focusing more. "Can we develop the Golden Triangle into an international class circuit?" he questions. "Right from arrival, to baggage, to the hotels, the roads to Agra, the buses, the sight-seeing, shopping, guides, upkeep of monuments, souvenirs, everything must be first-rate. This would invite investors too." He also pertinently points out that there is a feeling that lower hotel tariffs will automatically lead to a tourism boom. He feels what is required is a national attitude. "What has been done to create this awareness?" he asks. He also laments the common belief that tourism is an elitist activity confined to hotels, travel agents and airlines, rather than an essential part of the economy. Some interesting suggestions are made by a director of American Express. He believes India does not need to be apologetic about its infrastructural problems. "It can be positioned as a 'different' experience and still get tourists," he believes. "Look at Bangkok with all its traffic and pollution which still gets people." However, he believes the most critical requirement is for there to be comprehension with India of the needs of our different markets. "For instance how do the needs vary between a pensioner in Paris and a yuppie in New York?" he asks, "This is a monumental task and requires syndication of research. It will require a group to pool in its resources and do it. Thereafter we have to select our markets and focus on them."

In this endeavour the critical element will be the foreign airlines since they bring 75 per cent of the tourists to India. It is extremely encouraging that they are highly enthused about the potential offered by India, but a major impediment is the system of reciprocity whereby Air-India has to be given the same number of flights that a foreign carrier is given to India. Since Air-India is not exactly the world's favourite airline, they find it hard to fill even half the seats sometimes to the world's major destinations. So they are hardly in a position to welcome more flights. However, the Government is aware that this considerably inhibits tourist arrivals and we may be inching towards a more open policy. Lufthansa, for one, would be very pleased, "Since," says their Director, Corporate Communication, "the major problem we face is an acute shortage of capacity." They currently fly five times a week to Germany from Delhi and Bombay but would like to add Madras to their list and then increase the frequency. Air France too is pleased with the traffic that they have but would like to see the fares denominated in a neutral currency like the US dollar so there is an automatic increase in the fare linked to the evolution of the currency. Right now the Rupee is stable, but if there is a sudden devaluation we could lose a huge amount. That is why Nepal, Phillippines and many other are doing this.

Other senior officials also feel the future is "very very bright." However, they bemoan the fact that they can not get more counters at the airport and the ground handling is a monopoly that is frequently very slow and for which the airline gets blamed. Even an official of Japan Airlines (that left India about a year ago) is very optimistic. He explains JAL's withdrawal as being due to a global restructuring following heavy losses. But a company remains to look after residual interests. Basically he feels the airline is waiting to see how much Japanese investment comes to India but with the increasing interest of Japanese entrepreneurs the tourist will come. However, to encourage this, we need more Japanese speaking people, Japanese restaurants and concerted effort to create an awareness about India in Japan since not much about us is known there.

State Perspective

Tourism development and promotion is bogged down in the Northern States because of bureaucratic hassles and labyrynthine official procedures, controls and exorbitant taxes levied by the State Governments. These views were expressed at a conference of Tourism Ministers of the Northern States when the then Union Tourism and Civil Aviation Minister interacted with them and listened to the plethora of obstacles that came in the way of development and promotion of tourism in these States. There were free and frank discussions during which, besides the Union Ministers, State Ministers, officials and private tour operators also participated. The three-hour-long "post-mortem" of the problems that confronted the tourism industry, revealed that notwithstanding the Union Government's total support to the

State Governments, they have not helped tourist industry in the manner it was expected of them. For instance, the officials of Delhi Administration were frank enough to tell the Minister that tourism could not be declared as an industry in Delhi because in their perception the subsidy should go to the rural areas which need financial help and not to the five-star hotels in the national Capital. But Delhi officials were the only one who opposed the Government proposal to declare tourism as an industry. Himachal Pradesh, said the Governor's Adviser, had already declared tourism as industry and a host of incentives have been given to those interested in setting up hotels and other allied industries for the promotion of tourism in Himachal Pradesh.

It was, however, the Haryana representative who put the Union Government in a spot when he said that although his Government had decided to declare tourism as an industry yet the Development Commissioner of Small Scale Industries had conveyed in writing to the Government that under no circumstances tourism could be declared an industry and tourism development could not be subsidised. The Haryana Government wanted to have the Minister's response on this vital question, but even the Minster was shocked to hear this. The Tourism Secretary, however, said that in the first instance Haryana was not required to refer the matter to the Small Scale Industries Commissioner when the Government had itself said that tourism should be treated as an industry. Then it was the Adviser to the Governor of Jammu and Kashmir, who wanted to "explode the myth that with the advent of militancy, tourism in the State had ceased to exist." He informed the meeting that at least 10 lakhs more tourists have visited the State last year. He said tourism in Kashmir was not only confined to the Kashmir valley but Jammu and Ladakh were also attracting a large number of tourist throughout the year. Seventeen lakhs tourists had visited Jammu region alone. He said the three regions of the State have to be treated separately for tourism development. Good days would return to Kashmir again and he therefore wanted the government to maintain the infrastructure that existed in the valley and the Government should not hesitate in spending money on the maintenance of this infrastructure because when normalcy returned to the Valley, the Government may have to spend crores again if this infrastructure was not preserved now. 25 lakhs tourists had visited Himachal Pradesh including foreign and domestic ones. However, the Government needed to clearly define tourism and also review the Government policy about "heritage" tourism. At present the heritage tourist spots outside the municipal limits could be developed only and not those within the limits of the Municipal Corporations. This had put hurdles in the development of heritage tourism. The Minister, however, said that the only condition is that of Metropolitan limits and not the municipal limits, as was generally believed. The tour operators were, however, highly critical that the State Governments had imposed heavy taxes on commercial vehicles with the result they were finding it difficult to have remunerative business. Besides the financial aspect, the checkposts set up by the State Governments on the national highways and State highways were a nuisance to the smooth flow of transport carrying tourists. At a number of places tourists are harassed because the tourist buses are detained for hours by the checkpost officials. Another point that they highlighted was that recently because of Government's indifference to contradict news about cholera, as many as 26 charters had been cancelled which were to bring tourists from abroad. They urged the Union Health Ministry to contradict such baseless news immediately. Similarly it was also impressed upon the Minister that issuance of visas should be made easy for the foreign tourists in the interest of tourism promotion.

While conceding some of the points which had been made at the conference, the concerned Ministry was extending all help to the development and promotion of tourism without any discrimination. During the next five years nearly 5 million tourists would visit India as against 1.8 million tourists at present. For this we have to build a sound infrastructure. During the next three years the Tourism Ministry would spend Rs. 750 crores to develop airports. During the last fifty years, only Rs. 633 crores have been spent.

Finally, it is the official view that a real boost to the tourism industry will come when it gets all the benefits in reality and not in slogans. The States have to ponder over this vital issue to attract more investment from private sector particularly from those still to join the tourism sector. He also wanted tax structures to be rationalised because some of the States have levied exorbitant taxes, which impeded the growth of tourist transport and development of hotels.

Turning the Corner

India has never experienced such a tourist boom as she has had after the new economic policy of liberalisation. Foreign tourists have made India now one of the most-favoured destinations which is clear from the fact that during the year 1993 there were 605 charter flights to India as compared to 225 in 1992. Comparative figures show that 60,000 foreign tourists arrived in India in 1993 in charters as against 34,500 in the preceding year. Out of these 24,000 foreign tourists came to Delhi in 339 charters from all over the world. In December 1993 as many as 2.14 lakhs tourists came to India, the highest ever recorded number in a single month. This was despite the fact that foreign tourist traffic to India had suffered serious setbacks since 1991 particularly after the Gulf War, global recession, the Ayodhya incidents and its aftermath. There were bomb blasts in Bombay and Calcutta, earthquake in Maharashtra and prolonged Assembly elections in five States.

According to the Tourism Minister, the boom in tourist arrivals was continuing and the month of January, 1994 recorded an impressive growth of 28 per cent as compared to the figures of the same month last year. He said that the National Action Plan for Tourism aimed at increasing tourism from 1.80 million in 1992 to five million in 1997. For this, special promotional efforts were being made including the restoration of confidence in the traditional markets about India as a tourists', destination and also to develop new markets. As a matter of fact, the Heritage Tourism Plan was first conceived by Mr. Madhavrao Scindia when he was the Minister for Civil Aviation and Tourism. His efforts were being supplemented by his successor. As a matter of fact, for the first time the Tourism Ministry has made a serious attempt to attract foreign tourists in an organised manner. For this an official high-level delegation had already visited a number of countries where they had organised audio-visual presentation on "Images of India". The audience abroad also included the representatives of the travel trade, hotel industry, mediapersons, dignitaries, opinion-makers and NRIs. Already a number of NRIs have shown keen interest in India and they are ready to make huge investment in tourism industry. The delegation's visit to the European countries shortly after the aftermath of Ayodhya and the Bombay blasts had helped in restoring confidence in European tourists about India being a safe destination. During these visits the Indian delegation also laid greater thrust on projecting traditional tourism product, the new thrust areas such as adventure tourism, eco-tourism, heritage, hotels, new circuits and shopping were projected. The other points that were emphasised were improvement in flight schedules of Air-India and Indian Airlines, introduction of Air Taxi Services, simplification of visa procedures, and liberalised economic policy of Government of India was also projected for attracting foreign investment. The Tourism Ministry has also organised a two-day meet on overseas marketing in Delhi recently where all the officials associated with tourism promotion were invited from all over the country and abroad also. How to sell India to the foreign countries was one of the major areas of thrust during this conference which the then minister also addressed. He told these officials to explain to the foreign tourists that India is the safest destination as here tourist can have an easy access to each and every place.

It has also come to the Government notice that almost everywhere in the country the biggest menace that the foreign tourists counter is the beggars. While some of the States have already passed anti-beggary laws, there are many other States where beggars make life a nightmare for the tourists. Even in the National Capital, it is difficult for the foreign tourists to move about because they are harassed by the beggars whatever they go. Even there are beggars in front of the five star hotels. On the Janpath, it is difficult for the tourist to shop because at every step they have to drop a coin in the bowl or else they would be pestered.

The Government is seriously considering the possibility of prohibiting begging in Delhi but whether it be would done quickly is nobody's guess. The Tourism Department has also convened a meeting of all the Chief Ministers to review the Action Plan to promote tourist traffic in the country. The conference is expected to discuss major issues like expenditure tax, infrastructural development and identification of new sectors. A major decision that has been taken recently by the Government is to open the North-Eastern sector for the foreign tourists. According to the Home Ministry officials, in future there would be only a few "closed" areas in the North-East while all other areas have been thrown open to the foreign tourists. This is expected to give a big thrust to tourist industry in this part of the country and the stagnant economy of the North-Eastern States would also be accelerated. In the past, the North-Eastern sector was totally prohibited for the foreign tourists.

For the first time the Government has also signed bilateral tourism agreements with Israel, Korea, Uzbekistan and Singapore. This would help strengthen India's ties with these countries to further increase the tourist flow. The Ministry has also announced that tourist offices will be opened in Johannesburg, Tel Aviv and Tashkent shortly to tap the new tourist markets. Another step to promote tourism has been the issuing of "No Objection Certificate" to the small air-taxi operators to link remote areas in certain regions so that tourists from all over the world can have an easy access to the far-flung places of tourist interest.

Current Status : Tourist Boom Continues

Tourist arrivals in India have started looking up again after the setback received in the last quarter of 1994 following the plague scare. January recorded an increase of 2.5 per cent as compared to the same period in 1994, which itself was a kind of record. Anyone looking for hotel rooms at this time will vouch for the fact that traffic is booming in all the major centres like Delhi, Bombay and Bangalore. The picture is less rosy when it comes to destinations like Agra, Varanasi and Rajasthan. The explanation is that a boom in business traffic accounts for this situation. It is, however, certain that India is set to record a modest increase in traffic during the nineties. It will continue to trail behind high-growth regions like the Asia Pacific, but will be ahead of the world average and the rate of growth for South Asia. The traffic to India grew by 6.62 per cent between 1980 and 1990 while in the next five years it is expected to grow by 7.03 per cent.

In a way this modest growth rate should help us in building the necessary infrastructure to cater for larger numbers. A bigger tourist increase is forecast for domestic traffic which touched a figure of 81.0 million in 1992 with an annual growth rate of 18.4 per cent. This may rise faster thanks to the growing middle class and general growth of the economy following liberalisation.

The investment in the tourism sector during the coming years is expected to be around Rs. 1,000 crores annually—which however may not be adequate as the sectors like airlines and hotels need much more. The number of hotel rooms which at present are around 50,000 will need to be doubled as traffic by end of the nineties is estimated to be around three million against 1.88 million during 1993-94.

Yet another factor to be noted is that the earnings increased in dollar terms also by 14 per cent instead of showing gains in rupees only following the fall in the rupee's exchange value. This is considered significant and it also proves the point that business travellers coming to India are demanding better class of facilities and paying for it. Hotels in major centres will have to gear up to meet their needs. According to a senior representative of the ITC group, hotel chains in India have to earn money in metropolitan cities like Delhi, Bombay, Calcutta and Bangalore and invest in tourist destinations like Agra, Rajasthan, Khajuraho and Varanasi. It is, however, not widely known that even the best hotels in tourist destinations barely break even instead of making money.

The uncertainties of the tourist trade, unlike business travel, which is not affected either by climate, season or other factors, make investment in tourist destinations difficult. Although hoteliers are virtually lining up looking for new properties in destinations like Bombay, Delhi and other metro cities, it is a tragedy that after the boom of 1982 no significant new capacity has come up at these centres. The position is worse in respect of Bombay which has reached the saturation point despite the boom in areas around the airport. The lack of room availability in the long-run can affect our tourist plans seriously as Delhi and Bombay remain the most popular points of entry for foreign tourists. According to projections made, Bombay will require 675 additional rooms in the luxury sector and 2.500 in the moderate sector in the current year itself. The requirement for additional luxury rooms in Bombay by the turn of the century will be 2,000, 3,725 by 2005 and 6,000 by 2010. Delhi on the other hand will need 4,900 additional rooms in the luxury sector.

Even a destination like Jaipur will require 900 rooms in the luxury sector and 675 in the moderate sector by 2010 while in 1995 to 2000 it will require 500 and 425 rooms, respectively. The maximum growth is expected in Goa with demand for 650 rooms in the luxury sector and 700 in moderate sector between 1995 and 2000. Jaipur is another high-growth area. These projections are made on the assumption that the growth target of eight per cent in the domestic sector and seven per cent in international arrivals will be achieved. There is also an assumption that 25 per cent of the visitors will be business travellers who will ask for five-star accommodation. Yet another problem is regarding the poor availability of electricity and water at several tourist destinations The destinations which have poor facilities in these respect, besides environmental factors, include Agra, Jaipur Goa, Mysore and Varanasi. These facilities are good in Kovalam and reasonable in Banglore.

It seems possible to achieve the target of providing employment to 30 million people against 15 million at present. The factors in favour of tourism include the indirect employment multiplier of 2.358 which means that every single person employed in tourism generates employment of 1.358 persons in other sectors of the economy. But all these advantages are not of much help because the bureaucracy, the State laws and the desire on the part of the State Governments to earn a quick buck is destroying the industry. The tourist trade and the Government of India started three years ago a dialogue to get tourist coaches from abroad. Till today the talks have failed to achieve the results. The excise rules during the period have become more chaotic leading to closure of draft beer service in Delhi and high taxes on tourist coaches by Government in the South have made it impossible to deploy them.

The move to build new hotels has also not progressed because the Government is taking ages to bring about changes in the relevant law while the move to utilise properties of India Tourism Development Corporation more extensively has not made any headway because the criteria for disinvestment have not been finalised. Even the hotels for which the lease terms were finalised years ago—like the one earmarked next to the Oberoi—the progress has been negligible because of inter-department wrangling. Under the circumstances, the chances of building infrastructure fast enough seem rather slim. Old destinations are also losing their charm because of poor environment. The worst example of it is Agra while Goa is in danger of being overwhelmed because of the greed of the money-makers. Cities like Delhi are facing acute environment problem due to rapid increase in road traffic, and plying of vehicles which should have been long retired. Under the circumstance, the need for achieving a balance between growth and conservation cannot be overemphasised.

The problems of tourism also arise from the fact that despite strong pleadings by the trade and recommendations by bodies like the Yunus Committee, the department remains the monopoly of the Indian Administrative Service whose officials come for brief tenures and by the time they understand its working they have to leave. The result is that there is no continuity and policies change with every transfer of a key official. There is also a regular battle going on between the permanent staff of the department and those on deputation. As a result of this struggle, many key posts remain unfilled. The latest victim of this struggle is the ongoing controversy regarding holding of buyers' meet or an exhibition of tourism. While one section in the department is favouring holding of buyers' meet, the other is in favour of exhibition.

Both these activities have their own values. While one is expected to promote tourism in the country, the other is expected to get a better deal for tourists going abroad. Normally one would have expected the department to promote traffic into the country or support both. They, however, have created a major controversy by trying to hold both at the same time. The results is that not only the trade had got divided on account of it, but a wrong message has gone abroad that India with a small base is trying to hold two fairs while it has the infrastructure at best to support one such event only. With such waste of resources, one thing is certain, that both the organisers will have to fold up in the near future as the response will get divided and a world which stands overcrowded with such events will just ignore events in India. The unfortunate part is that instead of building on the success achieved in the past we are wasting out gains for lack of co-ordination and due to the inability to work together.

2

Tourism: India and the World

Introduction

It is often said with great conviction that "Tourism is the second largest industry—after Oil." But perhaps with the weakening of OPEC, Tourism has now become the largest industry in the world. We do not know. But is any case, the sheer dimensions of World Tourism are staggering.

What is very interesting is that this mass Tourism is really a very recent phenomenon. It is just about three or four decades old: in fact, post-World War II. The beginnings of Tourism were in the '50s and we are now in the early '80s—hardly thirty years. Like the Technological Revolution and the Computer Revolution, it is only about three decades old—and yet it dominates the behaviour, the perceptions, the activity and the economics of millions upon millions of people. It is one of the major sociological and economic phenomena of the 20th Century.

Therefore, it becomes all the more significant for the developing countries because the developing countries, in fact, are trying desperately to catch up with the rest of the world, economically; for various historical reasons, largely because of the colonial structure from the 15th to the 20th century, these nations have been left behind in the developmental process.

It has always seemed to me that Tourism is one of the very significant ways a developing nation (not all, perhaps, but some of the well-endowed developing nations) can make extraordinary progress in several fields, and obviously in the economic sphere. Balance of Trade and Foreign Exchange is, or used to be, one of the major problems of the developing nations. If Tourism can be creatively exploited, then a great deal of foreign exchange can flow in—without really having to export anything.

It is the most painless manner of earning foreign exchange, because you do not have to export, you do not have to sell your oil or your scarce resources. You can simply develop your infrastructure—and you can thereby earn vast quantities of foreign exchange which, in turn, can be used to strengthen the economic development of the nation concerned. So this is a major area of interest, in developing nations.

Then, the second major area of interest, of course, is the question of development within the nation itself—economic development. There is no doubt that Tourism (again, always with this proviso in mind: if creatively handled) can provide tremendous economic and employment opportunities in the developing nations.

One of the greatest problems in the developing nations is this question of unemployment, not only the uneducated but the educated unemployable. And Tourism seems to me to be ideally suited for absorbing the vast unemployed potential that we have in our countries, because of the multiplier effect, because of the fact that the Tourism infrastructure, from airports right down: transport, hotels, the handicrafts, entertainment, everything, is capable of absorbing so many employees. There are thousands and thousands of people in a single city who can be involved in the Tourism adventure, as it were. That is very valuable for the developing nations.

Similarly, if you come to other areas: Tourism can provide employment in the area of handicrafts and souvenirs, for example, not only to the new but also to the traditional arts and crafts of a nation.

This brings us to another aspect of importance: Tourism encourages and fosters the traditional arts and crafts of a nation, which would otherwise have died out. They can be re-created imaginatively and they can be utilized for Tourism. We know a lot of Folk Arts, for example the Rajasthan puppet theatre or various other types of art forms, can be developed for Tourism. Similarly handicrafts: there is, in the Indian experience particularly, a wealth of genius in our handicraft production. If you look at even a small object, the sort of devotion that goes into the creating of it, the exquisite artist is sheer genius. What we are saying is that we have no doubt whatsoever that a creative interpretation of Tourism can be a major positive force in developing nations.

Certainly, there are dangers—as there are in almost every sphere of endeavour. Tourism can lead to vulgarisation, it can lead to exploitation of all sorts, it can lead to cultural degradation. There have been such examples. The despoilation, for instance, of Ladakh. We have been very concerned with Ladakh. Now Ladakh was a beautiful place, and we for long resisted throwing Ladakh open to tourists. Well, subsequently the floodgates were opened. And information is that in effect the monasteries have been stripped. They have just been stripped because if a person is sitting in a monastery for 500 years in a tradition and a tourist comes and offers $ 100 for some work of art; $100 may be a very small amount for the tourist but for a poor person who is sitting in a monastery, $100 is 1000 rupees! Now Rs. 1000 is not what he will earn in three lifetimes. And you know they are very convinced about reincarnation. Therefore a vast number of *tankhas* and other art treasures have disappeared. It is all very well to pass Antiquities' Acts, but let's face it, it is really not possible to entirely prevent the despoilation. But that is the sort of thing that has to be prevented. In Nepal, the same kind of thing began happening: We think they have become more aware now, of those problems, in Nepal. But, Tourism cannot be looked upon as a sort of cultural counterpart to the earlier colonisation and imperialism. For four hundred years we have been dominated by the West, politically, and now, just because they have more money, they come and despoil our culture. That is not our approach to Tourism at all. That is too high a cost to pay for Tourism.

But Tourism can be very creative. It is up to us to decide whether it is going to be a blessing or a plight. And, if it is properly moderated, properly channelised, we have no doubt whatsoever that as far as India is concerned, it has been and it can be a blessing—because India is absolutely unique as a Tourism destination.

We are not talking as chauvinists, but as somebody who has travelled throughout the world to the ends of the earth, quite literally. We do not think that there is another single country which combines physical beauty with architectural, cultural and artistic glory, as India does. The physical glory, "Aze to Himalaya pariyantham". As you know, without the Himalayas, we would have been another Saudi Arabia. So "from the glory of the Himalayas down to Kanyakumari, where the three great oceans meet at the foot of India."

The architectural glory of India: of course, the Taj Mahal is the best known. But look at the other great works of Man, the Vrihadeshvihara temple, for example — that one temple of India is worth repeated visits. Then, the culture, the dance, the sculpture, the painting and so on. The wildlife: now the wildlife is disappearing but one is happy that a department has been set up for its conservation: some of us were involved with this. We think wildlife in India is still unique.

Then, shopping: which is important, for Tourism, and should never be underestimated. People tend to underestimate shopping. After all, when one goes abroad, one always likes to bring back souvenirs. And the shopping bargains in India, in spite of haggling and all the cheating (which goes on all over the world) are still some of the best bargains in the world. One other aspect which has struck us very greatly on recent tours abroad is this new interest in Indian philosophy, in yoga, in Vedanta. It is now no longer looked upon as some kind of fad; you do not have to be some kind of a nut in order to be interested in yoga or Vedanta. There are now thousands upon thousands of intelligent, thinking people who are concerned at the crisis of culture in Western civilisation, who therefore turn to a country like India for some kind of new insight. We do not know how many of you are aware of the incredible impact that the one film, "Gandhi" has had upon public opinion abroad. Touring extensively in the American continent this year, and in New York we happened to take a taxi, and the cab-driver said that he had seen "Gandhi" thrice. Now this was just an ordinary taxi-driver in New York. From intellectuals down to the man in the street, this one film has re-created a tremendous interest in India. Why? Because of the philosophy behind it.

So there is all this here. And a country like India, and generally, developing, countries, can derive great benefits of international goodwill on the one hand—and of national integration, on the other. Speaking of India, our nation itself is so big that even our domestic tourism involves a very large movement of people. If a patron saint has to be chosen, for Tourism in India, it can only be Adi Shankara. In the 8th century, Shankaracharya travelled the length and the breadth of this country, and established four great pilgrim centres in the four corners of India. In those days, there were people who would travel—and they were not rich people, they were the common people of India, the farmers, the peasants, the workers, and they would go to these shrines—and that built the warp and woof, as it were, of India's cultural unity and integration. And therefore, both in the sphere of international goodwill and in the sphere of national integration, Tourism remains a very positive and major force.

There are many problems, too. We will only highlight two or three points which have particularly struck us. One is that in India the major bottleneck now seems to be airports. When he was in charge of Aviation, a former ambassador and well-known cultural personality, had the privilege of being the only Minister in the world to sign Buckminster Fuller as an Architectural Consultant. That whole proposal for our airports envisaged that International airports were to be ready on 1st January 1980. We had worked it all out with the Airport de Paris and Bucky Fuller, and so on. But unfortunately, that has not happened. And therefore, today the greatest disaster in Indian Tourism is the state of our airports. When you travel all over the world and then come to India, you are struck immediately by the terrible state of our airports. He set up the International Airports Authority of India, he put it through Parliament, he had the Bill passed. We will not go into details, but unfortunately our airport development is very weak. If there is somebody here who is important in the Government of India now, you must realise that if you do not work on these airports, your Tourism is going to suffer a major nose-dive.

The second major problem which is now beginning to develop is this question of visas. We are aware of the security aspects involved, very acutely aware, as we come from a very sensitive State (Jammu & Kashmir). But at least for groups, for charters, unless we make some special provision for visas, if we reintroduce a great deal of restrictive formalities, it may have an unfortunate effect upon Tourism in India. And one notices with some concern, that the upward growth in our Tourism graph seems to have virtually levelled out over the last couple of years. It has straightened out and the growth rate is unlikely to improve. And may be one of the reasons is this question of airports and the visas for charters. (And, of course, the general recession in the originating areas, North America and Europe).

We would also like to make one other point, and that is with regard to Training. For a long time we have been talking about

Training in india—but our Training facilities are very inadequate. This is something we have long wanted to get off our chest, Indian Institute of Tourism and Travel Management which has been set up must be located in Srinagar. (Dr. Khushoo is a fellow-Kashmiri, and we think he will appreciate our reasons). We do not say this because we come from Kashmir but because, you will appreciate, Jammu and Kashmir State pioneered Tourism in India. We had a Visitors' Bureau in grandfather's time, when nobody had heard of Tourism in India, way back in the 20's. The first Visitors' Bureáu was set up in Srinagar. We do not think there is a single Central Institution based in Srinagar; and if the Centre cannot even base the Indian Institute of Tourism and Travel Management in Srinagar then what are they going to base there ? Therefore it is the logical choice, because this is a major Tourism area: you have the gardens in Srinagar, you have Gulmarg, another major area, next door, you have all sorts of infrastructural facilities.

Another thing about which we have a great grievance is that you have now a ghastly Convention Centre bang on the Dal Lake, a terrible, dreadful Centre. The location is very bad. May be the Centre is good from inside. They have put it right on the Lake which, if one may say so, is a strange thing to do; when you had the whole of the hills behind, there was no sense in putting this Centre on a lake which is already dying and which is already highly polluted. (However, pollution is another matter which we will not go into now). Nonetheless, you have the Centre now, for better or for worse. So you have the Conference facilities—in the most beautiful place in the entire world, with the possible exception of the Norwegian fjords. Switzerland is a favourite country outside of India; it is a marvellous country. But the Norwegian fjords are the only place in the world which have the sort of colouring and the configuration that Kashmir has. And it is a tragedy that we have to ask for the institute to be based in Kashmir: it would seem to be self-evident that it should be placed there.

To revert to the main scene: the major point is that Tourism is conceivably one of the great unifying and civilising factors in modern history. The 20th century is now coming rapidly to its close. Man, today, is at a crucial crossroads in his long and tortuous history on this planet. We are the "Third World"—but the First and Second World between them will probably succeed in blowing up the Earth before the end of the century. May be they will get the First and Second prize for that great feat. But in the expectation that they will not do it and we will survive, in an age when tension is growing, where the super-powers are shouting at each other over these terrible nuclear devices. Tourism is a positive force working for Peace. We do not know how many of you have read a book by Jonathan Schell called "The Fate of the Earth." We would suggest that everybody connected with Tourism reads it, because then you will be able to decide what sort of Tourism we will be able to have after the bombs have gone off!) we feel strongly that Tourism is one of the major forces working for Peace. If American tourists go to the Russian States and Russian tourists come to the United States, I think it helps in creating better understanding—whether or not politicians become receptive to that concept. We have no doubt, however that the people all over the world do not want a war. They want to live peacefully. And Tourism is one of the major forces that can bring about better understanding between people of different ideologies, different languages, different social and political systems. In the Vedas, we have an ancient phrase,"*Vasudeva kutmbakkam*", the "World as a family", the idea that the human race is a family. You have seen the most beautiful photograph ever taken—the photograph of planet Earth taken from the Moon. That shows the world as it really is, a tiny speck of life and light against the unending vastnesses of Outer Space. And those of us who live on this planet have a responsibility to preserve and produce it. And the people who live on this planet, regardless of their race, or their ideology, or nationality, religion, colour, belong to a single family: the Human Family.

3

Policy and Prospects of Tourism Industry

The tourism industry is a limitless industry with immense growth potential the world over, it is second only to the oil industry in terms to turnover. Tourism has a tremendous positive impact on the economic and social aspects of the host country. To reap the economic and social benefits of tourism countries are vying with each other to woo more international and domestic tourists. India is no exception, though its achievements are not astonishing.

Tourism is a major industry in India as it contributes to about 4 per cent of its GDP, employs about 14 million persons (directly and indirectly) and earns foreign exchange valued at about Rs. 4000 crore per annum at present (1992). Constant efforts are called for to enhance the Indian tourism industry to put it on par with international standards. India's share in tourist arrivals and tourism dollars is paltry, less then one per cent of world tourism. To grab a respectable share of the world tourism market, several imputs need to be harnessed and a planned approach adopted for the development of tourist attractions, accommodation and transport facilities.

The year 1992 was a watershed in Indian tourism since, for the first time, the country was on the threshold of reaching the target of two million tourist arrivals in one year. India achieved a record of 1.86 million tourist arrivals during the year.

Earnings from tourism were up, both in rupee and dollar terms in the last calendar year. The developments in the aftermath of the Ayodhya incident in December, however, affected the industry, as they led to several overseas cancellations by individual travellers and groups. Despite these developments,

India ended 1992 with an overall growth rate of 10.9 per cent, which was a marked achievement since world tourist growth was only four per cent during the year. The actual earnings from tourism in 1992 were Rs. 3912 crore, an increase of 34 per cent in rupee terms, while in dollar terms the earnings were 1414 million dollars—a rise of about eight per cent.

However, the stark truth is that even with nearly two million tourist arrivals, India's share in world tourism continued to be less than one per cent. Yet in terms of tourist appeal, India has all the climes, a whole range of animal species and four millenia of history, tradition and culture scattered across the country.

India is one of the best bargains for tourists in the Asia-Pacific region, according to a recent survey conducted by VISA International, the world's leading credit card company. In the VISA travel cost survey of 11 major cities, Bombay boasts the lowest food rates and taxi fares. Accommodation in a luxurious five-star hotel and fast food in India's business capital are also among the lowest in the Asia-Pacific region. Among the Asian cities such as Singapore, Hong Kong and Tokyo covered in this 15-item survey, Bombay came out the clear winner for the lowest prices for most items. These include soft drinks, camera batteries. taxi fares, hamburgers, accommodation, steak dinners and even basic necessities like toothpaste. The 11 cities in which the survey was conducted were Bombay, Bangkok, Tokyo, Jakarta, Kuala Lumpur, Seoul, Taipei, Singapore, Wellington, Sydney and Hong Kong.

New Policy

The new tourism policy has given a fillip to tourism. The policy involves the people who are actually in the tourism business such as travel agents and tour operators and the hotel industry—all in the private sector. As much as 95 per cent of the tourism industry is in the private sector and only five per cent is with the public sector including the India Tourism Development Corporation.

In a departure from the concept of selling India as a single tourist destination, India is now being marketed as a sub-continent with a myriad destinations. Trouble in one part of the country need not deter tourists from visiting another destination. No longer projected as a historic cultural destination, India is being presented as a year-round adventure destination, with each camping destination linked to a sport. For instance, Kangra with para-gliding. Diu with water sports, the Andamans with scuba diving and Goa and Kerala with water sports.

Infrastructure

A clear demarcation has been established between the Central and State governments in the development of infrastructure facilities. The states are to provide basic amenities in terms of roads, transport network, bus terminals, wayside amenities, electric grids, water supply and municipal services. On its part, the Centre's infrastructural support will be in areas like airports, airline services, railway stations, communication network including post and telegraph services and banks. Special attention is being given to pilgrimage centres to promote domestic tourism. A committee on pilgrim tourism has identified 19 pilgrim centres in 12 states for intensive development.

The Central government is formulating schemes costing more than Rs. 200 crore for developing 17 selected tourist circuits. A tourism Task Force has been created in the India Tourism Development Corporation to give a new thrust to camping tourism, both for domestic and foreign tourists. Special emphasis in being given in the new tourism policy to local fairs and festivals, setting up of craft villages, convention complexes, tourist complexes, wayside amenities and tourism-related activities.

Tourism infrastructure means a network of efficient domestic airlines, efficient and clean railways, comfortable modes of other surface transport and hotel chains. Facilities at most Indian airports are still inadequate while they are virtually non-existent at many lesser known and developed tourist attractions. Other infrastructure, like communications, are also not of international standards. These basic requirements to make India a major tourist destination have remained partly unattended to, even tough tourism was declared an industry in 1985.

There is a growing consciousness that India should not over-emphasise cultural tourism, but diversity into holiday and leisure tourism. In may, 1992, a Tourism Development Task Force was set up to help develop new, off-beat tourist destinations, promote adventure tourism through trekking, rock climbing, aquatic sports, aerosports, wildlife interest and beach resort tourism. Culture tourism has not been neglected and historical palaces and fortresses are being identified by the Task Force, which has carried out many feasibility studies in the states.

The Government's new economic policy has generated interest abroad, as the focus in the tourism industry has shifted from public to private sector participation, both domestic and foreign. The Eighth Plan does not envisage much of a state role or investment in tourism. Important schemes included in the plan for the industry rely on private sector participation through a variety of accelerated incentives.

Two areas which could specifically benefit from private foreign investment are hotels and transport. Some of the well-known international hotel chains like Hilton, Mariot and Four Seasons, which have avoided India in the past, could step in on their own or in collaboration with local entrepreneurs. In the case of transport, the government has already given permission to Indian private companies to enter into collaboration with foreign firms to operate rent-a-car schemes.

The Indian hotel industry is poised for rapid expansion with the number of hotel rooms in the approved sector expected to double in the next three years. Presently, three are 48,000 rooms in the approved sector and about 60,000 in the unapproved sector.

The key to unleashing India's tourism potential lies in liberalising the airline industry. Such a move would surely benefit the wider economy by paving the way for a tourist influx.

According Mr. O.P. Ahuja, President of the Association of India Tour Operators (AITO), India should encourage foreign carriers to expand their capacity in the interest of tourism. With more capacity, these carriers would then promote India in their own countries. Besides liberalising its airline industry, India could also attract more tourists by plugging into a major aviation hub close by, such as Hong Kong or Singapore, which could serve to channel visitors from major tourist-generating countries to India.

An IATA study pointed out that a 35 per cent capacity improvement could be achieved simply by improving facilitation procedures at Indian airports. Some peak traffic could also be diverted to non-peak periods or less crowded airports. Although the authorities recently simplified entry formalities for frequent travellers, visa procedures in general are still time-consuming. If tourism is to be fully exploited for greater economic growth, then such airport facilitation issues should also be resolved expeditiously at all international gateways in India.

National Action Plan

There are increasing signs that the government authorities have recognised the benefits to India of a vibrant tourist trade, the most encouraging so far being the National Action Plan for tourism announced in Parliament in May, 1992. (See Annexure-I for Summary of Action Plan.)

Many players in the industry are eagerly looking forward to the implementation of the comprehensive plans. These include the liberalisation of rules, expansion of support facilities, preservation of national heritage, and incentives to encourage local and foreign investments in the travel industry.

Notwithstanding the progress made by the industry so far, tourism is still in its infancy in India. It will remain so even by the end of the Eighth plan when 5.6 million tourists are forecast to visit India. Even then, India's share in world tourist traffic will not exceed one per cent. Yet tourism could well become India's single largest industry to terms of turnover, employment, both direct and indirect, and more than meet the current balance of payment difficulties. It has a spin-off effect on economic growth, including income and resource distribution, and promotion of national integration.

However, compared to other sectors, Indian tourism is doing quite well currently. Foreign tourist arrivals, which were expected to touch the record two million figure, are now expected to stop at 1.9 million by March, 1993. Were it not for the Ayodhya incidents and the airline strike, foreign exchange earnings from tourism would easily have crossed 1.5 billion dollars (Rs. 4,500 crore), according tourism industry sources.

Vast Tourism Potential

Tourism's natural potential is so high that even if things continued as they are, India could comfortably earn 3.3 billion dollars (Rs. 9,900 crore) by the end of the century. And if radical steps are introduced, doubling India's tourist earnings by 2000 AD is not impossible.

Consider the country's strengths in tourism. According to a 1991 Economic and Social Commission for Asia and the Pacific (ESCAP) rating of tourist attractions, history and culture were tops with 74.8 points. And as then Union Minister for Tourism and Civil Aviation Madhavrao Scindia had said, "Very few countries can offer a cultural diversity as vast as ours".

Being the country where the Buddha was born, India is a "must-visit" spot for cash-rich Japanese and Southeast Asian tourists. Geographically, too, few countries can match the sub-continent: snowy mountains, virgin beaches, rich wildlife, and of course, exotica of every kind.

The country's vastness holds out another advantage : the ability to absorb regional setbacks. For example, Kashmir, once the second-hottest attraction in India is also in the middle of an area that is witnessing an air traffic boom. A Boeing study states that the Asia-Pacific region will carry 52 per cent of world airline traffic by 2010.

In 1991, United States, which played host to 42 million tourists, topped the charts with earnings of 45 billion dollars (Rs. 1,35,000 crore). Closer home, Hong Kong (6 million tourist arrivals) and Singapore (5 million) earned 5 billion dollars (Rs. 15,000 crore) each, and China (12 million tourist arrivals) netted 2.8 billion dollars (Rs. 8,400 crore). India's 1.8 million tourist arrivals in 1992 accounted for a mere 0.40 per cent share of the world market.

If India wants to attain the 6.6 billion dollar target by 2000 AD it needs to work at it abroad, aggressively marketing Destination India. "At present, the 22 foreign offices of the Department of Tourism act only as information counters," points out Mr. Inder Sharma, Chairman, Sita World Travels. India's budget for promoting tourism abroad is only 12 million dollars (Rs. 36 crore)—a pittance, given the high costs of advertising abroad.

The trick lines in finding the right niches in the global tourist market, and going after them. For example, since the Japanese are one of the biggest spender-travellers in the world, the ideal thing would be to aggressively market the Buddhist circuit in Japan—as well as offer golfing holidays, a passion with well-heeled Japanese businessmen. Then, since India's main attraction is its heritage, the emphasis must be on capitalising on the potential of these sites, rather than trying to lure the tourist with beaches and mountains, which are available in other parts of the world too.

There is also immense potential in marketing convention tourism, which has an estimated annual turnover of 104 billion dollars (Rs. 3,12,000 crore). India currently earns a meagre 27 million dollars (Rs. 81 crore) from such traffic. India's diplomatic missions can easily help in building up this sector.

That India's allure is unbeatable is evident from the average time a tourist spends in the country: 27 days, comparable only to Australia. As a top official in the ministry remarks: "If you show them the way to spend money and get their money's worth, foreign tourists will gladly oblige. After all, that's what they're here for".

Poor marketing apart, the other big turn-off is the lack of proper tourist-supporting infrastructure. To start with, there are not enough international flights into and out of the country. According to Asian Travel Trade, India was served by 41 international carriers offering about four million seats each way in 1991. And the Department of Tourism estimates that 2.3 million Indians travelled abroad that year, leaving only about 1.7 million seats for foreign tourists.

The remedy is to open up the Indian skies to more foreign airlines. For, even Air India's plants to increase its fleet from the present 22 to 56 aircraft by 2010 will not be enough. In addition, Singapore, Hong Kong or Bangkok could be used as hub airports. For instance, India has eight weekly flights to Japan and 14 to the US. By comparison, Singapore international Airlines has 85 weekly flights to Japan and 51 to the US. A government-to-government aviation tie-up could result in more tourists flying in from the US and Japan via Singapore.

Airport upgradation is another urgent need. While Bombay and New Delhi account for 80 per cent of tourist arrivals, international entry points in the south will be necessary in future. An international Association of Travel Agents report states that a 35 per cent capacity improvement could be achieved at Indian airports simply by improving facilitation procedures.

There is also a lack of information available at airport counters for guiding foreign tourists, which invariably leads to visitors being taken for a ride by touts. The solution lies in installing computerised networks, which inform visitors on arrival what hotels are suitable for which budget, whether rooms are available, and allow immediate reservations.

Unfortunately, there is also a dearth of hotel rooms in the country. While the boom period for foreign tourists is between October and March, there is considerable domestic tourist movement, too, because of the Diwali and Christmas holidays during this period. As a result, foreign tourists often find themselves fighting with Indian tourists for accommodation.

Recognising this, the government's Tourism Action plan has initiated action and expects to nearly double room capacity to 80,000 by 1987.

The ESCAP reports states that foreign tourists view inter-city air, rail, bus and taxi services in India as very poor. The opening up of the domestic skies to private airlines can ease inter-city air traffic. As for buses and taxis, in order to meet the growing demand, the government recently facilitated the import of 500 air conditioned cars and 350 coaches by bringing down the customs duty from 275 to 50 per cent. But since nearly three times more the number of cars and coaches are required, such waivers must become the norm for the tourism industry.

Since tourism is a subject on the concurrent list—which means that both the Centre and the States can legislate on it—developmental projects are usually victims of Centre-State tussles. For example, Japanese-funded development of the Buddhist pilgrimage circuit in Bihar and Uttar Pradesh—both major tourist attractions—has come to a halt because of inaction by the Bihar government. A proposal to lease two islands in the Andamans received no international response because of the various conditionalities attached. To remove these irritants, tourism must become a Central subject—with a single—window for all clearances.

Drop in Arrivals

Hard hit by violence after the Ayodhya incidents and the Indian Airlines strike, the country's tourism industry urgently needs a reassurance campaign and aggressive marketing to get back on the rails.

Northern India was the worst hit. Arrivals dropped over December 1992 and have not looked up since.

Foreign tourist inflow dropped by 15.5 per cent this January compared to January, 1992. The figures for February fell by 12.1 per cent, according to data with the tourism ministry. In last January 180,000 foreign tourists arrived in the country, a figure which fell to 150,000 this January. In last February, 170,000 foreign tourists arrived, over 25,000 more than the figure for this February.

The governments of the United States, Japan and Pakistan have advised their citizens to avoid destinations in India. As a result, "a major forex earner is crippled," said Mr. Ahuja, President, Indian Association of Tour Operators. There has been a more than nine per cent decrease in the inflow of foreign exchange during the first two months of 1993 as compared to last year, he said.

South India, a known cultural tourist destination, was not directly hit by the recent disturbances and tourist inflow to the region actually grew over the past few months. While 121,131 tourists disembarked at the Madras airport in 1991, the figure rose to 146,330 by the end of 1992, according to the tourism department.

In the North, years of militancy in Kashmir contributed towards the development of the Himachal and Garhwal areas as alternative hill destinations.

"What is urgently needed is a reassurance campaign to put the industry back on track and aggressive marketing of India as a destination that is safe inspite of all the turbulence," Mr. Ahuja said. Instead of selling India as a single destination, different tourist destinations could be offered in segments, he said and added, "If there is turbulence in some areas, the focus could be shifted to other destinations, so that the industry does not suffer".

The Department of Tourism has taken up the matter of advisories with the US and Japan while a ressurance plan to portray India as a safe tourist destination which was taken up after the Ayodhya incident still continues, department officials say. Media persons are being invited from abroad—US, Japan and Europe—under this reassurance plan.

The Ayodhya violence also affected tourist inflow to Madhya Pradesh, Gujarat and Uttar Pradesh, the other states badly rocked by the year-end violence. The state tourism department in Madhya Pradesh has even stopped receiving figures of tourist inflow since December.

On the other hand, in Punjab and Haryana, where the impact of violence was not much, state tourism departments claim that the tourist inflow was not affected. About 4.3 million Indian and foreign tourists visited Haryana last year and the state tourism department expects a 10 per cent hike this year.

The ministry, recently directed the overseas tourism department offices to vigorously campaign and publicise the country's being 'a safe spot of tourism' However, inadequate infrastructural facilities continue to stand in the way of developing tourism further in the country, according to Mr. Ahuja.

Tourism Highlights

- Tourism is a major industry in India as it contributes to about 4 per cent of its GDP, employs about million persons (directly and indirectly and earns foreign exchange valued at about Rs. 4000 crore per annum at present (1992).
- India's share in tourist arrivals and tourism dollars is paltry, less than one per cent of world tourism.
- The year 1992 was a watershed in Indian tourism since, for the first time, the country was on the threshold of reaching the target of two million tourist arrivals in one year. India achieved a record of 1.86 million tourist arrivals during the year.
- The actual earnings from tourism in 1992 were Rs. 3912 crore, an increase of 34 per cent in rupee terms, while in dollar terms the earnings were 1414 million dollars—rise of about eight per cent.
- However, the stark truth is that even with nearly two million tourist arrivals. India's share in world tourism continued to be less than one per cent.
- The Central Government is formulating schemes costing more than Rs. 200 crore for developing 17 selected tourist circuits.
- Notwithstanding the progress made by the industry so far, tourism is still in its infancy in India. It will remain so even by the end of the Eighth Plan when 5.6 million tourists are forecast to visit India.
- Were it not for the Ayodhya in incidents and the airline strike, foreign exchange earnings from tourism would easily have crossed 1.5 billion dollars Rs. 4,500 crore, according tourism industry to sources.

Annexure-1

SUMMARY OF ACTION PLAN FOR TOURISM

(*i*) Increasing the share of the foreign tourist arrivals to the country in the Global Tourism Movement from the current level of 0.4 per cent to 1 per cent in the next five years.

(*ii*) Tourism will be so developed that foreign exchange earnings increase from Rs. 2,400 crore to Rs. 10,000 crore by the end of the century.

(*iii*) Employment opportunities would be atleast doubled when compared to the present level of 14 million employed persons (both directly and indirectly) by the turn of the century.

(*iv*) Besides uplifting the quality of life, it is aimed at fostering development even in areas where other economic activities would be difficult to sustain.

(*v*) Facilities to domestic tourists would be improved and expanded, particularly the budget category to ensure an affordable holiday for them.

(*vi*) Preservation and enrichment of environment would be made an integral part of tourism development.

(*vii*) While retaining the traditional image, diversification of the tourism product, particularly in the field of leisure, adventure, convention and incentive tourism would be encouraged.

POINTS OF ACTION

1. Improving Infrastructure

Efforts would be made to double the present capacity of 44,400 hotel rooms in the next three years. It, is proposed to withdraw the interest subsidy on all four and five star hotels and on hotels in metropolitan cities. In special areas and specified destinations, the interest subsidy will be increased to 5 per cent for all one, two and three star categories to stimulate their growth.

2. Heritage Hotels

To help encourage the growth of heritage hotels, the Government would give an interest subsidy of 5 per cent on loans advanced for construction of new heritage hotels. A new scheme would be launched whereby this category of hotels would also be given a capital subsidy of 5 lakhs or 25 per cent of the cost, whichever is less. For Havelis located in rural areas, there is an added incentive of a 10-year tax holiday from expenditure tax and 50 per cent from income tax.

3. Domestic Tourism

To encourage domestic tourism a new scheme for development of camping sites will be started specially for the low budget tourists. A scheme of paying guest accommodation will also be introduced in as many places as possible to provide affordable and hygienic accommodation, for both domestic and foreign tourists. Similarly, classification rules will be suitably altered to recognise apartment hotels as these also provide affordable holiday accommodation to domestic tourists. Further, rules will be amended to provide for recognition to operators engaged in domestic tourism.

4. Pilgrim Tourism

To help improve infrastructural facilities for tourists at pilgrim centres, a sum of Rs. 5 crore would be earmarked as central assistance every year to enable state Tourism Development Corporations/private entrepreneurs to set up or improve accommodation facilities, wayside amenities and transportation systems.

5. Craft Villages

Craft villages are to be set up in various parts of the country to provide a boost to the traditional handicrafts of these regions.

6. Cultural Tourism

Government is taking all necessary steps to have a tie-up with the zonal cultural centres for making arrangements at important tourist destinations to organise cultural evenings, sonet lumieres, craft bazars, food plazas, fairs and festivals all round the year. This would be done in co-ordination with the Department of Culture and the Archaeological Survey of India. Liberal financial assistance would be given to develop traditional fairs and festivals.

7. Travel Trade

To encourage participation of the travel trade in the tourism promotion activities, rules and procedures would be streamlined/ liberalised for recognising travel agents and tours operators.

8. Palace on Wheels

A new tourist train on the lines of the Place on Wheels is to be operated from the coming tourist season between Goa and Mysore.

9. Foreign Investment

A Sub-Committee is proposed to be set up to service the main Committee to concretise foreign investment in the tourism sector.

10. Special Tourism Areas

In the first instance 15 circuits/destinations have been identified for concentrated development both through central assistance and investment by State Government/private Sector. The Government, in conjunction with selected State Government, also proposes to notify a few special tourism areas for integrated development of tourism facilities.

11. ASTA

A scheme for giving assistance for specified tourism areas (ASTA) would be started to provide financial assistance for equity and other tourism related activities in such areas as are specified by the Government.

12. Island Tourism

Special emphasis would be laid on the development of Island Tourism in places such as the Andamans and Lakshadweep.

13. Human Resource Development

A national Culinary Institute will be set up to meet the requirements of trained manpower in the country. To correct the regional imbalance, regional institutes of hotel management and catering technology would be set up.

14. Marketing and Overseas Publicity

A Destination Marketing Strategy would be evolved. A tourist information service would be introduced to provide a computerised multi-lingual information to the tourists.

15. Convention Tourism

To encourage convention and conference tourism, fully integrated convention complexes are to be set up in the country. It would be the endeavour of the Government to set up a convention city with all facilities of international standards.

16. Trade Fairs

In order to promote tourism in India, tourism trade fairs would be held once in three years.

Table 3.1

Monthwise Tourist Arrivals in India

(Including Bangladesh & Pakistan)

Months	*1990*	*1991*	*1992*	*Percentage change 1991/90*	*1992/91*
January	1,77,984	1,44,173	1,77,477	–19.0	23.1
February	1,54,758	1,14,567	1,67,268	–26.0	46.0
March	1,49,653	1,30,178	1,48,559	–13.0	14.1
April	1,22,986	1,13,862	1,34,895	–7.4	18.5
May	1,07,989	1,09,988	1,23,446	1.9	12.2
June	1,11,033	1,14,658	1,24,385	4.2	8.5
July	1,43,973	1,49,215	1,60,971	- 3.6	7.9
August	1,33,941	1,41,830	1,53,529	5.9	8.2
Septemper	1,28,067	1,22,693	1,39,746	–4.2	13.9
October	1,46,263	1,58,942	1,74,622	8.7	9.9
November	1,51,241	1,74,304	1,89,573	15.2	8.8
December	1,80,276	2,03,098	1,73,182	12.7	–14.7
Total	17,07,158	16,77,508	18,67,651	–1.7	11.3

Source: Department of Tourism, Government of India.

Table 3.2

Foreign Exchange Earnings From Tourism

Year	*Earnings (Rs. in crore)*
1980	482.0
1981	1063.9
1982	1130.6
1983	1225.0
1984	1300.0
1985	1189.0
1986	1607.0
1987	1856.0
1988	2103.0
1989	2456.5
1990	2444.1
1991	2910.11
1992	3915.56

4

World Tourism: Cultural and Sociological Aspects

I

INTERNATIONAL PERSPECTIVE

In 1980 the "World Tourism Conference" was held in Manila to discuss the concerns of modern mass tourism throughout the world and to look for answers to questions which had come up everywhere. The then President of the Republic of India, His Excellency Dr. Neelam Sanjeeva Reddy, sent a message to the congress in which he said: "International tourism has grown in the recent past to rapidly that it has become one of the largest items of international trade today and has contributed immensely towards expansion of the area of friendship and goodwill among peoples".

In this message the President indicated the two main points of modern tourism: on the one hand important economic development and on the other cultural, social and religious influences. We have already read a lot of excellent contributions on the subject. This paper gives some explanations on the cultural and sociological aspects.

Tourism Imperative

When modern mass tourism started to spread all over the world everyone concerned with its individual sectors had hoped not only for economic benefits but also for cultural, social and political progress. "Tourism can be a vital force for world peace and can provide the moral and intellectual basis for international understanding and independence", said the Manila Declaration of World Tourism 1980. Many other speakers at different conferences and meetings in Asia, America and Europe promised a new world of welfare and brotherhood stimulated by tourism.

Disillusionment was inevitable. Forecasts and predictions of a better life, of international understanding and cultural exchange have not or have hardly came up to expectations. Cultural and social repercussions seem to have been negative rather than helpful.

Indeed, a mistake was made when the first comments and critical questions began to arise. The critics, intellectuals, religious groups, community workers, journalists and radical students, especially from the developing countries did not get places or seats on the official panels and at the meetings to explain and discuss their position at the time. For instance: At the 4th international tourism exchange in Berlin 1970 a meeting for experts on tourism and the developing countries was staged without any statement about social, psychological and cultural problems. Only the viewpoints of trade and industrial development were presented. Critical questions addressed to the chairman were appeased. Tourism seems to be embraced only as a chance of increasing foreign exchange earnings and as a promise of a great deal of new employment.

Consequently groups which had felt responsible especially for the cultural and social aspects of tourism, felt pushed out and there followed a period of isolation of commercial essentials and of confrontation with tour operators, hoteliers and travel agencies. Confrontation instead of co-operation predominated. This is still the case. These groups organized international meetings, published books and documents, organized exhibitions and started a worldwide movement. In Europe and the USA these groups are supported by the growing trend away from further industrial progress. Some young people in particular oppose this, reject the industrial lifestyle and condemm development in which old rural ways of life are changing to modern industrial patterns. They have been created their own style of alternative tourism. A wave of nostalgia is emerging and modern tourism has been indicated as one of the worst factors destroying good old cultures. We must not underestimate the influence of these groups. It does not seem to be at its height at the moment. I think it is important to have an explanation from this movement. Their arguments are found in all countries and often form public opinion. What is the current opinion of these groups about the cultural and social implications of tourism ?

The Pros and Cons

This movement has a long list of observations most of which are negative. They have said about *tourists:* The majority of tourists who travel to foreign countries, especially those from the industrialised to the developing countries are unable to understand what they see and unable to be good ambassadors of their respective nations. Goodwill is not lacking, but travelling and staying in external resort areas is a strain on behaviour which in turn prevents understanding and cultural learning. The tourist is fully occupied with learning his role in the tour group or in the foreign hotel and has no desire to establish significant relations with the host community. The tourist who goes out into the foreign community only plays the role of a casual observer of the society he passes through. He takes pictures of povery and assumes that there are simple solutions to the problem which his own country's know-how would have found. It follows that this sort of tourism supports rather than changes prejudice. Real contact with the host community is usually confined to shopkeepers, service personnel and beggars. In case of real contact with the local people and their problems, especially with poverty and sickness, the tourist feels threatened. They often feel a type of culture shock and react by turning to familiar patterns of behaviour like at home. The Americans long for hamburgers and the Germans for sauerkraut. No new understanding, no cultural learning an exchange, no educational effect, but greater consolidation of old cliches. Tourists are passengers in a mobile ghetto passing through the world, especially through poor countries.

The critical tourism movement said about *host communities*: There are two reactions by the indigenous population. One is passive but amused tolerance; the tourist is seen as a good-natured, rather bumbling foreigner with a camera slung around his neck, walking along the streets looking out like a hawk. The other reaction is aggressive; the tourist is seen as a symbol of neo-imperialism which in a new and subtle way threatens the integrity of the country's independent stand. The protest poet Cecil Rajendra who lives in Malaysia writes in strong terms:

"When the tourists flew in
we were asked
to be 'side-walk-ambassadors'
to stay smiling and polite
to always 'guide'
the lost visitor
hell, if we only tell them
where we really want to go!"

In other words the tourist is seen as someone who corrupts the lifestyle of the host community, especially of youth and children. They are examples of an easy and lazy life, fascinate the poor people, destroy the traditional lifestyle and project the behavior of a wasteful society in the midst of a society of want. In short, no progress for the society concerned, only problems. They said the following about service personnel:

Service Personnel and Employment

What about new employment? Does tourism help to improve the situation in developing countries? The movement criticizing tourism recognizes this as an argument which cannot be dismissed lightly. However, the real situation must be seen in a different light. Different facts must be differently qualified. The type of work which tourism offers the local population is unskilled, low-paid and servile. Since hundreds of people are looking for jobs they are under constant pressure to conform. This is a chance for management to exploit the workers in many cases. Some maintain that the cost of creating a single job in the tourism sector is extremely capital-intensive, investments being much higher than in large-scale heavy industry or small-scale cottage industry. It would be better to invest limited national resources in a sector which could produce greater employment possibilities. What has the critical tourism movement said about national feelings and culture?

National and Cultural Identity

National self-confidence is threatened. A country which seriously wishes to pursue international tourism as a national priority cannot do so without assigning some of its sovereignty in the industry. A country may run the risk of handing over its decision-making to foreign interests. This is the first stage of surrender of self-determination.

Another accusation is raised against modern tourism. A bastard culture is born of tourism. To begin with, it affects the old traditional hospitality of a country. In almost every country hospitality used to be a major virtue. Tourism exploits hospitality and turns the local people into a bitter and angry community that is greedy for money. Examples of this are Ball and Hawai. A foreigner is no longer a guest but a cow or goat that is to be milked.

There is also the decadence of art and artists. Artists soon learn that tourists cannot tell the difference between true artefacts and trash. So they begin to mass-produce goods by machine and sell them. The tourist buys them and comes away with anything. The local artists use both their time and skill to produce these trashy cheap items and they have no time to develop individual ideas along the lines of the traditional art of the country. When they try to do so, their products are not sold because "they are not typical of the country", says the tourist.

A final observation. The critical tourism movement stimulates discussion of one problem in particular: Prostitution tourism or sex tourism. Indeed, it is both a very difficult and serious problem. In magazines and newspapers sex tourism gets high publicity; sometimes it seems to be the only problem of tourism which exists. I cannot give details of the problems at this point. However, I believe with all humility-that publicity is far greater than importance and quantity in his field of modern international tourism. It is a serious matter, small-scale but grave, and we have to discuss it along with the other questions of tourism.

I should like to summarize: Many intellectuals, religious and national groups criticize modern tourism severally. We have to regard the movement seriously. The best way to do so is to be objective and co-operative and to use serious methods of exploring and staying various aspects of modern tourism. Some of the comments and observations are true, others are global statements and assertions, and some are not true. It is a problem to discuss the question with these groups.

Analogies in Tourism Development

The problems described above are world-wide. This is the latest situation in the development of tourism as a historical phenomenon. Several of the concerns even came up when class-tourism in Europe, *e.g.* travelling done by rich people of the leisure class, changed into mass tourism. It happened in Europe in the fifties. I remember a great deal of turbulence at that time when tourists from the cities began to invade the Alps. The problems were the same as they are now world-wide, though on a smaller scale.

Two different lifestyles also came face to face with one another. Urban people pushed rural people and disturbed the well-ordered village and rural way of life. The lifestyle of the farmers in the mountains with large families was modest and restricted to education and self-confidence. An affluent society comes up against a society of wants-conflict was inevitable. A lot of accusations and angry comments were made. One of our poets, Gerhard Nebel wrote in 1950: "Mass tourism is the nihilistic disease of the Occident, the modern form of plague". Other people said: Rural cultural will be destroyed, folklore bastardized, the young people irritated because they will no longer want to become farmers and live as their parents and grandparents had done. In 1958 we had an inquiry in Australian schools among ten-year-old pupils. They were asked to say what profession they would like to have. The majority answered: Tourists I Village communities were divided. On the one side the older people were against tourism often led by the local priest and on the other side the young people rebelled and tried to persuade the majority in villages or towns to accept tourism. Magazines and newspapers printed long articles on sex tourism, especially in Italy, at that time called "Amore" later "bums tourism".

In 1958 we organized one of the first meetings in Germany about these problems to find out what is true and what is wrong in the jungle of opinions. Our first result was that we had a lot of opinions and presumptions but no facts with scientific evidence. The second result was to organize an institution to promote tourist research. Our friends and we established the "Study Group of Tourism", an autonomous institution without segmental bias. And we began to work towards solving some of the problems.

After 25 years spent observing tourism in Europe, we would say that initially the basic problems were solved when the local population and service personnel began to have the same level of income, reputation and leisure time facilities as the tourists. Therefore, it is very important to develop internal tourism, especially for those concerned with tourism, parallel to external tourism. Internal tourism may be done in a modest way at first put it is important that such tourism exists. The idea amongst the local population and service personnel: I can also be a tourist whenever I like, relieved social tensions considerably. That is a first bridge over the ditch between the working class and the leisure class, educated and uneducated people, the rich and the poor.

What else can we do? Four catchwords for a programme are *Research, Information, Education and Relation e.g.* public relations as already known in many parts of the world.

Research Context and Content

Since 1958 many study groups for tourism have been established all over the world; other institutions which had been set up earlier extended their studies to include tourism. In the "annals of tourism research" published by Pergamon Press, New York, I counted about sixty institutions, almost all in countries where English is spoken. Institutions in countries where French, German, Spanish or other languages are spoken are not listed.

I should now like to give you an example of a scientific result, explored in psychological studies and by the "Travelling analysis" of the "Study Group of Tourism" concerning the question : What is characteristic of the tourist travelling to countries of the developing countries. I am confining description to tourists of my country but the outcome may apply to European tourists also.

The motives, expectations and behaviour of tourists travelling to the Far East differ considerably from the image which is given and spread by the critical movement against tourism. Two general observations, explored by psychological research, are important. The main motive for people to leave their homes is a negative feeling about industrial life. They want to escape for a new weeks from their routine, everyday life. They work very hard for eleven months, have many duties and rules to observe and also pay constant regard to neighbours and colleagues. The local population in the guest community often sees the tourist only in the role of holiday-maker. They forget that tourists are also poor prisoners of industrial work. Vacation and travelling is a chance to enjoy some liberty and forget about work. Which countries are preferred as destination is of secondary importance. The main motive for travelling is an "away from" and then later a "from to" fooling. The main motive of on behaviour on holiday is the desire to be free for oneself. The tourist wants to be free of the forces and constraints of home; he is dying to be his own boss. His 'ego' is accentuated a lot. This basic structure in the psyche of the tourist explains many of the following characteristics. The tourist is, in the first place, not a student, he is not an ambassador of his country, he is not a teacher and not a refugee nor is he an engineer nor a helper in economic development. The tourist is primarily a man who likes to be himself and secondly he can be a student, helper, ambassador or learner. When we respect this basic knowledge we may succeed in making tourists and locals friends.

What is special about the tourist who likes visiting the developing countries especially the Far East? In some ways he is different from the normal tourist.

Half a million people travel each year from my country to a developing country. Arrivals in India in 1982 amounted to about 50 thousand, two years earlier nearly 60.000, a low rate of 8.7 per cent (6 per cent of all Indian arrivals from foreign countries) ; 3.5 million people had already been on one or two trips to a developing country. In 1979 3.8 million Germans were interested in holidays in a developing country, about 60 per cent will really go to one, that means about 200.000 for India in the next year. The share of 30 year old tourists who are better educated and the middle and higher classes predominate. In a further phase we are expecting more people with a lower standard of education and lower incomes to travel to developing countries.

The majority of tourists are not only interested in the beach, the beer and the bowling but in being aware of the political, social and cultural features of the country where they are having their holidays. They are also willing to reduce their wants for comfort and luxury accommodation in favour of more intensive contacts with the indigeneous population and nature. A tourist who visits a developing country several times gets a realistic picture and loses his presumptions and prejudices. Usually a positive emotional relation is established. The interests of this tourist are much greater than those of normal tourists. The percentages vary according to the different questions of the research between 55 and 90 per cent. There are many chances of improving relationships between locals and tourists, if we are able to respect the liberty and goodwill of a tourist and if we are able to inform them in an objective way. There is an enormous gap between the tourist publicity of a country and the social and political reality. Tourist publicity tells only the good side. We must provide information in a better way.

Information Dissemination

A multitude of research and scientific knowledge is available. The problem is how to transfer information to the people concerned with tourism and to the tourists also.

Transfer to tourists :

Tourists plan their trips all through the year, most of them in January and February. That is the time for adult education to offer discussion, meetings and lectures. People are very interested in such opportunities. The mass media pick up the themes of these events and spread them.

Tourists on travelling :

The Study Group of Tourism has developed a special magazine for travelling tourists or those who want to travel, called. *The Sympathy* magazine. It provides information about foreign countries which are tourist destinations. We offer 10 *Sympathy* magazines on :

Kenya	Sri Lanka
Egypt	Indonesia
Thailand	Philippines
Tunisia	Jamaica
Mexico	China

We are preparing one about Turkey, too. The number of copies is about 400.000. The editor of these magazines is the "Study Group of Tourism" supported by our Government and religious and social organisations. The magazines are distributed by the "Study Group of Tourism", through official tourist organisations and agencies. A commission of experts with representatives of the respective countries plans and supervises the booklets.

Each magazine is addressed to tourists who have booked a trip to a particular country or are planing one there. It tries to build up sympathetic direct relations between the readers and the country concerned and to shorten the distance between them. This is done by information with the human touch, short stories and pictures.

The focus of all the articles and reports is on a country which differs to our own. That is a reason for being interested in more information. You can get it here.

The response to these magazines has been excellent. We have continued this type of information by making films which correspond in content to The Sympathy magazine. Three films have been completed on :

Kenya

Sri Lanka

Jamaica

Adult colleagues and academies use the films in performances and lectures. Some airlines also show the films in their programmes on board, especially on charter flights.

A first evaluation shows good acceptance by passengers. There is an important consequence.

As the information of tourists together with their experiences in travelling to foreign countries increases the claims of the tourists change considerably. In the first phase tourists seemed confident when they lived in hotels and areas like in a ghetto. Folklore shows were brought into the hotels and clubs and to the beaches. Tourists believed the performance was a true demonstration of local culture. According to this experience, tour operators developed the idea of tourist enclaves and confined the tourists to a relatively small area of the country, excursions being organized to follow beaten tracks and trails. Impact on the local people was kept to a minimum. But we are at the beginning of a second phase. We have an increasing number of well-versed tourists who are old hands at such things. They want to be closer to the country and its people. They want to live in it and not besides it.

I have given you the figures on interests of tourists. So this concept is no longer sufficient. Competition between countries involved in tourism has forced them to give their products more profile. You already find fine hotels up to the luxury class everywhere. One hotel or one area equals another. Competition will be won in future only by the individual ambience of a country and by non-interchangeable characteristics. We must find a new type of communication between tourists and locals beyond the enclaves and fenced off beaches while preventing all the negative influences of the first phase. There is a need not only to inform the tourists but also to inform the locals. We have hardly done any research on local populations we know very little about their motives, expectations and behaviours. We have a lot of opinions and comments without scientific evidence. We know various complaints and statements. That's not enough. Research is necessary, along with information and education.

Tourism Education and Training

Education can take the form of seminars, discussions and instruction of service personnel. A waiter should not only be versed in how to lay the table and how to wait on people but also know why he is doing that particular job. We must all learn a new concept of hospitality. Traditional hospitality sees the foreigner as a poor man, often homeless or destitute in some other way. Hospitality meant help without being paid and was a virtue. The new hospitality has an economic basis: the tourists pay and the local people receive. This structure is inevitable and not immoral.

However, the new hospitality also has services without a price: Kindness, sympathy and attention. When service personnel believe that all services are for sale, they destroy the basis of tourism. We still all need educating to adapt to this new form of hospitality.

Tour leaders and guides must also be trained effectively along these lines. Several large travel agencies of our country start their programmes this way in order to reduce conflicts in tourist area and to specialize their tours in competition with other agencies. Some have also done it for the sake of public relations.

Public relations :

Public relations means influencing two groups of society. One group is the politicians who make the decisions for tourist development. Most of them have recognized that tourism is an available instrument for a country's economic growth. They also know that there is no roll-back. Strong restrictions as in China, Vietnam, Ethiopia and Burma put tourists off and do not help progress. We must get through the problems and not stop before. We must find form a tourist policy which regards the interests of all : of natives, of industry and of tourists. These new policies must not only be brought into lines economically and technically but must also be harmonized as regards nature, the economic and technical demands of people, locals and tourists. Jost Krippendorf published a list of strategies for "soft tourism" compared with "hard tourism".

Hard tourism	*Soft tourism*
Developing without planning.	First planning developing later.
Scattered tilled areas.	Saving ground, concentrated architecture.
Promotion only by external promoters.	Participation of local people.
No regard for landscape and nature.	Regard for tradition and nature.

We have only picked a few items from the list. It is much longer and more comprehensive.

The other group for public relations consists of the journalists of the mass media. It is important to gain, their attention and their assistance. It is wrong to invite them to put on a show, make propaganda and advertise. Give them more contacts with local people.

Modern mass tourism is an important instrument for improving the economic welfare of the countries concerned. In spite of mistakes and problems it will continue on its upward march. It is important that cultural and social conditions are also improved. We can succeed by better co-operation, research, information, education and public relations.

II

SOCIO-CULTURAL PROBLEMS AND PROSPECTS

Although tourism has become of very great economic

importance to many Third World countries, its potential to contribute very significantly to better socio-cultural understanding among peoples and bring awareness of the essential common denominators of humanity has been almost totally ignored. From the outset, total concentration has been on the financial benefits. Consequently, almost all the studies both preparatory to planning tourism development or estimating the result have looked at the foreign exchange and employment contribution. The only socially relevant feature emphasized was its contribution to better international understanding. This is now widely questioned. Its real economic benefits particularly for Third World countries at a very early stage of development were not properly quantified and the impact of the modern "gold rush" on societies until recently outside the mainstream of world events, largely ignored. More recently, a number of more broad-based studies have come to some disturbing conclusions about the mixed contribution of tourism to developing countries and its impact on host communities.

President Marcos in 1980 at the opening ceremony of the 2nd World Tourism Conference in Manila speaking generally about developing countries, talked of "the means to transform material conditions of life" but warned that these were at best ambivalent in that they disturbed the equilibrium of our societies which "have become unmoored from our roots and our traditions trying desperately to find some synthesis". In affirming the need for "reformation of goals and directions" he outlined both the future potential and the approach to tourism in the coming decades. "International tourism as a force that fosters this kind of iteraction between peoples and cultures assumes, it seems to me, a far more significant role in the global scene than we usually allow. And I should think that the closer it identifies itself again with this mission, the more easily will its problems submit to resolution, and the more will it contribute to global community."

The hope for the future lies in the new generation of tourists many of whom have known up with greater interest in, and some awareness of other peoples and different cultures. A surprisingly large number come with considerable knowledge of the history and culture of the areas visited. Others equip themselves with one or other of the excellent guide books now available. Indeed in many areas, the official guides have found some of their less well informed explanations questioned and often corrected. It is unfortunate that almost no organisational effort has been made to enrich the book knowledge of such visitors through contact with local communities. Their local contacts are limited to the service elements—taxi drivers, waiters, shopkeepers, money-exchanging touts and other undesirable hangers-on interested only in extracting as much money as possible, by whatever means.

The Human Element

Somehow, the reaction of local communities has not been seen as relevant in viewing tourism as a panacea for economic improvement and progress of the people in Third World countries. Two extremely perceptive and attention demanding statements on this aspects of its contribution to development and modernisation provide an interesting insight into the impact of tourism on the individual characteristics and well being of communities in such host countries. They come from individuals at the two extremes of the socio-political heirarchy, the King of Bhutan and a Mayan tribal girl from the remote jungles of Quintana Roo in Mexico's Yucatan peninsula.

His Majesty, the King of Bhutan, after listening to extensive advice from international experts on tourism and economic development as a means of raising the GNP and of modernisation for his mountain kingdom, is reported to have responded that his concern was more for the GNH : "the Gross National Happiness of his people". The Mayan girl who grew up in almost unexplored isolation speaking only Mayan, learnt Spanish by her middle thirties because of tourism expansion into the virgin forests in which her people lived. Reacting to the erosion of age-old traditions and a simple life sedulously guarded and protected until the third quarter of the 20th century, she said, "Modern civilisation is like packaged bread—convenient but tasteless" adding sadly, "A people without links with their own culture are like animals.

Recent Developments

For more than a decade now, development planners, economists and sociologists have increasingly questioned the real economic benefits of tourism. There have been a large number of studies on the impact of mass tourism on the society, culture and environment of host countries. Significantly, the first concerns were in developed countries where scenic sites, historical monuments and recreational centres were endangered. The impact of the sudden explosive expansion of both national and domestic tourism has, for example, caused grave concern about the Alps in Switzerland and Australia, about the changing character of historic cities, about damage to the Japanese mountain environment and religious centres, and to the fragile island eco-systems of Hawaii and Puerto Rico. Examinations of the impact of tourism in Third World countries is developing more slowly, partly because of the visible economic benefit from foreign exchange earning, and the employment potential from tourism, particularly in remote areas not easily open to other forms of economic development.

This understandable emphasis on the economic advantages has resulted in the concentration on studies which look uni-dimensionally at the economic aspects. There is certainly an attempt to arrive at a cost/benefit ratio by relating the host country's financial resources from the countries of origin, plus the spread over a wider area of economic activity through the multiplier effect. All other costs including what can be collectively described as social costs, have only begun to be considered comparatively recently. Such after—the—event awareness is extremely difficult or almost impossible to correct. The immediate cost is to the special sites—coastal and mountain areas and historical monuments which provide the tourism attraction. In addition, overcrowded infrastructural development, pressure on limited civic resources, and the inflationary impact of high cost centres of affluence on prices of basic local necessities, all seem to have resulted in resentment by local communities directed against tourists. Many non-quantifiable costs also emerge, especially among traditional societies.

Socio-cultural and Political Considerations

The economic limitations can be rationalised in relation to the very substantial financial inputs from tourism. However, the socio-cultural and political consequences are not so lightly wished away. Many citizens in Third World countries fear serious socio-political consequences from the economic disparity caused by the creation of islands of extraordinary affluence amid oceans of deep deprivation and poverty. Those among the more affluent whose life styles are directly or indirectly affected including officials, could readily echo the sentiment from tourism centres in the developed countries: "We like tourist money but not the tourists". Paris, for example, empties of Parisians at the height of the tourism season with many pungent, "expletive expurgated" comments by the departing citizens. Concern about the consequences for the societies where tourism can and has added to local tensions has to become an important element in assessing the effect of tourism in host countries.

There is a noticeable impact on the younger generation in terms of dress, social behaviour—including greater interest in drink and drugs—and some vulgarisation of traditional dance, music and art forms. There can also be extensive dislocation of life-long individual economic activity. The earliest documented example was on the impact on the life of a Mexican farming-fishing community whose lands were swallowed up in tourism development. The resultant total dependence on the ebb and flow of tourists brought fluctuating benefits to a minority, and comparative deprivation to the rest. It also brought with it all the modern distortions of urban social life from massage parlours and sexual solicitation to gambling and criminal activity. This pattern has been repeated in many tourist centres such as Pattaya in Thailand. Though not fully documented, probably in the tourism development area south of Colombo as well.

Tourism has undoubtedly contributed much to a widening of mental horizons, particularly in Europe—not so long ago, the English Channel protected the British masses from their alien neighbours, the French, and *vice versa*. Now no region of the world is too remote for travel for any peoples. Very little cross cultural fertilisation has been achieved in Third World countries except in a few special categories. On the hand, there is visible evidence in some Caribbeana, South Asian and ASEAN countries that tourism has had a negative impact on local cultures and communities and has led to considerable increase in gambling, prostitution (male and female) and crime. In the ASEAN region, demonstrations against such tourism and the institutions promoting its undesirable aspects have received international publicity.

It is impossible to ignore the political implications as a result of the view that tourism is a form of neo-colonialism. A large number of studies have summed up the changed thinking on tourism "euphoria to xenophobia". Suggestions that it is "a new form of colonialism and imperialism is one extreme perception of tourist development and its effects ... found in the writings of Mathews (1977 : 21), Levitt and Gulati (1970), Lewis (1972), Bryden (1973) and Perez (1975) indicates that this perspective is not without foundation." .... According to some authors, the growth of tourism in these destinations has been only a change in the form and magnitude of travel without a major alteration in its colonial quality. Although the legal ties between metropolitan powers and tourist destinations has changed as many developing countries have received Independence, the economic relationship between them have remained essentially same. This condition has prompted the charge that tourism is a neo-colonial activity.

Three economic conditions substantiate this claim. Firstly, many developing countries have grown to depend upon tourism as a means of securing revenue. Many countries attempting to boost foreign exchange earnings have turned to tourism as a means of achieving this goal: Their success depends, in part, on their willingness to accommodate fully the needs of-tourists. The West Indies, for example, waived tax and import restrictions, developed appropriate infrastructures and relaxed environmental safeguards in an attempt to encourage the development of the tourist industry. In other words, their political and economic priorities and organisation have been directed towards the satisfaction of the demands of the tourists.

Secondly, the development of tourism may be accompanied by a one-way transfer of wealth from the destination area to points of tourist generation. A large proportion of expenditures and profits flow back to foreign investors. High leakages may leave little profit in the destination area. A large proportion of goods and services are consumed by the tourist are produced at the place of origin and, thus, most of the profits are transferred to these points.

Thirdly, the employment of non-locals in professional and managerial positions and the frequent existence of foreign, absentee employers have also provoked charges of neo-colonialism. These features also contribute to high leakages through the remittances of salaries and profits to the tourist generating countries. Bugni court (1977 : 2) writing specifically on African tourism, believed that these situations contributed to what he called 'tourism with no return'.

Perez (1975 : 141), Bugnicourt (1977 : 3) and Mathews also argued that tourism is neo-colonialist through the herding of local groups into 'reservations' for the purpose of entertaining tourists, and through the transformation of the relics of past colonial regimes, such as old tortresses and historic buildings, into tourist attractions. Similarly, cultural symbols of art, music, dance and literature—are exploited to cater to tourist curiosity and to make money".

The Indian Context

India, and indeed most of South Asia has been protected by a deep rooted conservative cultural tradition and the remnants of Victorian values. Visitor arrivals are very limited—India's around 850,000 per annum though estimated foreign exchange earnings are very substantial—estimates vary from Rs. 750 million to Rs. 1 billion annually. There are concentrations in some urban areas but the negative socio-cultural aspects are still easily controllable. Despite this, many current trends run counter to the host country's overall objective in promoting tourism, so it contributes to the maximum extent to the economic and the socio-cultural well being of the country and of its people and provides a rewarding recreational and cultural experience for the tourists. There are New Signs that tourism planners are giving adequate importance of the effect on local communities and already threatened environments or to enriching the cultural and recreational experience of visitors. The only index of progress seems to be statistical: the regular numerical increase in arrivals and estimates of foreign exchange earned.

Concentration on foreign exchange earnings and visitor arrivals or even on the employment aspect of tourism tend as an almost universal rule to concentrate the financial returns in the hands of those directly involved in the industry, and to a lesser degree, those indirectly benefiting from it. The vast majority are outside this magic circle, and too often, are adversely affected by growing socio-cultural distortions, and the local inflationary impact of concentrations of high spending tourists. The low spending category of foreign tourists at the base of the economic pyramid contribute marginally, but almost invariably have a negative impact on traditional life and moral values, besides being more a burden on the economy than an asset. This group has also contributed directly to the rise of drug addiction among middle class and college youth. It is an important factor in the emergence of India as a new centre in the global narcotics trade. Prohibition in India may or may not be a disincentive, but it brings the country into disrepute through open connivance of flagrant contravention of the law. It is also a catalyst in the expansion of currency law violation, smuggling, organised crime and prostitution.

Until recently, few international tourists visited our mountain and forest areas, but explosive growth is just around the corner. The international toúr operators who contributed so much to the expansion and damage to East African wildlife tourism now have their eyes on India and other South Asian centres. Domestic interest is growing steadily. More trekkers, mountain climbers and adventure—oriented tourists are planning to vîsit the Himalayas. Even our desert areas are opening to camel safaris. In addition, domestic tourism at a less affluent level adds to the stress on the natural environment, on the local economy and on travel and civic facilities, because of the very large numbers involved—the Indian Railways alone carry 10 million passengers daily.

There is ample evidence of the impact of the annual, seasonal influx of domestic visitors on the inner mountains. Around Naini Tal, Simla and other hill stations, the deforestation is largely to provide firewood for those who, escaping from the heat of the plains, still require indoor warmth to keep out the chill mountain air. Mountain lakes like Naini Tal and the Dal Lake are close to eutrophication. Less well known lakes in Kashmir, Anchar and Wular, are practically extensive marshes. The latter was once the largest in India—$12\frac{1}{2}$ miles dy 5 miles, and according to old records, "should be crossed early in the morning as dangerous storms sometimes arise later". The very rapid unplanned increase of tourism to Leh is a case of distorted development. Except for the very few individuals, local people have hardly benefitted. The cream off the top goes to people from the Kashmir valley, traders from outside and to travel agencies and hotel groups from urban centres.

Future Growth

The high rate of growth of the tourism boom has been

perceptively slowed down following the energy crisis which raised travel costs, the global recession and the declining growth rates in the countries from which most the tourists originated. Nevertheless, it is still considered that by the turn of the century, tourism will be the world's largest industry even at the projected slower growth rate of about 3.5 per cent per annum, compared to growth rates which have been as high as 15 per cent to 20 per cent. No less a person than the late, unlamented by many, Herman Kahn, the megadeath man, had himself predicted this. He had also with considerable presience, identified tourism's major dilemma in asserting that after nuclear power, tourism had the most devastating impact on the environment.

New Approaches

How government and private industry respond to these developments will have a major impact on both tourism's future, and on its contribution to the overall well-being of Third World countries. There clearly has to be an entirely new approach. This must consider all aspects of the financial and social costs, in relation to the benefits to host countries and communities, while retaining the constructive elements which have contributed to the growth of the tourism industry. There is of course, no standard formula to ensure constructive growth of tourism with the broad-based welfare of local communities in the host countries because conditions differ immensely. However, it should be possible to lay down to certain broad guidelines which can be adopted by individual countries to suit their special needs.

The Changing Tourists

Globally, there is an important new development which should spur corrective measures. An increasing number of today's tourists are themselves looking for a new kind of holiday experience. They still want to get away from their own environment but they also seek contact with and understanding of other cultures. The mindless exuberance of holiday makers seeking an inhibition—free holiday is changing. There is a strong urge to escape to natural areas, with a more intelligent interest in other countries and their peoples.

Once it was possible to develop a richly productive tourism

centre by providing familiar conditions on the formula "sun, sand and sea ... and sex". Everything was done in many areas to create a familiar environment. For example, a section of the Italian coast has prospered by becoming almost entirely German-predominant language and ubiquitous sausages and sauerkraut and German beer. There are many similar though not perhaps so extreme sites in Third World countries. This contributes almost nothing to social or cultural exchange, only producing short term and somewhat limited economic benefits. It is no longer so simplistic. Evidence is steadily growing that the new generation of tourists does not want this. They also do not want the kind of overcrowded, constricted infrastructural development which is what they are escaping from, and which also virtually excludes any contact with local people. To some degree, there is also embarrassment about excessive affluence amid poverty, and an increasing impetus to avoid centres where tourism has accentuated the negative social aspects.

Introspect and Retrospect

Tourism still holds out very considerable promise particularly in the spirit of the opening quotation from President Marcos' speech which places emphasis on better international understanding. Simultaneously, concern about the impact on local communities culturally and economically and of the increasingly threatened environments of the most Third World countries has become a critical factor. As future tourism movements may increasingly move into less settled areas and numbers may increase pressures on existing centres, it becomes extremely important to ensure the spread of the economic benefits as widely as possible, particularly to local people and to regulate movement and numbers with concern about the overall carrying capacity.

It will be presumptious of any individual to set out guide lines for the future but the reproduction of some crucial paragraphs from the Manila Declaration on World Tourism which represents the collective wisdom of the assembled nations may provide substantive material on which to base a re-evaluation of the existing operation and planning of national and international tourism:

"There are many constraints on the development of tourism. Nations and groups of nations should determine and study these constraints, and adopt measures aimed at attenuating their negative influence.

The share tourism represents in national economies and in international trade makes it a significant factor in world development. Its consistent major role in national economic activity, in international transactions and in securing balance of payments equilibrium makes it one of the main activities of the world economy.

Within each country, domestic tourism contributes to an improved balance of the national economy through a redistribution of the national income. Domestic tourism also heightens the awareness of common interest and contributes to the development of activities favourable to the general economy of the country. Thus, the development of tourism from abroad should be accompanied by a similar effort to expand domestic tourism.

The economic returns of tourism, however real and significant they may be, do not and cannot constitute the only criterion for the decision by States to encourage this activity. The right to holidays, the opportunity for the critizen to get to know his own environment, a deeper awareness of his national identity and of the solidarity that links him to his compatriots and the sense of belonging to a culture and to a people, are all major reasons for stimulating the individual's participation in domestic and international tourism, through access to holidays and travel.

Tourism resources available in the various countries consist at the same time of space, facilities and values. These are resources whose use cannot be left uncontrolled without running the risk of their deterioration, or even their destruction. The satisfaction of tourism requirements must not be prejudicial to the social and economic interests of the population in tourist areas, to the environment or, above all, to natural resources, which are the fundamental attraction of tourism, and historical and cultural sites. All tourism resources are part of the heritage of mankind. National communities and the entire international community must take the necessary steps to ensure their preservation. The conservation of historical, cultural and religious sites represents at all times, and notably in times of conflict, one of the fundamental responsibilities of the States.

In the practice of tourism, spiritual elements must take precedence over technical and material elements. The spiritual elements are essentially as follows :

(*a*) the total fulfilment of the human being,
(*b*) a constantly increasing contribution to education,
(*c*) equality of destiny of nations,
(*d*) the liberation of man in a spirit of respect for his identity and dignity,
(*e*) the affirmation of the originality of cultures and respect for the moral heritage of peoples.

Tourism development at both the national and international level can make a positive contribution to the life of the nation provided the supply is well planned and of a high standard and protects and respects the cultural heritage, the values of tourism and the natural, social and human environment."

5

Tourism Policy : Imperatives and Approaches

A RETROSPECTIVE SURVEY

Tourism : A Rationale

Whether a country with scarce resources should give high priority to tourism may depend on the options for economic development available to it. Nonetheless a majority of countries which have other options available to them still give reasonable priority to tourism *e.g.*, Mexico, Venezuela, Malaysia, Indonesia. However, India has always given it extremely low priority. In the last 25 years the budget allocations for the promotion and development of tourism have been usually less than half of one per cent of the Plan and non-Plan budgets, and even these modest allocations have remained party unspent. Of the 90 odd items listed on the Sixth Plan the only two items below tourism were Inland Water Transport and Lighthouses.

Many of you may remember the opening line of Mark Antony's oration in Shakespeare's Julius Caesar! "I have come to bury Caesar, not to praise him". During the last 40 years every Minister of Tourism has come to the annual travel conventions to do exactly the opposite. They have come to praise tourism and then they have tried to bury it. The fact that they have not been able to do so quite successfully is because of the resilient character of tourism. The low priority given to tourism in India could also be attributed to muddled thinking on the part of our decision-makers partly because they look at tourism mainly as a source of foreign exchange. In the last four years India had accumulated considerable foreign exchange reserves. So tourism did not seem to matter. What was not realised was that trade deficits can reappear, that the remittances from Indians working abroad which had become the main source of foreign exchange earnings were a passing phenomenon and the escalation in oil prices was likely to continue until the world could develop the other sources of energy at competitive cost. This is what precisely has happened now and our balance of payments situation is deteriorating.

However besides tourism's main recognised benefit of foreign exchange earnings, its other benefits *e.g.*, adding to the Gross National Product through multiplier effect, which is very high in the case of India, generating considerable employment in terms of investment, contributing to tax revenue mainly through indirect taxes, redressing regional imbalances, are no less important. It is a mistaken notion that tourism is a luxury activity which benefits only those engaged in the tourist industry. It has been established by the case studies of many developing countries that tourist expenditure percolates throughout the economy and benefits all segments of the community. Visitors to India spend on the average 27 cents of each dollar on purchase of goods, mostly produced by small scale industries. In many countries tourism had played a significant role in reviving and sustaining indigenous handicrafts and thus helped the village craftsmen. Finally, tourism has the additional advantage of not being subject to protectionist policies of industrial countries. This to some extent explains why the Third World's share of tourism is higher than that of trade—17 per cent as against 11 per cent. The 'Group of 77' which is now comprised of 120 countries have announced the goal of attaining 25 per cent of world trade by the year 2000. What is more likely to happen is that the Third World's share of tourism will come up to 25 per cent by 1990.

The increased leisure time available to industrial societies due to paid holidays and long week ends, higher family incomes and propensity to spend, improved educational standards and non-traditional attitudes among the young, better medical care enabling people above sixty to take long holidays after retirement, are factors which have made the growth of modern tourism an irreversible phenomenon. Tourism has shown far more resilience than international trade during the last six years of the energy crisis, increasing its share of world trade from 4.5 per cent to 5.5 per cent. India has enjoyed a comfortable balance of payments situation for the last four years but now there is a distinct downward trend. The North-South dialogue, the confrontation at UNCTAD and UNIDO Conferences between the industrial and developing countries, the New International Economic Order (NIEO) envisaged by the 'Group of 77' and the recent Willy Brandt Report, are all about transfer of resources from the rich to the poor countries. Tourism is after all a means, an easy one too because it does not overly exhaust indigenous resources, of transfer of wealth to the developing countries. The trade deficit for 1979-80 is more than Rs. 20,000 million, remittances from Indians domiciled abroad are tapering off and the cost of fuel imports is sky-rocketing to Rs. 50,000-60,000 million. Even at present receipts from tourism amount to more than Rs. 4,000 million—Rs. 3,500 million from tourist expenditure plus Rs. 600-700 million foreign exchange earnings of the two national carriers.

As explained in the next two paragraphs, if certain meaningful steps are taken it would be a realistic forecast that receipts from tourism would increase to Rs. 15,000 million (excluding earnings of national carriers) a year by the end of the present decade, which could conceivably balance much of the trade gap, as it has in several countries. In any case Rs. 15,000 million cannot be regarded as peanuts by any Government.

What Type of Tourism?

Almost 70 per cent of visitors to India so far have been coming from countries with high per capita incomes : Western Europe, North America, Japan and Australia. This does not mean that they are all high-spending visitors, nor that all visitors from elsewhere belong to low-income groups. Some of the most high-spending visitors, in fact, come from the Gulf and from Latin America. However, an analysis of visitors by income indicates that nearly half of them have an income of Rs. 200,000 a year or more, at current value, and less than 25 per cent have incomes comparable to Indian incomes of Rs. 75,000 or less a year. The official viewpoint that proportionately more modest income or 'budget' tourists have started coming to India should be treated with caution. There is no evidence that a new trend has set in. Secondly, the motivation of a majority of visitors is to see the country, its monuments, temples and scenic attractions, somewhat imprecisely described as 'cultural tourism'. Those with more well-defined interests *e.g.*, rest and recreation, trekking in the mountains, seeing wildlife, business and conferences, visiting relatives and friends, constitute minority segments. That would also explain why in the last 15 years there has been far greater increase in 5- and 4-star hotel capacity than in lower categories and at the same time the occupancy ratios of upper category hotels have been higher than those of the lower category. The observation made in the last survey of tourism conducted by the Hyderabad Staff Administrative College in 1976-77, on behalf of the Department of Tourism, that foreign tourists showed an increased preference for 3- and 2-star accommodation is not warranted by the income break-down of visitors or by occupancy figures. Eighty per cent occupancy in 5-star hotels was by foreign guests and many others stayed in 3- star hotels because accommodation in 5- and 4-star hotels was not available.

There is a large ethnic market of more than ten million Indians domiciled abroad which we have generally ignored. Many of them have now become affluent and would like to see their country of origin if they were assured of a warm reception. Lastly, all the places connected with Gautam Buddha's life are in India and Lumbini is just across the border. We could attract an immense number of Buddhist tourists. We have not provided even basic facilities in Bodh Gaya, Nalanda, Rajgir, Sarnath, Sahet- Mahet where Buddha died. Two of the largest segments of modern tourism are the mass movement in search of sun, sand and sea, and winter sports in the mountains. India has missed both despite its long sea coast and its mountains. Holiday tourism in India has remained practically undeveloped. Two surveys made by experts of Goa show that there are enough beaches there to absorb 250,000 tourists a year without environmental danger provided the development is well-planned. Goa alone offers more sea beaches than the wl .le of Sri Lanka and yet two beach resort hotels are finding it difficult to survive as against more than 50 hotels doing reasonably well on the west and east coast of Sri Lanka. There are other beautiful beaches awaiting development on the west and east coasts of India. There are only half a dozen seaside hotels in India, as against about the 50 in Sri Lanka. Pattaya, Thailand's sea resort, alone has 3,500 hotel rooms. All the Asian countries are fast developing new sea resorts. After 15 years of development process Gulmarg is still an amateur winter resort with just on ski slope of less than a mile long. It offers only rudimentary facilities for winter sports and has not attracted more than a few groups a year from abroad.

This implies that we have been concentrating on a narrow affluent segment of the total tourist market, thereby defeating our declared objective of providing modest priced facilities.

Regional Tourism

Of the 260 million international tourist movements in 1978, more than 85 per cent were intra-regional or inter-regional (regions as defined by the World Tourism Organisation). Nearer home more than 35 per cent of visitors to the ASEAN group originate from within the region. Fifty-eight per cent of 1.2 million visitors to Malaysia are from the three neighbouring countries. There is an emerging middle class in the newly industrial countries of Asia. India has not taken any initiative in promoting regional tourism. There are four times as many visitors from tiny Sri Lanka to India as those in the reverse direction. Towards the end of 1977 the Sri Lanka government allowed its citizens a travel allowance of $ 250 for visiting India which is not adjusted against the general foreign travel allowance. There was a dramatic increase of 102 per cent in 1978 over 1977 from Sri Lanka. We have not reciprocated this gesture.

Tourists coming from Western countries bring in a new lifestyle which over a long period may affect local traditions and social mores. Besides high spending visitors sometimes also create resentment among the local people, while visitors from neighbouring countries would have a cultural affinity with us and would not have any adverse cultural and social impact. They would also be satisfied with less sophisticated and expensive facilities. However, it must be noted that while tourism from industrial countries to developing countries can continue as one way movement over a long period, as indeed it has in the post-war era, regional tourism among groups of developing countries has to be a two way street.

To promote regional tourism India should allow a separate travel allowance of not less than $ 250, not to be adjusted against the general foreign travel allowance.

How Many Tourists?

The determining factor should be : What is the optimum number for which a country can provide facilities without unduly straining its resources? For a country of the size of India and resources, 765,000 visitors in obviously not the optimum number and it seems premature to discuss this question until we have reached the figure of, say, five million. After all there are many countries with less resources which are at present catering to more than five or even ten million tourists. If we aim at the right 'mix' of all types of visitors we could assume a growth rate in the eighties of 8 to 9 per cent in arrivals totalling to two million and 12 to 15 per cent in receipts. It would be unrealistic to forecast a higher growth rate, not only because India will not be able to gear up its facilities quickly enough but because the economic growth rate of industrial countries is slowing down. So will international tourism. In 1979 global tourism increased by four per cent instead of 7 to 9 per cent increases of earlier years. While a majority of visitors to India in the foreseeable future will continue to be 'cultural' tourists, in order to reach the figure of two million we shall have a much higher proportion of holiday, regional and ethnic visitors. A dozen sea resorts, if properly planned, can absorb half a million visitors a year without damaging the environment. Goa, which offers some of the most attractive beaches in Asia, alone can take in 200,000 or more visitors a year. The immediate problem is to motivate more tourists to visit India. At present hundreds of thousands are overflying India for lack of facilities available here. The fact that their stay in India is considerably longer than in other countries which results in larger volume is mainly because of the size of the country and its varied attractions, and need not be attributed to any special efforts that we have made to improve the quality of their travel experience. Considering what they have to go through on arrival and departure at our airports, the delayed domestic flights which upset their schedules, the rickety buses and cars we provide and the lack of evening entertainment the quality has, if fact, deteriorated. That is one reason why the percentage of repeat visitors is not high.

If we aim at the right 'mix' of cultural, holiday, business, regional and ethnic visitors we could reach the figure of two million tourists by 1990 yielding Rs. 15,000-16,000 million in receipts and possibly Rs. 5,000 million in tax revenue.

Infrastructure

To meet the needs of two million visitors we would have to

improve the supply position, would have to develop the necessary infrastructure and facilities as also change some of the existing policies in regard to tourism.

(i) AIRPORTS

(*a*) The concept of an international airport building has radically changed in the last 20 years. It is longer a transit shed but an end in itself. Thousands of passengers have to spend long hours at airports to catch connecting flights or wait for delayed flights. A modern airport building has to have restaurants and bars, large shopping areas, rest rooms, money changing, post and telegraph facilities, travel agencies and car-hire services for making surface transport arrangements, technological arrangements for the quick movement of passengers and baggage and for instant reservations. The four international airports of India not only lack many of these facilities, they are also highly congested and ill-equipped for passenger and baggage handling. A modern airport building with capacity to handle 3 to 4 million disembarking, embarking, and transiting passengers a year may cost in the Indian context not less than Rs. 1250 million. The terminals at Bombay and Delhi as now planned would be inadequate by the time they are ready. There is obvious need for a new airport building in Madras and for modernisation and expansion of the Calcutta terminal. The new airport in Nairobi which opened in April, 1978 with capacity to handle four million passengers cost $ 300 million. Singapore whose present airport, one of the best in South-east Asia currently handling three million passengers annually, has announced plans for a new terminal with capacity for 12 million passengers at a cost of US $ 800 million. It is understood that Santa Cruz airport, Bombay is already handling more than two million passengers and the forecast made by the International Airports Authority of India is that the international traffic at Bombay will touch 3.3 million by 1981 and at Delhi by 1984. The amount approved for the first module of the new Palam terminal, Delhi which is not likely to be ready before 1984 is indicative of poor perspective planning. We should plan for 1990 an air terminal at Bombay for 10 million passengers, Delhi eight million, and Calcutta and Madras four million each.

Assuming the differential in costs of construction between India and Singapore the cost of these four international terminals would be close to Rs. 8,000 million.

(b) Holiday tourism generally involves series of inclusive tour groups by charters and scheduled services. A major resort needs a gateway airport within motorable distance of 50 kms. Besides the four international airports we shall need in the coming years several new gateway airports where large aircraft can land as well as take off with full payload for non-stop flights from and to Europe. This would generally mean a runway of 10,500 ft. and not 8,000 ft. Regardless of the increased capacity of Indian Airlines it is impracticable to transport 500 passengers a day from Bombay to Goa and Trivandrum. Besides, the extra cost of the domestic sector would make the price of the 'package' uncompetitive with that for resorts in Sri Lanka, Maldives, Thailand, Malaysia, Singapore etc. To start with three gateway airports for Goa, Trivandrum and Srinagar should be planned. Immigration and customs clearance would also have to be provided. The main difference between a gateway and an international airport is that the former may not have all the 5-star facilities usually available at the latter.

(c) Both from the standpoint of development and marketing our 'product' a wide dispersal of tourists is a desirable objective. This would only be possible if we were to upgrade a number of domestic airports so that jets can land there. Bhopal, Bhubaneswar, Gaya, Indore, Mysore, Jammu, Cochin, Guwahati and several other cities would be obvious choices.

The amounts earmarked for airport development at present are totally inadequate. At a rough guess the cost of the international terminals, three or four gateway airports and upgrading or building of a score of domestic airports may be as much as Rs. 12,000 million. Since international and gateway airports are foreign exchange earners it should be possible to raise the money for their development internationally, and judging from past experience they could be self-financing.

(ii) TRANSPORT

(a) Air Transport

Perhaps the most negative factor which has kept away from India a large number of prospective visitors in the last few years was the lack of capacity on Indian Airlines. It is well-known that hundreds of groups every winter have cancelled their projected visits to India for lack of confirmation of air or hotel reservations on certain sectors of their itineraries. What is generally required is to marry air seats with hotel beds on certain sectors and in certain locations months in advance, and if both the domestic carrier and the hotels are running at 90 per cent or more occupancy the marriage does not materialise. The growth of domestic air traffic in India has been 20 to 24 per cent for the last several years, and yet the Indian Airlines' proposals to buy more aircraft were kept in suspense for years. A number of new aircraft are now on order but by the time they are delivered and are in operation further growth in traffic, mainly domestic, would have overtaken much of the increased capacity. The need for a Third Airline has already been accepted. With growing industrialisation there is also a need for air-taxis which could be rented like cars on hire.

The overall air capacity should not only keep pace with growth but keep ahead of it. The tourists constitute only 17 to 18 per cent of the total traffic within India. But their demand cannot be met unless the air transport capacity keeps pace with overall traffic growth, not merely to meet tourist demand but more importantly for economic and political purposes.

(b) Surface Transport

Most foreign tourists do not travel by rail in India because the process of making reservations is almost nerve-racking. Besides the Indian Railways are really not interested in providing sophisticated facilities for passengers. One can appreciate their difficulties because more than five million people per day travel by rail, not taking into account the commuters. Nevertheless, the Indrail Pass Scheme would not have been such a flop it the railways had made satisfactory arrangements for selling tickets overseas at the point of origin. One needs the temperament of Paul Theroux, author of the hilarious modern classic, 'The Great Railway Bazaar', in order to travel by rail through India. It is not meant for the average foreign visitors.

But a large number of foreign visitors would like to travel

short distances, one to two hundred kilometres, by road because it gives them an opportunity to see the countryside. There is hardly any other country in the world which claims to be in the tourist business and yet provides such poor quality of road transport to tourist. The so-called deluxe buses run by state governments or cars on hire can at best be described as third rate compared to what the same foreign visitors are able to get in other countries.

To make up for the past deficiency the immediate need is for the importation of a few hundred buses and a few thousand cars along with provision for spare parts. Secondly, to make the state governments agree to let private operators run road transport operating specifically for tourists, foreign and domestic, on the basis of inter-state permits.

(iii) PUBLIC UTILITIES

Public Utilities like adequate water and power supply, sewage disposal, communications (post, telegraph, telephone), road and rail connections, medical aid, are essential for all tourist centres but their primary users would invariably be the local people. It would be difficult to attribute a proportionate share of the cost to tourism development. Hence they are not dealt with in this paper.

Accommodation

There are at present about 19,000 rooms in 'approved' hotels, approved for tourists in the sense that they conform to certain basic standards laid down by the Department of Tourism. There is also considerable supplementary accommodation *e.g.*, tourist bungalows, rest houses, youth hostels and unapproved hotels available for both domestic and foreign travellers.

Nonetheless, it is generally accepted that in relation to the volume of travel, it is quite insufficient, particularly in large towns and during peak periods. The official estimate five years ago was that 15,000 more hotel rooms were required to be built by 1980, at the rate of 3000 rooms per year. In fact only about half that number have been added. To cater to two million visitors by 1990 we shall need at least 25,000 more hotel rooms. Assuming that for a balanced growth of tourism we need hotels of all categories and taking into account price escalations this would require an investment of about Rs. 7000-8000 million. An investment of this order would not be forthcoming in the public sector; nor will it flow into the private sector unless sufficient incentives are given to make the profitability of hotel projects competitive with that of other industries which enjoy substantial incentives.

Incentives

Perhaps the biggest hurdle in the way of hotel development is the lack of suitable sites in large cities of India, or if they are, the cost is prohibitive, as much as 25 to 40 per cent of the total cost. Hotels are not like factories which can be, indeed have to be, built outside the towns. During the last 25 years the town planners in India have rarely considered that hotels in downtown areas fulfil a social need of the community. Delhi is a classic example of not allowing hotels to be built where they are most needed, and allotting hotel sites six miles away from the city centre.

A study prepared by Word Tourism Organisation a few years ago showed that as many as 60 counties were providing various types of incentives to the tourist industry, more specifically to hotel projects. Because of substantial incentives given to hotels in Sri Lanka, 40 per cent of the total portfolio of the Development Finance Corporation of Ceylon was claimed by hotel projects during the period 1969 to 1976. As against this hotel projects in India got only 2.8 per cent of the loans give by the Industrial Finance Corporation of India (IFCI) between 1962-1977. What is required is that hotel projects, new as well as those needing expansion or renovation, should be given the same incentives as are granted to export industries from time to time. Hotels being capital—intensive should also be given what are called 'soft loans' by the financial institutions.

Many countries provide incentives to travel agencies and transport operators as well. The travel agents play a significant role as promoters and marketeers of the entire tourist product. They should be eligible for an import entitlement on their turnover and tax reliefs so as to encourage them to plough back their profits in enlarging their capital base. Some of the leading Indian travel agencies have shown considerable enterprise in opening overseas sales offices. But they have not been given the necessary encouragement and permission to maintain these offices is given grudgingly on a yearly basis.

Incentives result in loss of revenue. What is the cost to the exchequer of incentives and cash subsidies given to what are usually called priority and export industries? Estimates ranging from Rs. 15,000 to 20,000 million a year have been given in economic journals. It is not possible to estimate the cost of comparable incentives to the tourist industry, but if at a cost of say, Rs. 150 million a year it should be possible to stimulate an investment of Rs. 8000 million it would still be a much better economic proposition than finding a major part of the money from the public exchequer.

Air Policy

According to the 1976-77 Survey of Foreign Tourism 'package' groups accounted for only 8.52 per cent of the total visitors. This must be one of the lowest figures of inclusive tour groups for a country which announced the target of one million tourists by 1980. The corresponding figure for 1976 for Sri Lanka was 62 per cent. The main reasons for this wide disparity are the different air policies of the two countries and the predominance of holiday tourism in Sri Lanka. Sri Lanka followed an open skies policy, as many small countries do, while India has always followed a more or less closed-door air policy, a more restrictive air policy than even major countries usually pursue. When we aim at numbers our marketing objectives and strategy must change correspondingly. We have to allow group movement promoted by foreign tour operators and wholesalers who generally prefer to make back to back block reservations of air seats and hotel rooms. While in the interest of the national carrier it would not be feasible, nor desirable, to follow an open skies policy, nonetheless a more liberal policy is called for. Theoretically, there is no ban on charters but in practice they are discouraged; so are the initiatives of foreign carriers to introduce bargain and basement fares on scheduled services.

The air policy would have to be considerably liberalised because Air India as a small airline can at best carry 20 to 25 per cent of the total visitors. Two million visitors would mean hundreds of extra flights and not a dozen or less charters a year, which is roughly the average at present.

Investment Policy

Including the funds required to augment the Indian Airlines fleet and to start a third airline an investment of Rs. 30,000-35,000 million will have to be made in the next five to ten years in the tourism sector. It may appear to be an excessive amount but we have to make up for the cumulative neglect of the past many years, and to regain our competitive position against other tourist destinations. If an investment of this order is beyond our resources then we should allow foreign investment. So far foreign investment in the tourism sector has not been allowed, at any rate not encouraged.

Foreign investment need not be in equity; it could be in loans from commercial banks. In fact during the last ten years in most of the less developed countries (LDCs) far more external finance has flown in from commercial sources than by way of foreign aid or from international financial institutions like the World Bank or Regional Banks. Despite a creeping recession in the industrial countries international liquidity is not low and many friendly countries in a surplus situation are seeking opportunities for safe investment with a moderate return. Export credits are also available from industrial nations to finance the purchase of aircraft and other equipment. The Indian hotel industry has a good track record but foreign investment will be attracted on easy terms only if sufficient incentives are given to the hotel sector to create a favourable climate for investment.

It is a valid assumption that the tourism sector is self-financing; hence if funds of the order of Rs. 35,000 million cannot be found from local resources, foreign investment by way of loans, not equity, on moderate terms from commercial banks and other sources should be encouraged.

The Role of the Public Sector

It is universal experience that the private sector functions more efficiently than the public sector in enterprises which provide services. The growth of tourism in Europe and North America was from the grass roots; hence the public sector neither found it necessary, nor, as a matter of policy, advisable to run tourist enterprises. In many developing countries the process had to be reversed. The initiative had to come from the top and then spread to provincial and local levels. In India even though private enterprise, hoteliers, travel agents, tour operators, came on the scene in the early fifties, the public sector had a significant role to play in opening up new areas, to blaze the trail as it were. This indeed was the *raison d'etre* for establishing a new enterprise in 1964 in the public sector for operating the existing government—owned hotels and tourist guest houses and building new ones. The other compelling reason was to provide sophisticated road transport services to the tourist as an alternative to the nationalised road transport operation. Now there are two public sector corporation at the centre, the India Tourism Development Corporation (ITDC) and the Hotel Corporation of India (HCI), a subsidiary of Air India, which between them operate nearly one-sixth of the hotel accommodation units of the country. In addition there are about 15 Tourist Development Corporations in the states. The public sector has therefore come to stay. What is debatable is whether it should continue to expand and try to attain dominance in a service industry in the same way as it has achieved in the basic industries, the 'core' sector, to use the official terminology, particularly in view of the fact that the private sector is fully equipped and is willing to take risks in the development of new resorts. The public sector can still play a very useful role as a catalyst and in providing alternatives to the consumer against exploitation. At the state and local levels, in particular, there is immence scope for the public sector to develop the tourist infrastructure and reasonably priced facilities for domestic and foreign tourists.

In the 'mixed' economy of India both the public and the private sectors have to subsist side by side. But a complete review of their respective spheres is called for. The two main responsibilities of the Government, at the centre and in the states, are to develop the infrastructure and to regulate the working of the tourist industry.

Facilitation

The word facilitation in tourism terminology has come to mean 'facilitating the arrival and departure of foreign tourists'. The phrase 'tourist' based on an economic and not motivational concept was first defined by the League of Nations in 1937. This definition was affirmed by the Economic and Social Council of United Nations in its Resolution 870 (XXXIII). The Department of Tourism publishes it statistics on the basis of this definition which runs as follows:

> A tourist is a temporary visitor staying at least 24 hours in the country visited and the purpose of whose journey can be classified under one of the following headings:

(*a*) leisure (recreation, holiday, health, study, religion and sport).

(*b*) Business, family, mission meeting.

An excursionist is a temporary visitor staying less than 24 hours in the country visited (including travellers on cruises).

This definition has never been accepted by the Government of India except for statistical purposes. For instance, a foreign visitor can enter India without a visa up to a stay of 30 days provided he is coming for 'pure' touristic purposes, which means sightseeing, holiday, recreation but not for business or to attend a conference or even to see friends and relatives, regardless of the duration of the visit. The main problem, however, it not the dichotomy of meaning but the formalities that a visitor has to undergo on arrival and departure and the methods of dealing with him.

It is often said that the first impression is a lasting impression. The first impression of 88 per cent tourists who come by air is an extremely unpleasant one. It generally takes two hours or more to clear all the passengers of a flight arriving at our international airports when, considering how small is the number of passengers our airports handle compared to European airports, is should not take more than 30 minutes. There is a 'peaking' problem faced by almost every international airport, a number of flights land or depart in quick succession at certain hours. Obviously there should be sufficient staff at peak hours.

The passport is not merely checked and stamped but the immigration officer must compare the entries in the disembarkation card with the passport. Not only that, he must also make some notations on the immigration card while the passenger is waiting. All this takes 2 to 3 minutes per passenger while it should take less than half a minute. It may take 45 minutes for the baggage to arrive. The conveyor belts being too short to carry all the baggage the passengers have to keep on running from one belt to another to identify their baggage. The dual channel system—Green channel for passengers who have nothing to declare and Red channel for the rest—which was introduced with a great flourish a year ago has turned out to be a joke. The Green channel is just a number of customs counters with a green sign and all the baggage has to be placed on them for examination in the same way as in the case of other counters shown as

Red. The passport is supposed to be examined only once by the immigration but at our airports it has to be presented to the customs as well. Apparently the two departments do not trust each other and have separate Red Books.

In the case of departing passengers most countries have abolished the customs check and the formality of filling out the embarkation card. The baggage goes straight from the airline counter to the aircraft and only the passport is checked at the immigration counter. The departure tax does not have to be paid at a separate counter but is absorbed in the price of the ticket. The departure formalities at our airports are about the same as on arrival.

Apart from the fact that the arrival and departure areas are small and not air-conditioned there are no separate exits for passengers of each departing flight. Flights are delayed because the sheer process of cleaning several hundred passengers of 2 or 3 flights through a single security exit takes an inordinately long time. The courtesy of the staff employed at airports, health, immigration, customs, security and others is not in question. In fact they try to be both courteous and helpful.

What is needed in simplification of procedures, more staff, better trained and educated, and a co-ordinated 'drill' for quick clearance of passengers and baggage. This reform does not have to wait for the new terminals which may take years to build. The International Airports Authority of India may well be entrusted with the 'Authority' to bring about the necessary co-ordination.

Manpower Development

Almost 20 years ago the Government started setting up four Institutions of Hotel Management, Catering and Nutrition in Bombay, Delhi, Calcutta and Madras. The operative part seemed to be 'Nutrition' and hence they were placed under the control of the Department of Food, Ministry of Agriculture. Subsequently 14 Foodcraft Institutions were also established. In most countries it is the Universities that run Faculties of Hotel Management and Tourism. The institutions imparting training in hotel and catering at the craft level are usually autonomous and in many developing countries are supervised by the National Tourist Organisation of the country. This unusual arrangement in India still persists even though all the persons trained by these institutions look for jobs in hotels, restaurants and catering establishments. While 20 years ago no other Asian country had established institutions for training manpower for the hospitality industry, many Asian and even African countries now have established very good institutions. The institutions in India are still going on in a routine fashion with low-paid semi-trained teaching staff. No doubt these Institutes have acquired new buildings and equipment though for lack of facilities for practical training part of the equipment remains unutilised. Because the hotels need trained personnel the graduates from these Institutes are employed by them, but they find it necessary to give them practical training for a year or two before appointing them even in supervisory positions. For historical reasons the training is still heavily oriented to food production and bakery which is evidenced by the fact that numerically the staff for food production and bakery is as much as for all the other sections *e.g.*, reception service, waiting, housekeeping and so on. The large hotel chains of India now prefer to run their own training programmes of one to two years.

In the first place the farcical arrangement of their being linked to the Ministry of Agriculture must end. What is more important is to employ two or three experienced foreign teachers for periods of one year or more in each Institute so that the teaching staff can be put through a proper course of training. Catering education was something new in India and foreign teaching staff should have been appointed right from the beginning. The Institute in Delhi employed as Principal on a two-year contract the Head of the Hotel Catering School of Portsmouth, but with our usual attitude of self-assurance his contract was terminated while the new institution was still getting over its teething troubles. The salary scales should be revised upwards and the teaching staff of indifferent quality should be weeded out. The hotel industry would be only too willing to meet the extra cost. One of the best hotel schools which can serve as a model in the Utalii Hotel School in Nairobi. It was established five years ago by a Swiss company nominated by the Swiss Government as part of bilateral aid. It started with 20 Swiss teachers and as the local teachers progressively get trained the number of Swiss teachers is being reduced.

India also needs a post-graduate Institute for Tourism Management. The services of a foreign expert, Professor Robert

McIntosh, Dean of the Faculty of Tourism and Hotel Management of Michigan University, were obtained through UNDP. He furnished a scheme to the Department of Tourism seven years ago but funds for establishing the Institute have still not been sanctioned. Meanwhile the Philippines Government three years ago obtained the services of a few foreign teachers and the Asian Institute for Tourism and Hotel Management at post-graduate level has already been established on the campus of Manila University under a Filipino as its Principal.

Good management is the key to successful tourism. What is immediately required is to place the existing Institutions under the control of the Ministry of Tourism, induct a number of experienced foreign instructors who would reorganise the courses and train the teachers. Finally, establish a post-graduate Institute for Tourism Management.

Overseas Promotion and Marketing

India has established 22 overseas Tourists Offices and Representatives, more than any other Third World country has. Even Japan has less than a dozen overseas tourist offices. What needs to be reviewed is whether all these offices are necessary or whether some of the money spent on these offices could be diverted to other channels of publicity and promotion. What also needs to be reviewed is our entire tourist marketing strategy. For instance, the US market has been on the decline for the last five years. Since 1973 the West Germans have been spending more on travel abroad than the Americans. During the same period Japan has emerged as the third largest market of the world. Last year more than four million Japanese made overseas trips. Forecasts made by reputable experts, in particular by the Economist Intelligence Unit, a subsidiary of the Economist, indicate that by 1985 West Germany will account for 18 to 19 per cent of international travel, USA about 14 to 15 per cent, Japan ten per cent, France and Britain five per cent each, Italy four per cent, Canada, Switzerland, Scandinavia, the Benelux countries, Austria and Australia one or two per cent each. The new market of the Gulf is of considerable importance to India but in the long run is likely to make a marginal difference. I doubt if we have re-allocated our limited budgetary resources in accordance with the potential of each major market.

Air India's performance has been commendable and in the last ten years it has also been emphasising India in its sales promotion. But the interests of Air India may not coincide with the interests of Indian tourism, because Air India also needs to promote other destinations to which it flies. Besides the function of the National Tourist Organisation (NTO) is image-building, of an airline or a hotel is retail selling, selling itself. It was in 1968 that overseas Government tourist offices were placed under the control of Air India to ensure a combined operation. It was an ill-advised decision because the government offices must maintain their independent identity if full co-operation and support of foreign carriers which bring in three quarters of the foreign traffic is to be secured. This does not mean that these offices should not support Air India, but supporting is one thing and merging the identity is another. It does not help Indian tourism if the Government tourist office in Frankfurt is housed in the premises of Air India.

Finally, the personnel appointed for overseas offices must be selected for their ability to communicate and adjust to foreign environment, their flair for promotion, and not because of seniority or to give representation to a caste or a community, as is the present practice. Not only foreign environment but which environment? One man may be a misfit in London but not in the States, or he may be able to communicate with the Germans but not the French. After all we carefully select the personnel for the foreign service out of the total IAS list. Why not apply the same considerations to the foreign service in tourism?

The overseas Government tourist offices should be delinked from Air India, revert to *status quo ante* and maintain an independent identity. It would also be advisable to engage the services of one or more tourism experts to make an overall assessment and advise the Government on the structure, location and personnel of its overseas tourist offices and its future marketing programme.

Domestic Tourism

Domestic tourism in India reminds one of Mark Twain's comment on the weather: Everyone talks about it but no one does anything about it. Its sheer size in India defies measurement. How can you do anything meaningful about something whose dimensions are not known? Ten million people travel daily by rail and road. How many of them can be defined as tourists? Five million pilgrims are reported to have visited Ardh Kumbh; Tirupathi Devasthanam's takings last year amounted to Rs. 6,500 million. Domestic tourism moves on its self-generating momentum.

A policy decision was taken at the time of framing the Second Plan in 1956 that domestic tourism would be primarily the responsibility of the state governments. Considering the limited human and material resources of the Department of Tourism it was, and still remains, a sensible decision. The centre can at best act as a catalyst. That is not to say that domestic tourism is not important. It is, because it provides a base for the edifice of tourism. Because of the wide disparity of incomes the foreign and domestic tourists may need different types of facilities but no resort can subsist on foreign tourists alone. Kashmir Valley does not hum with activity in the summer because of 55,000 foreign tourists but because of the much larger influx of 550,000 Indian visitors. The same is true of Khajuraho, Goa, Ellora, Ajanta and so on.

The immediate approach could be to promote the orgainsed sector of domestic tourism consisting of all those who are entitled to paid holidays: civil servants, employees of public and private sector companies and offices. Their number alone would be close to 40 million out of the 225 million adult work force of the country. The law should be amended so that leave travel allowance to private sector employees becomes tax-deductible for travel to any place and not only to their home town/village, as is the case at present.

This approach may be objected to on the grounds that it favours the somewhat privileged section of the community and not the weakest sections. Idealistically the objection is valid, but in the given circumstances, to start with the organised sector seems to be the only practical approach.

Co-ordination

In no country can tourism be promoted and developed by the government alone; it has to be a joint effort by the government and the industry, particularly in developing countries. Nor within the framework of each government can the official tourism organisation (NTO) do it alone. Tourism permeates so many activities in the public and private sectors that several governmental agencies have to become involved in its development. Hence the need for co-ordination. In a country with a federal structure co-ordination is also necessary between the centre and the states. Over the last 30 years various countries have experimented with evolving co-ordination machinery, suited to their genius and administrative systems. In India more than 20 years ago, a Tourism Development Council on which the centre, the states and the industry were represented was set up. Later a Cabinet sub-Committee was set up for a brief period and also a Secretaries Committee which functioned quite effectively.

The Estimates Committee of Parliament while examining this problem came to the conclusion that the present organisational set-up of the Department of Tourism was not attuned to developing tourism. It suggested that "an effective and efficient Central Organisation has to be set up to formulate well thought-out proposals and policies for the development of tourism in the country with proper co-ordination and liaison between the central organisation, the state tourist organisations and the business community involved." In 1969 the Minister of Tourism asked the Indian Institute of Public Administration (IIPA) to make a Management Survey of the Department of Tourism. The IIPA in an elaborate report submitted in July 1970 recommended "the creation of an independent tourism organisation under a Tourism Board which would have autonomy of operation but its Chief Executive with top professional competence would retain the rank of Secretary in the Ministry of Tourism and Civil Aviation to handle co-ordination with Ministries of the Government of India and with State Governments, ensuring thereby that the incumbent has both sufficient flexibility, and the authority vested in him." This problem was also referred to a UNDP team which made an extensive report on Tourism in India in 1969-70. The team suggested that an autonomous National Tourism Commission with wide financial powers be established. Apparently, a Tourist Board but only with advisory functions was appointed. Over the years the Tourism Development Council, the Secretaries Committee, the Tourist Board have all lapsed. Now there is no co-ordinating machinery.

The situation has changed and the solution of yester-years may not prove effective today. But the need for co-ordination still exists. What matters is that the co-ordinating body must have leverage in the government. Regardless of whether an autonomous organisation is created or not what is equally important is that the Department of Tourism with the present hierarchical structure is restructured to make it more functional.

Consumer Preference

The Consumer is King. The product is fashioned to meet his wants and preferences. However, tourism is different from other export activities because the consumer of the goods and services comes to the exporting country rather than goods and services being delivered to him at home. Thus personal contacts are established between the visitors and the local people. The consumer preference may therefore have to be balanced against national traditions and goals. The visitors may want to indulge in gambling in a casino or visit a massage parlour, sometime a euphemism for other activities. If this runs counter to the national ethic the consumer preference may have to be ignored. No country need have tourists entirely on their terms; on the other hand no country should impose its own values or fads on foreign visitors. Prohibition is only one example of this. Knowing that more than two-thirds occupancy in 5- and 4-star hotels is by foreign guests, it was a display of insensitivity to close the bars in these hotels for almost three 'Dry' days in a week. A more subtle aspect of disregard of their preferences is not to provide them with the type of food they are used to or the entertainment they can enjoy.

Food habits are ingrained and so is the taste for music, dance and other performing arts. It is not easy for anyone to appreciate dance or music in a foreign idiom. Many of us find the finest opera in Europe a refined form of torture, though we may not like to admit it, or having spent $ 30 on a ticket we may not like to leave the show after the interval. A foreign visitor during a two weeks stay may like to sample Indian food but he can not eat it all the time. He finds it hot, greasy and monotonous. This is also linked up with the problem of gastro-enteric upsets among visitors, a problem that we generally like to push under the carpet and not talk about. The problem is not peculiar to India but the incidence of 'tummy upsets' is sufficiently high to have become a deterrent to visiting India. Mexico, where the incidence of tummy upsets among tourists is also quite high, used to dismiss it as a joke, 'Montezuma's Revenge'. But now considerable medical research has been undertaken and many new health measures have been enforced.

The stress of sightseeing day after day, change of environment and climate may be contributory causes but the importance of serving the foods that the tourist is used to and the observance of strict hygienic standards in our catering establishments cannot be too strongly emphasised.

The only form of entertainment available all the time in Indian cities is the Indian films. In the absence of subtitles in foreign languages the tourist cannot appreciate them even if he chooses to see them. We have no regular theatres for visual forms of entertainment—dance, ballet, opera, for which the passing visitor can make advance reservations or buy a ticket on arrival at a day's notice. The usual recourse for his travel agent is to include the Sound and Light show at the Red Fort in his itinerary (which is why I installed it in 1964). But one need have no illusions that *Son et Lumiere* is after all 'canned' entertainment, not meant to be artistic.

This situation prevails in most of the Asian and African cities. Consequently most hotels provide a variety of entertainment, both national and Western, the latter being more universal. The Indian hotels as a rule do not for several reasons. First, the best visual form of Indian entertainment *e.g.*, dance, is almost entirely classical, and no first rate dancer would be willing to perform in a hotel while guests are eating and drinking. We have not quite evolved light entertainment which is sophisticated and artistic and acceptable to foreign audiences. Secondly, heavy entertainment taxes have been levied by many state government on all forms of entertainment in hotels. Thirdly, the import of first rate foreign artistes has not been allowed for years because of restrictions on foreign exchange and work permits.

So what do the 70 per cent visitors to India who mainly come for sightseeing do in the evenings? They sit in their rooms and drink or can be seen in hotel lobbies bored to tears. While tourist expenditure on shopping in India is one of the highest in the world, on entertainment it is one of the lowest, almost negligible.

Tourism and Environment

Modern tourism has often been blamed for causing environmental damage. In the context of tourism it is an omnibus phrase which embodies not only pollution but also distortions of local land- scape or native cultural and social traditions. Miami Beach, Waikiki Beach (Hawaii) Torremolinos and Costa Brava (Spain) are often quoted as examples of damage to the landscape caused by mass tourism. It is true that uncontrolled construction of high rise hotels and condominiums has ruined the landscape of several areas Pattaya in Thailand is an example of how a sea resort should not be developed. Fortunately for the last few years there is far greater awareness of the relationship between tourism and environment. The Ceylon Tourist Board have made a rule that no hotel building on the seaside shall rise above the coconut treetops, which is another way of saying that the maximum height of hotel buildings shall be about 35 ft. It is now an accepted concept that tourism planning should not be treated as *sui generis* but as an integral part of overall physical and economic planning. Some of the new resorts *e.g.*, Phuket Island in Thailand, Sentosa, an offshore island of Singapore and Puerto Azul near Manila exemplify this concept. Tourism in many countries has heightened the awareness of the local people of the value of their own heritage.

Tourism is the modern version of interaction between different cultures but its scope and effect have been exaggerated. Tourists tend to be highly concentrated in a local or regional centre of attraction rather than spread throughout the host country. Tourist resorts in the Third World have frequently been created in the form of semi-isolated ghettos. The process of acculturation, which means that when two cultures come into contact for considerable duration each becomes somewhat like the other, takes place only in places like the Caribbean where tourists outnumber the entire local population; in the Bahamas and Bermuda in the ratio of eight to one. But in practice the host societies have been influenced far more than the visitors. It may have similar effects in Seychelles, Maldives, Bali and South Pacific islands when tourism develops on a mass scale. But considering the size of India and its population, 800,000 tourists hardly present any such danger, nor for that matter two million by 1990. Besides, countries like India with a well-entrenched cultural tradition are much less vulnerable to the social and cultural impact of tourists coming from highly industrialised societies than those with a weak social and cultural fabric or primitive communities.

This is not to underestimate the value of planned growth of tourism. It is of utmost importance that we should adopt all the necessary measures to ensure that tourism does not spoil the landscape or disrupt the local traditions of new areas like Ladakh and other parts of the Himalayas. But we should be far more aware of the immense damage that has been caused to our lakes, rivers and forests by industrial waste and uncontrolled urbanisation. The Dal Lake in Srinagar was 10.5 sq. miles in 1907 and now it is 10 sq. kms. It has been mainly damaged by encroachments, lack of sewage disposal and past neglect on the part of local authorities. The rejuvenation of Dal Lake will cost several million dollars according to the findings of an Expert Committee which surveyed the lake two years ago or else in 25 years from now it may be a memory or a bygone era. The point to drive home is that relatively small investments in prevention at an early stage are more effective than subsequent remedial actions which are inevitably highly expensive. What is required is that for all new projects environmental experts should be associated in the selection of sites and provision of safeguards against pollution which should be built into each development project. The cost of preventive measures is not likely to be more than one to three per cent and should therefore be acceptable to promoters and to the governments of developing countries. In pursuance of this philosophy the World Bank is the first lending agency which has started screening new development projects for their environmental and health implications. The post of Environmental Adviser has since been expanded into the Office of Environment and Health Affairs (OEHA) in the World Bank. It is suggested that the Indian financial institutions like IFCI, ICICI, IDBI, LIC and so on should also scrutinise industrial and other development projects in the same way as OEHA is doing in the World Bank.

The major problem therefore is not tourism but the conflict between industrial development and concern for environment. How else can one explain the location of a giant refinery at Mathura and not somewhere else away from Agra or the Silent Valley project or for that matter many others all over the country?

Conclusion

While reliable statistics for the last 25 years of visitor arrivals and breakdown by nationality, age, sex, points of entry and so on are available, there is considerable lack of economic data on tourism. Forecasts of arrivals, foreign exchange receipts and tax revenue in this paper, therefore, are based on past trends in the seventies, the economic conditions likely to prevail in the main tourist generating countries and the capability of the Indian administrative machinery for expansion of the tourist infrastructure and managing its growth. The assumption of 15 per cent annual growth rate in arrivals made by the Ministry of Tourism is not likely to be realised, not only because of the above mentioned factors but also because the percentage growth rate must decline as the base of Indian tourism widens. For lack of economic data estimates of employment, direct and induced, generated by tourism and its contribution to the Gross Domestic Product have not been worked out.

6

Tourism Promotion : State and Regional Perspective

State Tourism : A Background

Different states are being advised to co-operate with one another in mapping out places of interest which could attract foreign tourists and present the group circuit to the tourism ministry which in turn would publicise this through Indian diplomatic missions abroad. This process would help states to cut down on expenditure to project tourist attractions in their states alone. Besides, it would help travel and tour operators in India and abroad to offer foreign tourists a choice of circuits in groups of states in different parts of India. This was the main thrust of the two-day state tourism ministers conference held in New Delhi late last year. In addition, all states which have not yet declared tourism as an industry are being encouraged to do so in recognition of the fact that tourism is the biggest money-spinner with the largest, employment potential.

Some seven or eight years ago, there was a proposal that the central tourism ministry would help states project abroad their tourist attractions. However, that never got off the ground. Now, the modification is that instead of 'selling' any one single state, it would be a group of states that would be projected as potential sites for visits by foreign tourists, be they in the realm of wildlife, temples and monuments or adventure skiing, rock climbing, surfing and hang-gliding.

Foreign tourists arrival during the first six months of the current year was 9.38 lakh, up by 19.5 per cent compared to the same period last year. Foreign exchange earnings during this period touched Rs. 2,313 crore. In terms of dollars the increase was about 21.5 per cent.

Addressing a meeting of the Parliamentary Consultative Committee attached to his Ministry, Minister for Tourism and Civil Aviation had said there had also been an impressive growth of charter flights to India. During the first six months of the previous years, 534 tourist charters were received as against 605 charters received during 1993. The Minister informed the committee that the endeavour was to attract five million tourists by the turn of the century. He, however, admitted it would not be easy to achieve this target unless transport and tourism infrastructure was improved and better facilities created for tourists with active co-operation of State Governments. Tourism had already been declared as a priority sector for foreign investment and proposals for foreign equity amounting to Rs. 720 crores have already been cleared by the Government. It had been decided to take up vigorous joint promotion in the overseas markets by the Department of Tourism, Air India and Indian Airlines. It had also been decided that Air India give a push to promotional tourism where the Department of Tourism had not set up its offices and *vice-versa.*

As regards aviation, it has been stated that the entire Vayudoot operations had been pulled out from other parts of the country to concentrate its operations only in the North-Eastern region. 12 airports being developed as model airports would be ready for operation by December next year.

Industry States

All States and Union Territories of India are expected to give industry status to tourism, thereby catalysing development of tourism infrastructure. At present, 14 States treat tourism as an industry. According to a survey conducted by Top Tourism Bulletin, a new magazine launched in New Delhi recently, foreign and private investment aggregating to Rs. 500 crore is expected to flow into the tourism infrastructure over the next few years. The projects include new hotels, recreation centres and transportation facilities.

Other measure in the offing include free and concessional availability of land for the development of remote tourists resorts, leasing out small islands around Lakshadweep for tourism and the unhindered movement of tourist coaches throughout the country. More attention should be paid to domestic tourism while the quest to increase the country's share in international tourist traffic continues, former Prime Minister P.V. Narasimha Rao told tour operators, hoteliers and airlines executives at a national travel convention recently. Opening the 11th annual convention. of the Indian Association of Tour Operators (IATO) at Vigyan Bhavan, Mr. Narasimha Rao said that it was good to woo foreign tourists but equally important was inland tourism as people needed to know more about their own country. To revive interest in domestic tourism, Mr. Narasimha Rao suggested that the tourism and other Ministries should draw up action plans for boosting student travel and pilgrim tourism. The tourism and travel industry should speedily build up infrastructure for promoting all categories of tourists in the country if India has to get its rightful share in the world tourism traffic, he said, adding that it was time "we give a fillip to domestic tourism which has not been receiving the right attention. The opening ceremony of the three-day convention was attended by then Union Civil Aviation and Tourism Minister and Minister of State for Tourism, besides several other dignitaries. The convention's theme was "Indian tourism-challenges ahead".

The concerned Minister reaffirmed the Government's full support to IATO, and asked the industry to maintain quality standards and "see tourists not just in terms of money but in terms of human values." He also said, "We must see that the tourist comes to our country as a guest and leaves as a friend," pointing out that the Government had taken various measures in the past to ensure that tourism became a major economic activity.

The IATO, president urged the Prime Minister to give the tourism industry the status of an "exporter". He said that the tourism industry should also get the same benefits as enjoyed by the exporters. It was because of the tour operators that there was so much trade in items like gems, jewellery, carpets, etc. Several sessions on different issues of the tourism industry, held during the convention worked to evolve a strategy to take up the challenges the country faced in this sector. Emphasising the need to promote domestic tourism, the former Prime Minister said that travelling to various parts of the country and understanding its diverse culture was the best way to have national integration. Mr. Narasimha Rao said to the industry that they must keep in mind that the benefits of liberalisation, of which they had also been beneficiaries. They should also go to the people living in areas where their projects were coming up. "You cannot have an island of affluence in a sea of poverty. You must think of this too. The benefits must flow to the people", he said. According to him, tourism was one industry which had both social and economic benefits. Learning about the cultural diversities and lifestyles of different people helped in promoting international brotherhood among the millions who travel all over the world really build up an ethos of integration and relations. On the domestic side special attention should be paid to provide a more sophisticated ways, like chartered flights, for pilgrims. He called upon tourism planners to tap traffic from Buddhist countries like Sri Lanka to revive the centres of Buddhist tourism. Tourism promotion did not mean just providing "creature comforts", but providing a truly distinctive cultural feel of the country to foreign tourists.

The tourism industry should also consider projecting different areas to be developed as tourists destinations for people with different motivations, as some may come for religious reasons of for cultural or scholastic reasons. "Creature comforts" like good hotels were not all that the industry should concentrate upon because these were the same all over the world. India's famous fairs, its festivals and the bazaars which generated in enormous amount to the economy should be revealed to the tourist.

The meeting was taking place about ten days after another travel industry meet, which was described by its organisers as an exhibition. That show, known as the ITE, according to the captains of the industry, did not have many buyers as participants. Infact, president of the Indian Association of Tour Operators (IATO) who had given his support to the ITE, when asked said, "the organisers had promised a lot but they could not deliver. I was totally dissatisfied with the ITE show." In fact, many participants at the ITE show are planning to sue the organisers. One such angry participant is the Tourism Authority of Thailand. TAT's presentatives, MS Vasudhra Sondhi and Ms Nidhi Sharma said, "We did no business—there were no buyers, we just kept on distributing pamphlets to people, including women and children, who looked like as if they were on a picnic." Similarly, the representative of the Israel Tourism Ministry was also said to be very upset with the show. Meanwhile, soon after the inauguration of South Asia Travel and

Tourism Exchange (SATTE) by the Union Civil Aviation and Tourism Minister, business sessions would be organised for both buyers and sellers on what India could offer as a destination to foreign tourists. A large participation of international tour operators, some of them coming for the first time, shows their keen interest in India as a destination, and this is the time to diversify and sell new packages and themes. The idea of SATTE was catching up worldwide, like similar international travel trade meets. "Instead of going abroad," he said, "Indian buyers and sellers can now do business in the country itself and an added advantage is that the foreign buyers can feel the country and see its rich culture themselves. So far, our hotels in winters are full as foreign tourists generally arrive during that period, and during summers, our hotels are empty. The Indian participants at SATTE will attempt to offer good packages and incentives to woo foreign tourists even in summers".

In the experts' opinion, the Government should replace the word "tourist" with a better word "visitor" as was the practice in many countries. "This way, you get a clear picture of how many foreign visitors come to India every year.

State Tourism Ministers Conference

The States Tourism Minsters' conference, which was held in New Delhi in mid-95, decided to set up regional tourism boards to identify regional travel circuits to boost tourism in the States. The regional directors of the Department of Tourism will be the nodal officers for such boards. Infrastructure development in the States and intensive promotion in overseas markets would be concentrated on these identified travel circuits. The Tourism Ministers' conference emphasised the need for promoting massive foreign and domestic private investment to develop tourism infrastructure. The Department of Tourism, as a nodal agency, will be establishing an "investment cell" at the Centre to help publicise the investment plans of various State Governments. The campaign will be publicised through advertisements in overseas and domestic markets and communications through Indian missions abroad, Air India offices, India Investment Centres and offices of the Department of Tourism. The States have been asked to submit their "tourism master plans" and investment schemes to the Centre within a month's time, so that a campaign strategy can be evolved.

Cultural and Heritage Aspects

One of the highlights of the Tourism Ministers' conference was due importance to be given by the State Governments to develop pilgrimage, cultural and heritage aspects of State Tourism products. The Ministry of Railways has been requested to connect and establish rail links between various important pilgrim centres throughout the country. The meeting felt that one of the major irritants in inter-regional tourism promotion is the multiple tax structure for surface transport in various States. As such, it has been decided, in the first phase, to constitute a committee under the aegis of surface transport ministry consisting of representatives from the Department of Tourism and the State Governments of Tamil Nadu, Karnataka, Andhra Pradesh and Kerala, to finalise methods and ways and means for introduction of single-point tax collection for tourists coaches to help free flow of tourist movements in southern States. Recommendations of this committee will form the basis for similar procedure to be adopted by other States.

The State Tourism Ministers' conference, which was attended by representatives of almost all the States, including 16 Tourism Ministers, passed unanimously 13 resolutions to help forge a "united effort" to boost tourism in the country. One of the resolutions said that a few State Governments which had not yet declared tourism as an industry, may do so immediately and all the concessions and incentives provided to the industrial sector would also be extended to the tourism sector.

Foreign Participation

The $ 1.5 billion France-based Club Med is soon setting up its sales and marketing networks in India. The company which offers self-sufficient 'villages' for tourists worldwide is also planning to open its resorts in the country. According to the country manager—India of Club Med, the company at present is scouting for local partners to open four to five resorts in the country. While project details are yet to be ironed out, the company expects an investment of well over Rs. 150 crore for each resort. But before it caters to the inbound tourists, it is all set to tap the outbound tourists. What the company has in mind is not just to cater to the family or to honeymoon couples but also cater to the burgeoning Indian corporate sector. "We are aiming at the upper middle class like expatriates and corporate executives," the executive clarified. The company definitely sees a big potential market for outbound tourists that has surfaced with the new foreign exchange policy. Club Med's optimism reflects in the fact that it plans to seek the patronage of domestic tourists in India.

In the Asia-Pacific region, Club Med manages 12 resorts and has sales and marketing offices in the main markets in this region. Its destinations include Phuket (Thailand), Cherating (Malaysia), Bali (Indonesia), Male (Maldives), Mauritius and Lindeman Islands (Australia). To further its presence in this region, the company has chalked out plans not only to open resorts in India but also in Burma, China, Indonesia, Japan and Vietnam through joint ventures. The company boasts of introducing the most eco-friendly technology in its new projects. In fact, the company endorsed the World Tourism and Travel Council Environmental guidelines in 1993. It may be pointed out that the company is one of the largest resort chains to enter tourism business in India. The company was originally a non-profit organisation formed to give young people an opportunity to enjoy relaxation and sports activities and to promote cultural exchanges between people of different classes and nationalities. After 44 years the company has now more than 105 resorts worldwide. Club Med has now become an international company which is listed on the stock exchanges in Paris, New York and Luxembourg. Club Med resorts offer the same village concepts worldwide. This includes access to and diverse range of activities from sports and entertainment to theatre, dicotheques, planned excursions and trips.

The company offers an assortment of marine sports like scuba diving and snorkeling. Members are also provided access to archery facilities, tennis courts and many other facilities.

Heritage Development

The scheme of converting old properties like forts, palaces, castles and *havelies* into tourist hotels without changing the peculiar individual character and maintaining the architectural ambience and decor was launched by the Union Tourism Ministry in 1991. This was done not only to increase the tourist accommodation, keeping in view the new-found interest of tourists in India, to protect vintage properties, lying dialapidated and ruined and thereby conserve the rich cultural heritage inherent in old-world charm. Further, since the owners of these palatial mansions do not have sufficient money for the maintenance and renovation of these properties, the Centre decided to provide capital investment subsidy on these. The various benefits include, among others, income tax concessions under the Income Tax Act and priority consideration for its various requirements like telephone, telex and LPG etcetera.

Unfortunately, for a scheme which was launched with much fanfare and envisaged to have bright prospects, it has found few takers. The response of different states has not been very promising. The result—despite India being studded with countless magnificent forts and palaces, four years later, we have only 29 "heritage hotels", for that is what these tourists resorts are called. Except for Rajasthan that boasts of having 18 heritage hotels approved by the Government of India, momentum is lacking in other states. Some states are still in the process of recognising such properties while others have decided not to pay any attention to the matter. So far, 25 such properties have been recognised in Himachal Pradesh and 52 in Orissa. In Gujarat, four palaces have been approved for conversion into heritage hotels. The state of Jammu and Kashmir is not paying enough attention to this proposal for obvious reasons and in Punjab nothing has come up as yet due to either "lack of interest or communication"—someting that Deputy Director General, Department of Tourism, Government of India, disagrees with. Says he, "This proposal was discussed with FHRA (Federation of Hotels and Restaurant Association) at the time of its launch and was well covered by the national press. There are many favourable factors which worked towards its success in Rajasthan," he adds, pointing out how Rajasthan is dotted with a large number of such heritage properties and a good tourist inflow.

But then, even other states are well endowed with such properties and this argument cannot be agreed upon fully. The official further comments: "In any case, private properties have to come forward, as it is the owners who are the active participators. The government merely has to assist." Behind the good response shown by Rajasthan lies some hard work done by the Rajasthan Tourism Development Corporation. According to the Tourism Secretary of Rajasthan, information was disseminated through a number of booklets pamphlets, magazines and directories which were distribuied among travel agents and tour operators. "Of late, we have also produced a CD which provides information about heritage hotels, including the kind of menu offered Tourism is an important sector in Rajasthan and one out of every three tourists come to this State. We give priority to tourism as we do not have any other sectors for earning revenue like commerce and industry, as is the case with other states," he explained. "Incidentally, this kind of thing was going on in Rajasthan much before this scheme was launched. Initially the owners of *havelies* and *thikanas* used to keep tourists as paying, guests. The first impetus to this came from the palaces of Jodhpur and Jaipur that were developed into hotels in collabora- tion with big industrial houses like Tata and ITC in the seventies. Tourism has been a great hit with foreign tourists, now they are interested in living the lifestyles of common men".

Development Dilemma : The Case of Mussoorie

Can the tourists' romance with the "queen of hills" be saved from turning into a sour experience in the wake of frequent power failure, scarcity of potable water and haphazard construction boom? This question casts a shadow over the serenity and charm of Mussoorie. The number of tourists in 1995 registered a decrease despite the oppressive heat wave lashing the plains. Admitting this, secretary of the Mussoorie Hotels Association said that the basic infrastructure of roads, water and power is the same as was made by the Britishers about nearly half a century ago. Moreover, the hotel construction boom in the recent years has caused haphazard growth of the town. He added some of the entrepreneurs were merely interested in usurping the subsidy which the State Government provided to them for constructing hotels. Some of them later sold these hotels which were constructed without keeping in mind the economic viability and town planning.

The water supply was transferred from the Municipal Board to the Garhwal Jal Sansthan. The Sansthan failed to tap new water sources to augment the current inadequate water supply but continued to charge bills on the basis of minimum charges irrespective of the fact that the required quantity was seldom supplied. Similarly, the power substation, supplying electricity to the town, was not upgraded despite substantial increase in demand. To cap it all, people have accused the UP Electricity Board staff of highhandedness. Some residents complained about the encroachments on the roads of the town, particularly the Mall Road (The Mall) which used to be the pride of the city. These dwellers and hawkers get away by paying a petty amount to the Municipal Board. A large number of Tibetans also occupy stretches of this road. The residents of the town also complain about the callous attitude of the Mussoorie Dehradun Development Authority (MDDA). Though this regulating agency corners enough money from the town on account of development charges and compounding fee it has not contributed to its development except for constructing a parking lot and a lake on the outskirts of the city. According to a member of the Municipal Board, the number of hawkers increased since the elected board came into being. He said that the Board used to have 154 sweepers in 1950 when 1,30,000 tourists visited Mussoorie in a year. The number of tourists has gone up to 20 lakh but the strength of the sweeper remains the same and 50 per cent of them do not work at all.

The abolition of toll tax during a particular government dealt a blow to the income and resources of the Board. It used to collect about 40 lakh per annum as toll tax. Now it has to depend on the irregular grant from the State Government. It was admitted that 90 per cent income of the board goes to meet the salary bill. Regarding water supply, the Jan Nigam was responsible for water providing the infrastructure for the water supply while the Garhwal Jal Sansthan is a service body. In the absence of these two bodies the consumer suffers. Besides the State Government treats the Mussoorie Municipal Board at par with the Chutmalpur Municipal Board in Saharanpur district on the basis of population. Though, it used to be recognised as the 'A' class municipality, due to its special character, it is now treated a 'C' class Board. He said if the town has to retain its charm, the State Government or its agencies should undertake housing construction activities in Mussoorie and ban private construction besides solving the water and parking problem. An environmentalist opined that proper management of tourist traffic should be undertaken. He said the town should be permitted to develop in accordance with the carrying capacity. He alleged the authorities were complacent. Talking about the decrease in the number of tourists during the last summer season, he said that certain basic amenities must be provided and Mussoorie should be developed as gateway to Garhwal tourism.

The Rotary Club has come forward to help in solving civic problems. Recently, the Rotary district governor dedicated a scheme to bring water to three hamlets within the limits of the town. Talking about the ambitious project, secretary of the Rotary Club of Mussoorie said 8,000 feet-long pipeline was laid to take water to three hamlets from the spring at the cost of Rs. 60,000.

"Up Air", a private airline supported by the State Government, would give the much-needed boost to tourism, especially in the hill regions, With an investment of over Rs. 100 crore. Tourist places like the Jim Corbett National Park, Dhudwa National Park, Kumaon and Garhwal hills and Buddhist religious places like Kushinagar will now be more accessible. The airline has already procured three 52-seater Fokker aircraft and will initially have flights to the Himalayas in Up-Pantnagar, Pithoragarh, Dehradun, Delhi-Agra-Lucknow sector and the Buddhist Gorakhpur and Kushinagar circuit.

The State Government will provide all infrastructual support of building airstrips and other logistic facilities and will get one per cent share out of the total earnings of the company. The tourism department is planning to introduce the flight bookings into the computerisation network of major hotels and other agencies "to make it more accessible and make it a part of the package tours." The tourism department is giving top priority to develop the Buddhist circuit.

Himachal Pradesh

The Himachal Pradesh Government has expressed its unhappiness over the "step-motherly" treatment being meted out to the State as far as development of tourism is concerned. Tourists are visiting Himachal Pradesh in large numbers because of prevailing situation in Jammu and Kashmir. But, the Central Tourism Ministry is not helping the State to develop and tap the potential available here. Recently Chief Minister Virbhadra Singh told a senior mediaperson that during the first five plans, the State was completely ignored. No financial or other type of aid was given to Himachal Pradesh. As a result, the tourism potential has not been fully exploited. During this last tenure as Chief Minister, Mr. Virbhadra Singh said be tried to persuade the Centre for increased aid. Though the State got some financial assistance for specific tourism-related projects, that was not enough to attract tourists in large numbers. "Whatever tourists we are getting is because of the facilities created by the State Government," he added.

Citing an example of discouraging tourism, Mr. Virbhadra Singh stated that the Centre had withdrawn the Vayudoot facility to Shimla giving a setback to tourism. "The Centre, on the other hand should give subsidy on air travel as is being given to passengers going to Kashmir or North-Eastern regions," he emphasised. The Chief Minister said that the Government was planning to introduce helicopter services in different parts of the State in a bid to promote tourism and the department could be a big revenue earner. Mr. Virbhadra Singh, who has ambitious plans for promoting tourism, expressed anguish at the Centre for not developing the railway network in the State. "Not even an inch of railway line has been laid in the State since Independence," he pointed out. He demanded immediate laying of broad gauge lines on the routes where feasibility reports had been completed so that more and more people could come to the State. "The Railways will also help in transporting goods and lessen pressure on roads," he added.

The Chief Minister clarified that his Government's policy was to promote tourism through the private sector. He said that the Tourism Corporation and the Tourism Department would help in exploring new areas of tourism and build infrastructure there so that more and more private parties could be attracted to set up facilities in those areas. The State Government is keen to promote adventure, cultural and religious tourism. The State Government has decided to bid for Asian winter sports meet near Manali in the next few years. It has been decided to set up a few ropeways for the benefit of tourists going to different parts of the State.

Mr. Virbhadra Singh plans to fully exploit the vast tourism potential in the State and hopes that the Centre will come forward to assist him in this direction.

Tourist Flow to Nepal

There is a considerable decline in the inflow of foreign and

Indian tourists to Nepal. Nepal's law and order situation has already affected the tourist sector. Communists agitation in 1993 has had an adverse impact on the arrival of the foreign as well as Indian tourists, and the trend continued unabated this year also. Earlier, tourism industry used to be the number one revenue-earning industry in Nepal, but it has been relegated to second spot as carpet industry reigns supreme these days. Government failure to remove the insecurity complex from the mind of tourists severely affected this sector. Another reason is the Nepalese Government's decision to raise the visa fee. Naturally, tourist strongly resented such measure keeping in mind the lack of infrastructure facilities, lack of cleanliness in the Capital and pollution, etc. The Government had doubled the visa fee from $20 to $40 which came into effect from September, 1993. There is no space for small-income tourists in Nepal who mainly come from India. Cheap lodgings are a matter of the past. Even the pilgrims who come to have the *darshan* of Lord Pashupatinath are facing immense problems. In 1993, total number of Indian tourists who visited Nepal was 83,632 whereas foreign tourists formed major chunk of overall arrivals—2,10,205. According to sources, 26,033 Indian tourists reached Nepal during January-April 1994.

In spite of all these nagging problems, casinos are doing a brisk business in Kathmandu and other cities. Casinos in Soaltee Oberoi, Everest Yak and Yeti and Annupurna have been major attractions for well-off Indian businessmen who come to spend their easy-earned money. These Indians confine themselves to these cations and keep gambling throughout the nights. Earlier there used to be only one casino in Soaltee Oberoi but now three more licences have been issued by the Government and roaring business is being done in these casinos which had been estimated to be around Rs. 500 to Rs. 600 crore every year. Roual Nepal Airlines operates many week-end flights between Bombay and Kathmandu which is quite popular amongst Indian businessmen because they can come on Friday and return to their work on Monday. The Director General, Tourism Department, told this author that they are planning traditional type of the infrastructure for the tourists including trekking, river rafting and mountaineering. He said, "We had planned to preserve the heritage sites in Kathmandu which could form the centre of attraction for the foreign tourists."

Karnataka

Ten tourism promotion projects totalling Rs. 4 crores have been sanctioned for Karnataka by the Centre, for 1994-95. Speaking to mediapersons at the seminar on Tourism for Economic Growth, in the city on Thursday, Union Minister of State for Tourism and Karnataka Tourism Director said these projects included sound and light programmes at Basava Kalyan, Srirangapatna and tourist complexes at Aihole, Patadkal. Basavakalyan and Karwar. Under the equity scheme, an elephant safari will be started at Mathaudi. Two 52-bed Yatrinivas (tourist hostels) would be set up at Dharwad and Gulabarga at a cost of Rs. 50 lakhs each. Such hostels had also been approved for Hanumanthnagar in Mandya district and Sabdatti and construction had already commenced. Rs. 37 lakhs had been allocated for developing the Bangalore golf course and Rs. 30 lakhs for the golf course at Mysore. Of these Rs. 10 lakhs each had already been released and work was underway. The Minister pointed out that Karnataka's share for tourism had been increased from Rs. 1.7 crores in 1993-94 to Rs. 4 crores in 1994-95.

Inaugurating the seminar organised by Associated Chambers of Commerce and Industry of India (ASSOCHAM) and Greater Mysore Chamber of Industry (GMCI), the Minister for Tourism observed that despite the thrust given to tourism in the recent years by the Government, the situation was far from satisfactory. There was an immediate need to develop infrastructure, place greater emphasis on cleanliness and revamp work culture for attracting more tourists into the country. She expressed regret that foreign tourists balked at bringing their families to India due to the unhygienic conditions they experienced here. She said that despite several incentives—like subsidy on loans for three-star hotels set up in places other than the four metros, capital subsidy for heritage hotels, income tax and expenditure tax exemptions for hotels in rural areas and pilgrimage centres—the industry was still clamouring for more incentives and subsidies "No industry can ever survive on incentives and subsidies. The industry should be able to make reasonable return on investment without Government assistance to sustain their operations," she said. She also expressed concern over the unwillingness of the private sector to move away from major cities and open up new areas for tourism and said it was an unhealthy trend.

Non-availability of land at reasonable rates was often being mentioned as a major constraint in the setting up of hotels.

The Andhra Pradesh Cabinet which met here today approved the proposal to extend certain concessions to motels and hotels for the development of tourism. As per the proposal, new hotels and motels constructed in the tourist centres would be given investment subsidy. They would also be eligible for 25 per cent rebate in power tariff for a period of three years and sales tax exemption for five years.

The Government has formulated a two-pronged strategy to attract Buddhist tourist traffic from foreign countries. The strategy includes marketing and publicity campaigns through Indian tourist offices in Japan, Malaysia, Singapore and Thailand and strengthening of existing infrastructural facilities along identified Buddhist travel circuits in Uttar Pradesh and Bihar, according to an official announcement here on Saturday. To bolster these efforts, the Government has signed a loan agreement with the Japanese Overseas Economic Co-operation Fund (OECF) to the tune of 9,244 billion Japanese yen for infrastructural development in Uttar Pradesh and Bihar. The Government has also signed a loan agreement with OECF to the tune of 3,734 million Japanese yen for a conservation and tourism development plan for Ajanta and Ellora in Maharastra. The National Park Service (NPS) of the United States has been commissioned to prepare a concept plan for Buddhist heritage sites at Bodhgaya, Nalanda, Rajgir and Sarnath. Buddhist centre and sports connected directly with the life of Lord Buddha include Bodhgaya, Nalanda, Rajgir and Vaishali in Bihar and Sarnath, Kushinagar, Poparawah and Sravasti in Uttar Pradesh. More than 1,46,000 Buddhist tourists from Indonesia, Japan, Sri Lanka, Thailand and Taiwan had visited India last year.

Delhi Tourism plans to go in a big way into the travel trade by getting the IATA membership so that it can sell train and air tickets to tourists and travellers. The IATA members get bulk tickets for sale on commission from airlines and railways, CMD of the Delhi Tourism and Transportation Development Corporation in an interview here today said that the Delhi Tourism was neither going in for privatisation nor disinvestment but would like to have "level playing field" with other tour and travel operators and therefore, was seriously exploring the possibility of getting membership of Indian Association of Tour Operators so that it could sell airlines and train tickets. "If the bottomline is performance and profits, then we have to play the same kind of game," she added. She also said that Delhi is very much part of the Golden Triangle of Jaipur-Agra-Delhi. Of the 1.8 million foreign tourists arriving in the country annually 62 per cent come to Delhi and spend on an average four to five days. Besides, Delhi receives about a crore of domestic tourists every year. Tourism is one of the most important economic activities and a service industry which has tremendous potential for growth but it is being viewed more like an activity and less like an industry. It's time we went about dealing with it more systematically. Tourism is given a low priority today and treated as a peripheral subject. India which has potential for adventure tourism, culture tourism and holiday destinations has to be sold with much better packaging and marketing to specific target groups; trying to sell everything to all tourists in a vast country like India was not right.

As for as Delhi was concerned, there were certain advantages like communications were good, being well-connected by rail and road it was one of the main gateways to India, it had basic infrastructrue for tourists, but the major disadvantages for the city were its multiplicity of agencies with which co-ordination had to be done for any tourist project, too large population with other problems of metropolises like slums and beggars, and there was hardly any land available for any major tourists project. "Fifty or hundred acres of land is just not available for our purpose we have to confine our creativity and imagination," it has been said. The tourism budget of the Delhi Government was just Rs. 20 lakhs for 1994-95 though the Corporation has asked for more than a crore from the Government in the revised estimates, as equity participation. Major projects should be commercially viable, projects like amusement parks or water sport activities. They need not be subsidised by Government. Delhi tourism can play a very "pivotal role" by taking advantage of the city's inherent strengths. The Corporation planned to have several major tourist complexes in Delhi which would serve as recreational areas both for tourists and Delhites with amusement parks, water, sport facilities, picnic spots, theme parks (like a park with fossil models). A committee had been set up to go into the details of this project. Presently DTTDC had three areas earmarked for the 12-hectare Bhalswa Jehangirpuri Lake, Shahdul Ajab village near Sainik Farms and an area near Palam.

With a Rs. 20 lakhs grant from the Government of India, they planned to have public conveniences at Qutab Minar, Humayun's Tomb and Safdarjang Tomb. Another Rs. 25 lakhs had been given from the Government of India for the sound and light project at Purana Qila. A Japanese restaurant in South Delhi near Lado Sarai was also on the cards, besides the only hotel project, a medium budget hotel near Hotel Oberoi Inter-continental for those who cannot afford five-star luxury. Pre-servation, conservation and beautification of lesser known movements was also a major project and one stage taken up is the Bhooli-Bhattiari section on the Ridge. "Delhi Haat" is another major attraction which shows a mini-India, bringing handicrafts and cuisines of various states under one roof. This "haat" is how a cultural show-window of the entire country.

Tourism is fast catching up in the Himalayan States of Uttar Pradesh, Himachal Pradesh, West Bengal and Sikkim, where new tourism promotion strategies are being evolved to attract both domestic and foreign tourists. This is bring done to open new vistas of employment for lakhs of people who are unemployed or under-employed.

The Sixth Himalayan Tourism Advisory Board, which held a two-day conference at the popular pilgrim centre of Rishikesh, took stock of the tourism development and identified new areas which need immediate development. The focus this time was however on the development of hill tourism in Uttar Pradesh, a state which abounds in opportunities for adventure tourism, trekking, mountaineering, skiing, river rafting, water sports, aero sports and rescue arrangements. Besides promotion of botanical excursions, pilgrimage during off-season and expansion of tourist activity, improvement in the existing arrangement for pilgrimage were also discussed. For the integrated development and promotion of tourism in these Himalayan States, eco-friendly Master Plan has to be evolved. All illegal constructions at the tourist places should be stopped immediately by all the State Governments. During visits abroad one had been informed that a lot of tourists wanted to visit India but there were no facilities available. Authorities had been laying stress on the State Governments with tourism potential to build tourism infra-structure so that tourists when they come here are not put to any inconvenience.

In view of the modern technology there were not enough

avenues for employment for boys and girls but there are great opportunities for self-employment in tourism. For the Governments it was not possible to provide jobs. Even in small countries where the population is not much Government has not been able to provide jobs. But development and promotion of tourism can take care of the employment problems.

Tourism was one of the major foreign exchange earner. Last year the Government earned Rs. 4,000 crores foreign exchange and it is hoped in the coming years the amount would touch the 10,000 crore mask. There has to be a co-ordinated effort for tourism promotion. Tourism does not mean building hotels and earning money, it was first of all a source of brotherhood and international understanding. Foreign tourists are our best ambassadors because they preach more about our country than anybody else. Conceptual paradoxes, lack of synergy among various Government departments and also the private sector, has retarded tourism promotion all over the country, although the various organisations, Governmental and private, engaged in tourism promotion have been inviting tourists from all over the world to visit India. The Government as well as private tour operators may hold annual jambories to discuss the problems of tourism trade and pass quite a number of resolutions, but unless a worthwhile tourist infrastructure is provided at all the tourist spots, tourism promotion in India would remain a far cry. This author was recently witness to the three-day Indian Association of Tour Operators Convention here when viewpoints from the private sector as well as the Government side were expressed as to how to promote tourism in the country. There were suggestions galore from both sides, but whether the promises made by the Government at the convention would actually be fulfilled is still in doubt because the promises made at the earlier such conferences are yet to be honoured.

Khajuraho is far removed from the humdrum of city life and to reach it one has to travel in buses or cars as there is no railway station at Khajuraho. It was however an airport and there is a daily Indian Airlines flight to this place from Delhi which though is not a dependable one. The plane quite often overflies Khajuraho leaving the passengers stranded. This happened even during the three conventions of the ATTO in which officials of the Indian Airlines were participating and the Minister for Civil Aviation and Tourism had inaugurated it.

The worst thing that can happen to a tourist station like the Khajuraho is lack of communications. Once you are in Khajuraho you are cut off from the rest of the world because telephone and telex connections are fragile. There are only two lines with Delhi which remain occupied all through and the tourists find it difficult to contact their people anywhere. STD is not available because there are only two lines. During the convention also the communications system remained out of order for quite some time and those who wanted to use STD facility were at bay. The Communications Department provided the microwave facilities last year in Khajuraho, but still there is no air-conditioned room with the result that the system goes out of order frequently. For the foreign tourists it is a nightmarish experience although the place provides the best of the tourist sights.

Incidentally the big hotels are taking full advantage of the tourists rush. At least two five-star hotels are doing a brisk business which are being run by renowned groups. Besides them, more hotels are coming up, both big and small, and it is expected by the turn of the century Khajuraho would be one of the most sought after tourist centres in India. A town of nearly five thousand people is fast expanding on all sides and one can see a number of sites along the road which have been booked by hoteliers and other industrial houses. Curiously, Khajuraho is a recent phenomenon because these centuries-old temples were only discovered nearly 50 years ago.

Kerala

Kerala beaches and resorts are to be put on the international tourist map and the centre has announced schemes worth over Rs. 2.5 crores. Rs. 30 lakhs each has been allocated for beach resorts at Paravoor in Kollam district and Chertala in Alappuzha district. A sum of Rs. 30 lakhs has been provided for a lake resort at Akkulam. In addition, Rs. 20 lakhs will be spent on setting up waterside amenities at Changanassery and Rs. 15 lakhs each on wayside amenities between Cochin and Thekkady and between Kochi and Thrissur. The Centre has also cleared Rs. 43.12 lakhs for the upgradation of KTDC's Hotel Samudra. Speed boats will be bought at a cost of Rs. 45 lakhs to be used from Kochi, Veli, and Kumarakom. One of the main areas which the Ministry of Tourism was looking at was setting up golf courses and market them as a tourism destination. With this in mind, an amount of Rs. 36 lakhs had been allocated for a golf course in Thiruvananthapuram, of which Rs. 26 lakhs has already been released. Work on the beach resorts will start in 1994 itself as these were part of the 1993-94 proposals. But the State Government will have to identify places it proposed to take up for development next year.

The central allocation of Rs. 2.43 crores for 1993-94 was much higher than the Rs. 1.14 crores sanctioned last year. The Ministry had held discussions with the Chief Minister, the State Government officials and other agencies in the field. Appreciating the Government's efforts in the tourism sector, it is noted that a lot needed to be done if Kerala was to become a tourism destination. And for this, public participation was quintessential for attracting foreign tourists. It was urged upon the State Governments and the concerned local bodies to be co-operative in keeping the city clean. Regarding Bekai, a sum of Rs. 2 crores had been released so far. The land acquisition process was on and a consultant would be appointed soon. The design for the project would be ready within six months. The authorities ruled out State or Central Government participation in the Rs.1000 crores Bekai project. Hotel chains like the Taj, Oberoi and Welcome groups had expressed keen interest in putting up hotels in Bekai.

Constraints and Drawbacks

Tourism a potential area for Kerala's economic growth that can also absorb a large number of unemployed people, is moored in the doldrums thanks to the flawed planning, the State's travel industry sources believe. Successive governments that have ruled Kerala ever since its birth in 1957 have not paid adequate attention to the sector since development of tourism for them meant "gajamelas, food festivals and traditional dances," according to a noted general secretary. Infrastructual development had never been the priority of the governments as is evident from the government spending on plan and non-plan expenditure all these years, instead more emphasis was being given to the social services sector. It is time for the government to shift from creation of 'relief' type of employment to building up of durable productive assets in rural areas, said Kerala travel industry sources, adding that tourism could flourish in the state and absorb a large number of educated unemployed.

"Destination Kerala 1993-94" launched recently by the Kerala Government, has the development of roads, waterways in and around 15 selected centres, the public transport system, power, water supply and communication facilities on its agenda. Besides, the government has also called upon educated, unemployed youths to set up self-employment ventures in this sector. However, the state (not having made any additional budgetary provisions for the programme), is likely to be concentrating on co-ordinating the existing schemes of the various departments to ensure focussed development of the chosen destinations. "But that is not enough," banking sources said, adding that with a per capita income below the national average, the unemployment problem requires massive investment in the private sector and the only potential area is tourism. Priority has always been given to the social service sector in Kerala and as a result development of basic infrastructure lagged behind. Kerala's increased non-plan expenditure in the absence of corresponding increase in the income had resulted in a drop in plan expenditure. This has virtually slowed down the economic growth, besides accentuating financial crisis, said banking sources who are of the opinion that the situation would become worse in the coming years because of the flaws in the planning process and the priorities and programmes adopted.

The main agencies which promote tourism in the state are the Kerala state Tourism Development Corporation (KTDC) and Department of Tourism. They had together spent Rs. 2.49 crores for tourism development during 1990-91. In addition, Rs. 65.54 lakhs was spent under Central assistance. KTDC which operates 11 hotel units, two Yatrinivas and eight hotels had an accumulated loss of Rs. 7.98 crores in 1991. Of the 11 hotel units, only three had an occupancy rate of about 60 per cent while in the others occupancy often remained below 40 per cent. Lack of facilities of international standard is the reason for poor occupancy rate as none of these hotels have five star or above ratings.

Development of backwater tourism and water sports facilities, apart from all other natural spots all over the state, would help prolong the stay of foreign tourists in Kerala said a tourist operator. "Unless we sell Kerala as a tourism package, the state is not going to gain much," he said, adding that "More hotels of international standards, accommodating different classes of tourists should come up." Development of better roads, and telecommunication, power and water supply facilities are also imperative for attracting tourists to the state. The state is ranked fourth among the recipients of financial assistance from the Tourism Finance Corpporation of India for hotel projects in the country—Tamil Nadu got 25.3 per cent and Goa 10.3 per cent, followed by Karnataka (9.7 per cent) and Kerala. The State Government claimed that its efforts had made a perceptible impact on the tourist inflow to the state. There was a 27 per cent increase in the inflow of foreign tourists to the country last year, according to hotel industry sources. If Kerala is able to provided adequate infrastructural facilities (mainly uninterrupted power supply, better roads and communication facilities, and more hotels), more tourists might visit the state. According to KTDC sources the Government should encourage private sector to develop hill stations and other spots where they own vast stretches of land such as tea estates in the higher ranges, who could develop and promote tourism. There should be a co-ordinated effort by the government, hotel industry, tour operators, financial institutions and the public.

However, there is much reason for optimism. The proposed Veli-Akulam development project, estimated to cost Rs. 500 crores, is set to transform the touristscape of Kerala, converting it into the dream vista every foreign tourist visualises. The project aims to develop 500 acres of the Veli-Akulam lakefront after draining the lake. "A clean lake is the first priority for any major tourism initiative," says KTDC director. Apart from a marine pathway—much like the marine path in Kochi and jogging avenues, the project will have 10 'star' hotels of various categories with 1,500 rooms in all, capable of accommodating charter tourists and offering multi-country gourmet cuisine. There will be two five-star hotels with 250 rooms each and three four-star hotels and five three-star hotels. The Government will notify 550 acres of land under the Town and Country Planning Act. The required land of 400 to 450 acres will be bought on negotiation or by acquisition. The proportion of saleable to non-saleable area is 1 : 1 making the sale value of land to be arrived at by doubling the actual purchase value and adding the cost of infrastructure development.

Facilities and Attractions

As an inevitable concomitant of any major tourism project, the Veli-Akulam package will include golf courses, water sports facilities, convention halls and sophisticated parlours for herbal massage and ayurvedic treatment. Floating restaurants, house-boats, an aviary and a handicrafts village are also planned. Golf courses and convention halls have been conceived anticipating a spurt of Japanese tourists in the wake of the economic liberalisation. But what will bestow the poineer imprimatur on this project is the proposed water train. The four-and-a-half kilometre Veli-Akulam water stretch can be negotiated in a water train which will have initially four bogeys and will seat 160. More bogies will be added later. The water train, with rails laid in water, is friction-free. The experiment has already been approved by the Department of Science and Technology. If the experiment is successful, it would cover the splendid waterways of Kerala and give a boost to domestic tourism as well. It will take at least a year to examine viability. The work will begin by December and the project is expected to go on stream in eight months. A miniature water rail now exists in the Science and Technology Museum in Thiruvananthapuram.

The project is conceived as a joint venture, mostly contributed by the private sector. Water is inhibiting the charter tourists now is lack of hotel rooms. The project is believed to guarantee an year-round availability of 300 rooms. Time-share resorts, a relatively new concept for Kerala, will also be available to the project, giving investors rooms except during peak season. For once, the project anticipates no financial hitch with developers rushing to foot the developmental bill. TCI has agreed to underwrite the whole project. Local developers like the Great India Tours, Kerala Hotels and local builders like the SI Investments, Choice and Bhageeratha Investments are also offering finance and technical expertise.

Though Kerala was never hit by the plague that terrified foreign tourists, it experienced a fall in tourist arrivals. It had set an ambitious target of 10 lakhs tourists by the year 2000—not an impossible target. It is only around a lakh now. But the plague led to many cancellations. The development of the Veli-Akulam project, along with Bekai, the Nedumbassery airport and the Island development can pitchfork Kerala into a tourism high. By 1997 the infrastructure will be ready and the tourist target will hit the five-lakh-mark. The authorities plan to bring in charters by 1996 itself. East West Hotel can provide 400 rooms. Samudra and ITDC are planning expansions.

Assams—The Underexplored North-East

Tourism in Assam has been affected more by its unsettled law and order situation than the restricted area permit (RAP), official sources have said. The number of tourists from abroad in particular started to decline during the often turbulent Assam agitation, and things never looked up afterwards. At present, the rise of the ULFA and increasing tribal militancy continued to keep foreign tourists away from the state, according to travel agency sources. The State Government has been trying hard to change things. Its most recent move is to introduce more buses between Assam and West Bengal, in a bid to bring in more tourists. It has been trying to persuade the Centre to lift the RAP, which the Centre has agreed to only days ago. However, it may be seen that the RAP did not hurt tourism, but law and order did. For instance in 1979, when the RAP was in force, Assam received 2,320 foreign tourists. A year later as the anti-foreigners' agitation began, the figure fell to 1,000. Then came a sharp fall, and between 1981 and 1992, the figures of foreign arrivals ranged from 23 to 595. Only the state had a share of 0.39 per cent of foreign tourists visiting India in 1971, but this fell to 0.01 per cent in 1989.

At present, most hotels in Guwahati except for two or three more expensive ones that cater to corporate demands and group bookings, report low occupancy rates. Kazairanga and Manas continue to draw tourists especially from other states. But there seems to be no move to make spots like Haflong or Jatinga more presentable as tourist destinations. The major reason perhaps being their location in the tribal belt. While there was occurred a drop in the number of domestic tourists as well, this fortunately for the Government compares favourably with the reduction in foreign arrivals.

Given these basics, there seems little likelihood either of Guwahati's conversion into an international airport despite persistent demands from political circles or the introduction of a weekly international flight from the region. It would be seen that even Shillong, the other major tourist spot, does not receive as many visitors as before as troubles and disturbances over the years have taken their toll.

Air-India authorities recently made a survey to assess the potential of the region for international traffic. The findings were discouraging. "To start an international flight a week, one must be certain of at least 250 firm bookings. There is no possibility of this happening from this region," said a travel agency spokesman. Even the Indian Airlines authorities have no plans to increase the number of flights from Borjhar airport to other area at the moment. An IA spokesman said, "There was a time when Borjhar handled 14 flights daily. This is no longer the case. There are no immediate plans to link Guwahati directly with the south or other regions. We will resume flight to Agartala and Imphal very soon. However, there are no areas where we make any profit." The introduction of private air services to the region has not affected the IA's volume of business, it seems. The overall number of passengers remains more or less the same.

The then Finance Minister, Dr. Manmohan Singh's participation in seminar on investment opportunities in tourism in the north-east raised the hopes of local enterpreneurs, but the minister had nothing more than a professional lecture to deliver. In his address, Dr. Singh dwelled upon the role that the private sector could play in boosting the tourism in the seven states of the region. "The tourism industry requires a lot of flexibility. From our past experience, we have learnt that its expansion in the form of hotels and other facilities should be left in the hands of private enterpreneurs rather than the State Governments", he said. He also advocated better co-operation between the Central Government and the State Governments on the matter. Incidentally, Dr. Singh never referred to the withdrawal of Restricted Area Permit (RAP) without which foreign tourists cannot enter any of the north-eastern states. The Inner Line Permit (ILP) required by the Indian visitors to Mizoram, Arunachal Pradesh and Nagaland too is an unnecessary hurdle to free movement within one's own country.

In his address, the former chief minister talked about Assam's tourism policy. The policy envisages provision for a number of schemes. Through this scheme, several private entrepreneurs have been already assisted in setting up about 15 standard hotels in Assam. The State Government has also decided to declare Kaziranga as a 'Special Tourism Area' as per the National Action Plan for Tourism. Proposals regarding the establishment of a crafts village and holding a tea festival in the

State have already been submitted to the Central Government.

The Meghalaya Tourism Minister was the most vocal of all the speakers. He said that the Centre had ignored the region. "A major stumbling block is the lack of exposure," he said. He also drew the Finance Minister's attention towards the fact that besides Assam, no other state in the north-east has any major industries, this means that tourism can become a major source of revenue for them. But, to make this possible a relaxation in air fares and luxury tax will be required. It is pertinent to note that in last year's budget, the luxury tax was brought down from 20 to 10 per cent. Surprisingly, none of the distinguished speakers referred to the on-going anti-foreigner agitations is almost all the seven states. This factor has posed a big hurdle to the free movement of non-tribals and is also affecting tourism. To investors, under the prevailing circumstance in the region, who but a romantic can envisage of a flourishing tourism industry?

ModiLuft plans to increase its foreign exchange earnings to Rs. 200 crores in 1994-95. The earning for the year 1993-94 has been Rs. 10 crores in foreign exchange. The private airline has with the help of Societe International Telecommunications Aeronautics (SITA), a Paris-based company, programmed a computerised reservation system to increase the flow of tourist traffic. Under this communication system, passenger and travel agents from any part of the world can make their reservation for ModiLuft flights within India. The airline has also set up office through general sales agents in London, Paris, Dubai, New York, Frankfurt and in South-East Asia.

Federation of Indian Chambers of Commerce and Industry (FICCI) has suggested that tourism should be made a central subject and accorded the status of export-oriented industry to give a vital boost to this sector which can generate a foreign exchange earnings of Rs. 10,000 crores by 1996-97. A Position Paper on tourism, prepared by FICCI, says that with the earnings from tourism pegged at Rs. 10,000 crores in the next three years and Rs. 14,000 crores by the turn of the century, tourism along with the allied sectors can generate 3.3 lakhs jobs per cent year which is more than the entire manufacturing sector.

Travel Trade and Tourism

The 42nd convention of travel agents in the country made a call for greater interaction with the Centre and State Governments to create and implement a co-ordinated development plan for tourism in the country. The convention which returned to the Pink City after 35 years since the last one was held here in 1957, was organised by the Travel Agents Association of India (TAAI). Its was attended by more than 950 delegates including many from abroad. Though there were in-house meetings, the convention was formally inaugurated by the Tourism and Civil Aviation Minister. The valedictory session was presided over on World Tourism Day by the Director General of Tourism.

The TAAI also decided to work towards an integrated action plan for the future and felt it was necessary to evolve a resource arrangement between the centre and states on the one hand and the private sector on the other, to work towards boosting tourism in the country. The convention also resolved unanimously to work towards the creation of a federation comprising all segments of the travel and tourist industry, to provide a common platform to further common interests. It was decided to form a joint forum with the board of airline representatives (BAR) to discuss common issues. A steering committee was formed with three representatives each from the BAR, the TAAI and the Travel Agents Federation of India to initiate dialogue on bank settlement plan (BSP), guarantees and other issues.

It was decided to press for increased commissions on domestic and international tickets and it was noted that Indian Airlines had introduced a productivity—linked commission scheme. The convention described as a major achievement the decision of the Tourism Ministry to direct hotels to discontinue the practice of charging dual tariffs. The convention expressed dismay at the undue delay in setting up a national distribution company for Indian travel agents, for which discussions between national carriers and the computer reservation system vendors were in an advanced stage. They said this delay had resulted in depriving the Indian travelling public and travel agents of a host of services aimed at improving efficiency and productivity.

A high-powered 30-member Japanese delegation said on Friday that Sakura Bank besides expanding and exploring opportunities to make substantial investments in various areas, to start with the bank has decided to make considerable investment in the tourism and infrastructure sector. The very fact that his is the second such visit in three months and the fourth of a high-level team over the last four months, was indicative of the increasing Japanese interest in the emerging Indian economic co-operation and investment opportunities.

It was emphasised that this mission having come with certain specific and indentified proposals to crystallise them into concrete business tie-ups and will bring the Indo-Japanese co-operation on the accentuated scale. Nomura securities and Sony Corporation already having made their presence, will soon set up joint ventures with Indian partners. The volume of Japanese direct investment could only be increased by joint efforts from both the sides and the Japanese private sector was now making efforts to understand the post-liberalisation scenario in India to forge long-term ties. Japan was committed to continue aid to India at present level. However, Indian business sector need to convince of their reliability, profitability and stability of tie-ups to the Japanese counterparts.

Punjab—Gateway to the Northern Himalayas

Since the loss of its leisure-time retreats to Himachal, Punjab has had alow very tourism projection. The situation had been compounded by the disturbed conditions since the mid-80s. The return of normalcy has revived travel-related activities particularly concerning business. The holiday-maker may not find places of quietude or relaxation in the state. The main attractions are the urban centres where people go for pilgrimage, visiting families or relations, sometimes for shopping and the special culinary offerings. Fairs and festivals and educational institutions do attract people on very short visits. Travel in Punjab revolves around Amritsar, Jalandhar, Ludhiana and Patiala, the four major cities in the state. Reflective of the revived economic activity in these cities is the thriving business of hotels in these centres as also the resumption of international flights from Amritsar.

Of course, Amritsar with the sacred Golden Temple and Durgiana Mandir and its location as a gateway town, Jalandhar, reputed for its industrial establishments and historic monuments, Patiala with its magnificent forts, palaces and gardens and its proximity to Anandpur Sahib, Bhatinda, Faridkot and Kapurthala which boast of a replica of Versailles Palace—are all destinations for visitors. The Punjab Tourism authorities are now concentrating on developing the Haryana-type of wayside facilities for travellers. Of all the listed centres, it is Ludhiana where most segments of the travel industry foresee a spurt in activity. This has been underscored by the findings of a major firm of consultants in the hospitality services, professional Hotels, which is a joint venture with the Singapore-based American chain Radisson and Scotts Holdings and Alpha Consultants in Delhi. The consultancy division offers, among other things, market surveys, loan syndication, concept planning, project-management and other related services, has found considerable potential for hotels and tourist services. Though it does not meet the conventional description of a tourist destination, Ludhiana has several factors contributing to the possibility. It is basically an industrial town with over 2,500 establishments spread over three industrial estates—textiles, bicycles and spares, hosiery equipment, readymade garments are broadly the products of these units. At least four hundred of them fall in the medium and large category. Buyers, sales agents and sales executives of allied products, visit these establishment. Besides new entrepreneurs come to look at the market for starting new units. In other words, the industrial estates in themselves at present offer scope for expansion of business travel and establishment of facilities like accommodation, transport, eateries and entertainment.

A measure of Ludhiana's prospects of being the focal point for the business travellers is the decision of most private airlines to operate scheduled flights. One service is already in operation. Though the foreign traveller may not be heading for Ludhina now, there is a substantial business of NRIs returning home and either staying at Ludhiana or passing through it. The professional Hotel's survey notes a change in trends with more NRIs using hotels which offer living standards to which they are accustomed. At present there are nine hotels in the city with a total of 244 rooms catering to the upmarket clientele. The tariffs range from Rs. 275 to Rs. 600 for single occupancy and from 300 to 1,050 for double occupancy. But only two hotels, Cityheart and Grewals, are in the approved two-star category accounting for 66 rooms. It is the high rate of occupancy not only in these but in all nine hotels which enhance the possibilities of more hotels coming up. It is also to be noted that since the visitors are mostly Indian or Indian abroad on business and family trips, the occupancy is not just seasonal. At least three hotels, the survey notes, enjoy 100 per cent business round the year. The break-up is : NRIs 20 to 25 per cent and business travellers making up the rest. There are at present no three, four or five star hotels and as per the general norms of the business, occupancies of five per cent and above in the prevailing tariff range are conducive to the demand of rooms of higher category. While one five-star property is under construction, a Delhi-based hotelier has plans for a 100-room project.

The survey reinforces its optimism on new hotels by citing the growing floating population which comes by air, rail and road on business stopover. Incidentally, when Vayudoot was operating a daily flight, Ludhiana was among the stations with a high utilisation factor. The annual air traffic was 12 thousands plus. Even then a private operator had started his service. As for rail connection, Ludhiana is served by 34 trains daily from different parts of the country. Of these, 21 trains are AC first and second class and passengers in these classes coming from relatively short distances like Delhi are potential customers for star hotels. The consultancy firm which was engaged to assess the market and determine the demand for three to four-star hotels held discussions with the managements of the existing hotels on their client profile and growth plans as also with the local authorities and executives of industrial development organisations on the potential of expansion of business. It came to the welcome inference that Punjab is well on its way not only to mere recovery but set for a major economic leap that is *sine qua non* for the growth of hospitality services, with their multiplier effect. Business travel brings in its wake and own spin-offs like weekend resorts, clubs and golf courses.

The creation of demand for services in Ludhiana is confirmed by the survey is typical of the conditions in other urban centres and their neighbourhoods for different reasons. International traffic to Amritsar as a gateway point and a pilgrim centre has been going up gradually. Cultural tourism could revolve round the Patiala complex. In the context of the improved economic scenario, the tourism authorities would do well in persuading entrepreneurs to invest in travel-related infrastructure like amusement parks, entertainment centres and wayside facilities.

Regional Tourism : An Overview

Any analysis of principal tourism markets and successful

destinations points to one common feature: most of the arrivals are from within the region. This is true of Western Europe, North America, Asian and East Asia. Only South Asia is different in this regard. The reasons are not far to seek. These are political and economic. Besides, India is the only country which has not only common borders with other nations of the region but is also a multidimensional tourism product. True, India receives a substantial number of visitors from two neighbours, Pakistan and Bangladesh, but few if any are tourists in the accepted sense of the term. Even the Department of Tourism maintains separate statistics about them. They go almost in all cases to visit relations. This cannot be held to deny the relevance and the potential of regional tourism. The SAARC had initiated moves to overcome the constraints but the progress in this direction has been painfully slow, if not nil.

The rationale for promoting regional tourism is very simple. Long-haul travel needs larger incomes and longer stays from home. For instance, out of every 100 Canadians going overseas 75 head for the next door USA and two to Mexico. The ratio of Americans who account for the World's largest travelling section is no different. A vast majority of them go to Canada, Maxico and the Caribbean. Because of cultural congruity and competitive airfares Europe too gets a fair share of the North American market. Asia gets only 10 per cent of the American outbound traffic. The picture is the same elsewhere. As much as 75 per cent of tourists visit countries in Western Europe and in the case of Germans going on holiday to the rest of the region is as high as 89 per cent. In the case of Japan where the government encourages its citizens to travel abroad, 11 million of them go on holidays. By 2000 AD this number is likely to reach 20 million. As of now 50 per cent of the Japanese visitors go to heighbouring Korea, Hong Kong, Singapore, Thailand and the Philippines. Inter-regional traffic accounts for 80 per cent travel within the Asean region, particularly Malaysia and Indonesia which are tourism success stories.

Notwithstanding the limitations inherent in the South Asian region an enlargement of the regional concept is bound to bring in gains from travel-related activities. Now the tourist movement within the region involves apart from India, Nepal, Bhutan, Sri Lanka and the Maldives. Nepal receives the largest number of Indian visitors because of easy accessibility and the absence of travel restrictions like visas and foreign exchange. Bhutan for its own understandable reasons like concern for ecology is very selective in tourism arrivals. Both Nepal and Bhutan would naturally prefer high-spending foreign tourists who also bring the valuable dollars. In the case of the Maldives and Sri Lanka, thanks to overseas operators, India is a convenient add-on or a two-in-one experience. Nepal, however, is a very natural extension to India. In all these cases, however, the thrust is on foreign tourist arrivals instead of intra-region movement. In the present context the situation may remain the same—limited intra-region tourist movement—until the political realities change. The two major countries are India and Pakistan and one does not have to go deep into the causes of restricted tourism between the two countries.

The others are too small which naturally expect more affluent Indian tourists. Which is why there is a need for enlargement of the concept. For a long time, the Central Asian Republics of the former USSR had been sending a large number of visitors to India. Even after the break-up of the Soviet Union, the traffic flow has continued although the tourist profile may have changed. If earlier it was for sightseeing now it is for shopping. The previous visitors may have spent more on hotels, the current ones spend all in the market place. In any event, for historic and cultural and political reasons the Central Asian Republics will remain a potent force in India's reckoning of regional tourism. Facilities and concessions extended to promote regional tourism under the aegis of SAARC or bilaterally should be made available to the people of this area.

Not long ago the then Pakistan Minister for Tourism, lending support to greater and freer movement of tourists in the subcontinent in fact, suggested enlargement of this concept to take in the whole region including Afghanistan, Iran and Central Asia. At that time conditions looked better, but new and harsher realities have overtaken, at least in respect of Pakistan and Afghanistan. For these reasons, the enlarged tourism region, apart from Central Asia, could be extended to the Indian Ocean rim. This has been facilitated by the rapid change which have swept South Africa and brought that one-time prohibited country into the global mainstream. These Ocean rim countries are all extremely tourism-fertile and contain both generating markets and destinations. Economic synergy in the region is possible through such movement to the benefits of all concerned. New airlinks have to be forged and packages developed. The liberalisation of the economies in almost all countries in the region has already given a boost to business travel. Leisure travel cannot be far behind. The principal air carriers in the region could take the initiative and form a grouping with other countries' carriers.

The Resources Question

The Department of Tourism has initiated a proposal to set up a tourism venture fund to provide interest-free or low-cost funds for tourism-related projects in the country. The venture fund is planned with a corpus of around Rs. 2,000 crores, with the Tourism Finance Corporation of India (TFCI), mutual funds, and the public subscribing to its equity. The Directorate of Tourism have already made a detailed presentation to the Planning Commission and the proposal has been favourably received. Addressing a tourism conference organised in New Delhi by the Federation of Indian Chambers of Commerce and Industry (FICCI), a senior tourism official said the Government would soon come out with a nationwide policy, suggesting as to how paying-guest accommodations should be treated by the Centre and the State Governments. At present there appears to be a lot of uncertainty on how income from such accommodations should be treated for the purpose of tax, rent and other levies.

Addressing the conference earlier, the then civil aviation and tourism minister said his ministry, in consultation with State Governments, would soon initiate a "massive publicity campaign" overseas in consultation with the State Governments. The campaign, he said, would ensure greater tourist arrivals to India and educate investors on the high returns offered by tourism projects in the country. The ministry had recently set up a committee comprising finance and tourism ministers of four southern states to suggest a model for the rest of the country, that would facilitate larger flow of domestic tourists from one state to another. The minister suggested that there were some irritants to domestic tourism today due to certain levies imposed by some state governments. These, he hoped, would be removed with the adoption of the uniform nationwide model which is being worked on by the commitee.

The inflow of chartered flights to the country had gone up considerably during the last four years, from less that 40 charters to over 1,000 in 1994. New terminal buildings with immigration and customs facilities were on the anvil at several airports, particularly in the north-east, to attract more charters. Referring to the modernisation programme for Delhi and Bombay airports, the authorities have said the project would be completed by the end of 1996, and increase the flight-handing capacities from about 10 flights per hour at present to about 40-45 flights per hour in Delhi and 30.35 flights per hour in Bombay.

West Asian Pipeline

India is making a major effort to woo tourists from West Asia through a high-profile participation in the first Arabian travel mart held in mid-1995. In all, more than 300 organisations from 52 countries will be represented at the four-day mart, the first dedicated travel and tourism show for the region.

The Indian participation was co-ordinated by the India tourist office in Dubai and Air India. Indian exhibitors included leading hotels, travel agents and tour operators. According to Ahmed Addul Azeem, assistant director of the India tourist office here, out of the 18 lakhs tourists who visited India in 1993, 1.36 lakhs were from West Asia. United Arab Emirates (UAE) accounted for more than 28,000 of these. The inflow of tourists to India from this region had recovered from the setbacks suffered in the wake of the Ayodhya and related events.

India's foreign exchange earnings from tourism in 1993 amounted to $ 1.2 billion. Arabs were among the highest spenders. The Indian stand at the show had been designed to resemble a *qila* (fort) and *darwaza* (gate), similar to the old bastions and battlements in India. The stand had been designed and pre-fabricated in India and flown here by Air India. The stand depicted the many attractions of India as a tourist destination, including its monuments, palaces, mountains, beaches, wildlife. sanctuaries, adventure tourism facilities, festivals and handicrafts. The effort was to promote India as a safe, reasonable and persuasive destination.

In recent months, the tourist office has been making efforts to publicise India as a summer holiday destination. In response to these efforts, several groups of tourists from UAE, Saudi Arabia,

Bahrain and other Gulf states are slated to travel to India this summer. Civil Aviation and Tourism Minister had visited seven countries in the region in 1995 at the head of a high-level delegation, which made elaborate presentations on India's tourist attraction. Efforts are also being made to publicise sophisticated medical facilities available in India, given the large number of Arabs who travel abroad each year for treatment. Nearly 10,000 trade visitors from Europe, United States, West Asia and the Far East attended the travel mart, which was now being planned as an annual event.

"This excellent response is clear evidence of the importance the global travel industry now places on West Asia and the Gulf in particular," Sheikh Ahmed Bin Saeed Al Maktoum, head of Dubai's civil aviation, told reporters. It also emphasised the growth of the industry within this region. Much of Dubai airport's traffic—estimated at 5.7 million passengers a year—was sustained by inbound and outbound tourists. "The exhibitor spread is one of the most varied of any travel and tourism trade show," said David Hammond, a spokesman for the organisers of the show. He said the exhibitors were drawn from Asia, Europe, America, Australia and Africa. The product profile covered major hotel chains, tour organisers, airlines, national tourist boards, car rental companies and specialised design houses. The industry wants to come to his region to meet not only the travelling public, but also the growing indigenous travel and tourism sector. Overseas exhibitors are looking to form long-term relationships with the regional travel trade and further the growth of both inbound and outbound traffic.

Residents of West Asian region, especially Gulf states, travelled more frequently and spent more money abroad per head than most other groups; everyone wanted a slice of the West Asia trade. The travel mart was surrounded by all the razzmatazz normally associated with the high-profile tourism industry. Among other things, a special golfing tournament—the Arabian golf classic—has been organised to coincide with the exhibition, while a leading travel agency has sponsored a visit by Euro-Disneyland's Mickey Mouse to the show. There are also many competitions with prizes ranging from trips to various resorts to a trip to the World Cup football final. Tour operators in the region put together regional trips for the large numbers of travel buyers from around the globe. Several seminars and workshops were organised to coincide with the exhibition. The travel mart will be held next year in Bahrain as part of an effort to rotate the venue among Gulf states.

Travel Tax

Government has streamlined the rules relating to the levy and collection of inland air travel tax and foreign travel tax that came into effect from September 1, 1995. The changes that were made in the 1994-95 budget are stricter and designed to ensure collection of the levies in a more effective manner. According to the changed provisions, any delay in the remittances on account of inland air travel tax and foreign travel tax, due to the Government treasury from the airlines will be liable to an interest rate of 20 per cent per annum over the delay period. A special provision has also been made for levy of interest on amounts of inland air travel tax and foreign travel tax that were due to be paid but have not been paid by the airlines till the introduction of the new interest clause from September 1. No interest would be liable if such arrears of tax are paid by September 30. Government has also imposed penalties on non-payment of tax amounting between one fifth and three times of the amount not paid. This penalty will be in addition to the interest for delayed payments.

The new provisions also leave it to the airlines to indicate on the ticket the amount of inland air travel tax collected from passengers on the ticket. Failure to comply with this rule would attract a penalty of Rs. 500 for each such ticket that does not bear the amount of tax collected from the passenger. For delayed filing of returns, the rules make the airlines liable to a minimum penalty of Rs. 2,000 that may extend to Rs. 20,000 and to a further penalty not exceeding Rs. 500 for each days delay in filing the return.

Moreover, the period for filing the returns has also been reduced from 60 days to 30 days after the close of the months to which the return pertains. Even the form of the return for inland air travel tax is revised.

Expressway Scheme

The Centre is considering a proposal to build 10,000 km four-laned "expressways" with private investment to the tune of Rs. 60,000 crores. This project, when executed, will change the face of the highways in the country and accelerate development tremendously. The $ 20-billion project covers six corridors of the country. They are Amritsar - Chandigarh, Kanpur - Calcutta, Visakhapatnam to Madras, Madras-Bangalore-Bombay-Delhi, Delhi - Hyderabad - Thiruvananthapuram - Kanyakumari and Bombay-Calcutta. The project will take a final shape by the end of 1995 when the international contracts will be finalised.

Nine countries—Britain with nine gigantic private companies, Canada with 15 contracting companies, the US, Japan, Malaysia, Singapore, Germany, Macedonia and one of the former Soviet republics—have come forward to take up the expressways project in India in a big way. The investing private companies, as per the understanding, will take 16 per cent of the expressways revenue to the extent of the area contracted by them, for a period of 30 years. After the expiry of the time agreed upon the foreign companies will hand over the expressways to the Indian Government. Setting up of expressways will generate massive employment opportunities to the rural poor. Main- tenance of the roads will also be taken up by the contractual firms. Even if the project involves inconvenience to the displaced villagers, they will be adequately compensated. One has to look at the national needs, 50 years ahead.

Another new project the Ministry is actively considering is the proposal to make a special kind of rake by the Indian Railways with private parties investment to transport "loaded trucks" with fuel or any substance to far off places. This measure will reduce traffic on the roads and ease the national highways apart from minimising road accidents. Fuel consumption will not only be reduced, but transportation by railway rakes will work out to be cheaper than any other mode of transport.

The Kakinada port on the East Coast and Kharwar on the west coast are being taken up for development. Private parties will be involved in berth construction, while only breakwater and channel construction will be taken up by the Government. The satellite port will materialise in three years. Development of inland transport and coastal shipping is on the top of the agenda of the shipping and transport ministry.

ITDC Plans

The India Tourism Development Corporation (ITDC) will shortly go in for a marketing and management tie-up with one or more international group of hotels and undertake a massive modernisation plan for all its 34 hotels around the country. Disclosing this the ITDC chairman and managing director said that international tenders for the foreign tie-up have already been floated and final decision would be taken in due course. It will also consider similar tie-ups with renowned car rental agencies for offering better services to its daily clientele of 1,00,000 in the network. The ITDC has also embarked on a massive programme of human resources development (HRD) and upgradation of facilities in its network of services, which include hotels, duty-free shops, travel and tourism, to further its existing profitable performance. For instance, after about 15 years, a cadre review was done and hundreds of persons at various levels given promotions, in addition to several profit-linked incentives. This emphasis on HRD has paid rich dividents in terms of a record profit of Rs. 24 crores during last year and hopes of achieving a gross profit of Rs. 38 crores by March 1995. Profitability with service is the keyword in ITDC and with this aim in mind, the ITDC is pumping in about Rs. 20 crores to give a facelift to all the 34 hotels in its chain very soon the chain shall be able to offer services on par with any five star hotel in the private sector.

With a view to lure the corporate clientele, the ITDC has added a convention hall with a capacity of 500 to the Kovalam Ashok Beach Resort, in addition to 12 new cottages at the Temple Bay Ashok Beach Resort in Mamallapuram. Tie-ups with the Government and private airlines are also being considered towards this end. Regarding the ITDC's duty free shops at the Bombay and New Delhi international airports, they would soon offer a wider choice of imported goods to the customers on lines of such shops worldwide. Maharashtra and Gujarat offer the greatest domestic tourism potential for over 280 million tourists who travel within the country. Out of these, nearly 90 million comprise pilgrims.

There is an urgent need to find new niches in tourism marketing to continuously project India as a healthy, pollution-free and adventure filled destination, in addition to highlighting its rich cultural heritage and scenic splendour. This has been brought out in studies conducted by the industry journal, *Top Tourism Bulletin*, to suggest measures for overcoming the present temporary setback in tourists arrivals and any biases which arise in the future.

There are more than 1,000 zero-pollution tourist spots located in different parts of the country. Recent biometeorological findings indicate that so far as a healthy atmosphere is concerned. India has an edge over other tourist destinations because of its unique spring-cleaning by monsoon rains, purified air and abundant sunshine. Take garden destinations in India, the country offers limitless floral fare with over 2,000 nature parks, flower valleys, rain forests, well laid-out gardens and floral retreats. It has its fair share of the quarter million flowering plants on the planet. From Kashmir in the north to the Cape in the south. There is no package tour that cannot include a memorable excusion to a park, garden or a flower show.

Retaining and enriching its richest traditions of classical entertainment and authentic folklore, the country is fast developing a complete array of facilities for modern recreation and merriment. Unlike in other ancient societies where traditional arts have retreated to the archieves, India of the yore lives with full gusto hand in hand with the throbbing modern. This gives a unique choice to tourists to have the best of the East or the West or both. According to the journal, India has a big potential for emerging as a popular venue for international events in business sports and culture. Interviews with leading sportsmen and organisers showed that India could prepare to bid for the Olympic early next century.

The former Prime Minister, P.V. Narasimha Rao, expressed concern that India had not been able to increase its share of tourism in the booming tourism traffic in the world. Speaking at the first ever National and Regional Hotel Awards, at a glittering function here, the Prime Minister called on the private sector, to match the Government in funding tourism promotional campaign abroad and also stressed upon the capital market to show adventure by investing in long-term gains for building tourism infrastructure. Mr. Rao also urged the private sector and the hotel and trade industry to take advantage of the recent concessions announced by the Government to build up the tourism industry.

Asserting that India had an enviable position in the world, as the bounties of nature have much to offer the tourist the former Prime Minister asked the tourism industry to exploit this to make tourism the largest foreign exchange earner in the country. While developing tourism traffic, Mr. Narasimha Rao urged the travel and hotel industry to woo "serious tourists" like writers, poets and artists by offering them destinations and facilities to different destinations. He stressed upon hoteliers and travel industry to improve the quality of tour packages to maintain an edge over competitors in the region. Mr. Rao said, the summer season which was lean as far as tourist flow was concerned, had to be packaged attractively to get more foreign tourists.

Calling upon the tourism industry to be consumer-conscious, the former Prime Minister cautioned the industry against "short delivery", saying that within the resources, efforts should be made that every tourist went back completely satisfied.

Minister for Tourism and Civil Aviation said, it was a matter of dismay that the international media tended to give precedence to negative news from India, while ignoring the positive developments.

It is widely believed that once the regional initiatives are taken, accessibility to another vast market becomes possible. This is Latin America. It must be noted that Latin America is closer to Bombay *via* Durban. Today a visitor from Brazil to India takes the circuitous route through North America, Europe to reach here exhausted after an arduous change of flights. Direct air connections from India to South American countries through South Africa could also open new trade routes. Thus it promotes inter-regional traffic on the existing pattern of traffic between North America and Europe. The immediate objective of tourism planners, however, should be to push thrust on developing tourism on the enlarged tourism canvas.

Contribution of Railways

Highly encouraged by the success of the Palace on Wheels, the Railways are now going to offer five more such tourist circuits to the private sector with a view of give the much needed boost to tourism, both domestic and foreign. For these who have enjoyed the luxury of the Palace on Wheels are in for a surprise because the metre-gauge Palace on Wheels is now being replaced by a similar saloon on the broad-gauge. Since the Delhi-Jaipur-Jaisalmer-Jodhpur-Bharatpur-Agra-Sawai Madhopur metre-gauge has been converted into broad-gauge this train is now being shifted to Gujarat, while a 21st century Palace on Wheels will be introduced on the Rajasthan circuit by January next, according to a well-informed Railway Ministry source. The Gujarat circuit would be Delhi-Jaipur-Ajmer Chittaurgarh, Udaipur-Verawal, Ahmedabad Delhi. This Palace on Wheels will be run by the Gujarat Tourism Development Corporation which was earlier being run by the Rajasthan Tourism Development Corporation.

The five tourist circuits which are being offered to the private sector are :

1. Calcutta-Gaya-Varanasi-Bhubaneswar-Puri-Calcutta.
2. Bombay-Aurangabad-Nanded-Secunderabad-Hyderabad-Pune-Bombay.
3. Delhi-Jaipur-Agra-Gwalior-Jhansi-Varansi-Lucknow-Delhi.
4. Goa(Madgaon)-Mangalore-Mysore-Hospet-Bangalore-Goa.
5. Bangalore-Mysore-Kodaikanal Road-Kanyakumari-Trivandrum-Cochin-Mettupalayam-Bangalore.

The Railway Ministry has already decided to offer these five circuits to the private sector. An announcement about this would be made shortly. Railway Minister had already approved the proposal. Modalities in this connection are already being made and the Ministry would soon invite proposals from the private sector. As a matter of fact the Palace on Wheels concept has become quite popular with the foreign tourists.

The tourists actually get the luxury of a five-star hotels and they do not mind paying US dollar 200 a day (about Rs. 8,000). Since it is luxurious journey, the foreign tourists prefer to travel by the Palace on Wheels rather than undergo the trauma of air travel. Actually this concept has become very popular in the developing countries. Besides, this does not require any big investment. Encouraged by this there is demand from all over the country, particularly from the south, to start such circuits there also. Therefore, keeping the demand the Railways have decided to operate in all eight circuits, six of them on the broad-guage and two on the metre-gauge. The new Palace on Wheels will be the 21st century train which will have all the luxuries expected of a five-star hotel. The Palace, unlike the present one, would have more rooms and amenities.

7

Tourism Traffic and Facilitation

I

BARRIERS AND BOUNDARIES

Rousseau said this in the political sense in the eighteenth century. The pity is that it is still largely true in many parts of the world in respect of freedom of movement across the frontiers of the states and in some states within their own borders as well. The aims concerning freedom of movement have two distinct aspects that need to be considered. The first is mainly concerned with the mechanics of travelling, the rules and regulations pertaining to issuance of visas, and health, immigration and customs controls. This is generally defined as facilitation, facilitating the movement of travellers across the frontiers at points of entry and departure. The second aspect which is more fundamental to freedom of movement arises from restrictions imposed on travel by governments for political and/or economic reasons. It is not relevant here to discuss these restrictions because of political reasons. Besides, the more common feature of such official restrictions is to limit the opportunities for travel abroad of their own citizens because of economic reasons such as an adverse balance of payments situation. The irony of the present situation is that while the technological revolution in means of transport and increased discretionary incomes have made it possible for millions of people to travel perhaps not more than 30 governments allow complete freedom of travel to their citizens. All the rest of the countries which are members of United Nations and ostensibly subscribe to the provisions of Article 13 of the Universal Declaration of Human Rights impose restrictions on travel beyond their frontiers, and some even within them in varying degrees and of various types.

Facilitation–Historical Background

Restrictions on freedom of movement are usually placed during an emergency. The world had not experienced a global war until 1914 and it is not surprising that there were less restrictions on travel until 1914 than there are today. Travellers then did not have to carry elaborate passports or obtain visas to go from one country to another. Of course travel for pleasure was the privilege of the leisure class, the landed gentry and the newly established economic elite. During the 1914-18 was restrictions were imposed as a war time measure. But it is characteristic of bureaucratic practice that restrictions once imposed are not easily lifted, even when the reason for having done so has disappeared. However, travel became relatively free of restriction in the inter-war years and recorded a high growth rate even though air transport has not yet been introduced. The second World War was far more global and intensive than the first one, the restrictions on freedom of movement consequently more severe too. The war brought about a technical revolution in aviation and ushered in the era of air transportation. There was pent-up desire among the people to travel abroad after six years of confinement within their national boundaries. The age of modern tourism had begun, but the travel barriers, *e.g.*, passport and visa regulations, frontier formalities on arrival and departure, were not dismantled. The main exceptions were the British Commonwealth countries which by an unwritten convention, had never imposed visa requirements for travel among themselves and the countries of Western Europe which unilaterally abolished visas for US visitors. The flow of American traffic over the North Atlantic was considerably strengthened by an imaginative aspect of Marshall Aid which helped the reconstruction of the tourism plant of Europe as a measure for reviving its shattered economy. A significant event of this post-war era was the re-establishment of the International Union of Official Travel Organisations (IUOTO) in 1946 in London. Freedom to travel and removal of travel barriers were given a prominent place in IUOTO's new declaration of objectives. Otherwise, the 1950s and early '60s was perhaps the worst period in regard to facilitation. The fact that many countries had attained independence from colonial rule during these years made little difference. On the contrary, many newly independent countries considered it a matter of prestige to impose stringent entry and departure procedures. It was not uncommon for an intending visitor to have to undergo the following types of formalities during this period :

(*a*) visa application to the filled out in triplicate.
(*b*) application referred to the Home Government for clearance; hence delay of one to two months in obtaining the visa.
(*c*) E/D card in duplicate or triplicate both on arrival and departure.
(*d*) customs declaration in writing and physical check of contents of baggage both on arrival and departure.
(*e*) currency declaration in writing and surrendering the declaration form on departure showing all transactions made during the stay.
(*f*) health declaration showing where the passenger had been during the previous nine days to ensure that he had not passed through a Yellow Fever area.
(*g*) registration at a police station within 24 hours of arrival.
(*h*) reporting departure to the police 24 hours in advance.
(*i*) income tax clearance certificate before departure to show that the visitor had not engaged in any gainful activity during the stay.

It was against this background that WTO's predecessor, IUOTO which enjoyed a consultative status with the United Nations decided in 1958 to hold a Conference on a technical level to discuss two main aspects of international travel and tourism : first, relaxation, simplification and standardisation of,rules and procedures with regard to passports, visas, immigration, customs and health formalities: second, to give tourism its rightful place in the economic and social development of member states and to evolve a development strategy for tourism's future growth. The Conference held in 1963, in Rome, made detailed recommendations in regard to travel formalities that were acceptable by consensus to all countries present at the Conference. Some of the European countries considered these recommendations somewhat restrictive in scope because they had already relaxed frontier formalities beyond what the Conference had recommended. Nevertheless, they served the highly useful purpose of providing a benchmark to a large number of countries which were exposed to the modalities of international tourism for the first time. The Conference helped them in their efforts to relax and simplify the formalities obtaining in their countries.

The next significant step in IUOTO's campaign for freedom of movement was that, at its instance, United Nations declared 1967 as the International Tourism Year. Two of the main objectives of this were (a) to rouse awareness of the value of tourism among the peoples of the world and (b) to make a special effort to relax formalities attendant on international travel. The IUOTO presented a report on the status of Facilitation at its Conference held in Tokyo in October 1967. A comparison between the situation obtaining in 1967 with that ten years earlier showed that substantial progress had not been made even though the whole range of official travel formalities had been somewhat simplified. However, many of the relaxations were granted on a regional or sub-regional basis. Some modes of transport, civil aviation in particular, had profited from special measures both in respect of individual and group travel. It was noticed that some of the measures were of temporary nature to mark the observance of 1967 as the Tourism Year. But it is interesting to observe that, just as most rules once made are not easily changed, the relaxations granted for the period of 1967 by many governments were made permanent thereafter. For instance many countries, for the first time, exempted visitors from visa requirements for periods ranging from one week to four weeks for the duration of the Tourism Year but have continued the exemption ever since. Similarly the procedure of reporting to the police on arrival and departure, was abolished by most countries and not restored again, while the oral instead of written customs declaration became almost a universal practice. Also those countries which had imposed the unusual measure on temporary visitors of having to obtain a tax clearance certificate before departure had gradually withdrawn this formality.

Facilitation—Present Status

It is not feasible, nor altogether necessary, for this conference to go into minute details on Facilitation. In this paper it is intended to touch upon only those aspects which in a broad sense tend to inhibit the growth of international tourism, particularly air travel which is playing an increasingly important role in international travel. Undoubtedly a large number of countries in the last decade have progressively reduced a variety of official formalities in regard to issuance of visas and frontier checks arising from health, immigration, customs and currency controls, even though as in the earlier decade, a majority of countries have reduced the formalities only on a regional or selective basis. For instance, it was reported by the International Civil Aviation Organisation (in the Seventh Edition of Annex 9-April, 74) that by the end of 1973, 52 Contracting States had eliminated entrance visas in respect of nationals from 50 or more countries. It was also noted that 17 of these states were in the Western Hemisphere, 21 in Europe and the Middle East, nine in Africa and only five in East and South Asia and the Pacific. By the end of 1978, 92 states and self-governing territories had reported to WTO that they did not require a visa from visitors coming for 'tourist purposes' from a certain number of countries for a stay usually ranging from 15 days to 90 days. Of these, approximately 24 each were in the Western Hemisphere, Europe and the Pacific and 20 were in Africa. It is significant that Asia and the Pacific region and Africa which were lagging behind had improved their position relatively since 1973. To this list may be added at least a score of other countries which may not have reported to WTO.

Presumably it may be surmised that only a few countries have abolished visas for temporary visitors universally. The visa requirement is usually waived on a reciprocal basis by bilateral or multilateral agreement. But since the tourist movement in a large measure is from the industrial countries with high income levels to the developing countries, many countries have abolished the visa for visitors from North America, Western Europe and Japan unilaterally. Thus visitors from a dozen or more leading tourist generating countries not only can travel freely among themselves but also to the rest of the world.

Visa

The phrase 'tourist purposes' is significant in this context because in the case of some countries it implies a dichotomy of meaning. The most annoying part of the visitor's experience on arrival and departure is that this dichotomy sometimes runs through all the rules and regulations governing immigration and customs procedures. In other words the rules and regulations published by governments and reported to international organisations like WTO, are hedged in by reservations which are not always mentioned, with the result that the actual procedures on the ground are far more complex and tiresome than would appear on paper.

According to IUOTO/WTO definition, which has been accepted by United Nations, a 'visitor' is any person visiting a country other than that in which he has his usual place of residence, for any reason other than following an occupation remunerated from within the country visited. A 'tourist' is a temporary visitor staying at least 24 hours and the purpose of whose journey can be classified as follows : (i) Leisure (recreation, holiday, health, study, religion and sport) (ii) Business, family, mission, meeting. But there are several governments which accept this definition only for statistical purposes and not in regard to visa, customs and other controls. The exemption for tourist purposes is thus applicable only to those visitors who come for pleasure or holiday, and not for other purposes such as business negotiations, attending a conference or even to visit friends and relatives. Nor is it usually applicable to returning foreign residents of the country. Another example of the reservation to the visa exemption is that it is usually subject to the condition that the passenger is holding a confirmed reservation on a returning or onward flight. The visitor may like to have a flexible programme or may not be in a position to determine the date of departure before embarking upon his journey. It is an unnecessary imposition because he is obliged to make a hypothetical reservation and then on arrival at the destination to go through the procedure of changing it to another date and may be to another carrier. There are some countries which exempt a visitor for tourist purposes from a visa provided the visit is not repeated in less than three to six months. The exemption from visa should be for all temporary visitors, irrespective of purpose of visit, and not hedged in with other conditions : secondly, the period of exemption should normally be in excess of the average length of stay of visitors to the country concerned. In any case it would be in the interest of all countries to waive the visa requirement for short visits of three days to one week, because there is a steady growing volume of international air travellers who wish to break their journey in one or more countries, for only a few days for a variety of reasons, *en route* to the country which may be the main destination. If they are required to obtain entry visas for such brief halts prior to departure they may forego the transit visits.

Passport

It should be considered the basic right of a citizen to be granted a passport by his government enabling him to travel abroad. This is generally recognised by all governments except in the case of persons considered undesirable *e.g.*, suspected of smuggling, or terrorist activities or those against whom criminal charges are pending. The concern of this Conference, however, should be with the process of issuance of passports. In many countries it may still take a person three to six months to obtain a passport because the authority to issue this passport in not decentralised. Hence the passport issuing officer sends the application to the police authority of the applicant's place of residence for character report. The enquiry may then be directed to the police authority of the applicant's native place. In this long channel of communication, weeks or months may pass and the applicant may give up the idea of travel abroad.

As in the case of visas some countries on a regional basis have now started accepting other identity documents such as a passport expired within the last five or ten years, a driving licence with a photograph, or an identity card which some countries require their citizens to carry on their person or one which may be specifically issued by a local authority for travel abroad. But such identity documents are of no use for travel to those countries which require a visa. Hence the passport remains the universally accepted document which makes even more necessary that the procedure of its issuance should be simplified and made more expeditious.

E/D Card for Air Travel

About 20 years ago ICAO recommended a standardised Embarkation? Disembarkation (E/D) card with only seven entries to be adopted by member states. It did not contain particulars of passport number, date and place of issue, date and place of issue of visa, nor purpose of visit and intended duration of stay. Even the size of the E/D card was prescribed to match the size of the standard passport so that it could be placed in it. The entries were in particular order so that international travellers would get used to filling them out easily. The card provided information on matters in which carriers are interested but which were not of interest to immigration and customs, *e.g.*, particulars of passport and visa, dutiable articles and so on. Nor did it provide information for statistical purposes *e.g.*, purpose of visit, expected length of stay. It is not surprising that a majority of countries have not accepted the standardised E/D card; consequently, a passenger is confronted with E/D cards of all shapes and sizes.

The latest recommendation of the Facilitation Division of ICAO is that the E/D card should be abolished. This agrees with one of the basic concepts of facilitation, that it must take precedence over the need for statistics and not necessarily use E/D cards or the frontier check as a means of collecting the data pertaining to tourism. In any case, information obtained from E/D Cards regarding purpose of visit and intended duration of stay is sometimes misleading. Since many countries give preferred treatment to visitors who come for 'pure' tourism, the passenger is likely to mention tourism as 'purpose of visit' even if he is coming for other reasons, and he would generally mention a longer stay than really intended. A majority of countries still use the E/D cards as the primary means of compiling data on tourism because they have not been able to develop reliable sampling techniques or other methods of compiling data. It is also not realistic to believe that many governments would give up, at any rate in the near future, the E/D card as a source of information for security purposes.

Assuming that the E/D Card is likely to be retained for several years to come for purposes of security as well as a source of statistics, it is suggested that a more elaborate card should be introduced so that greater uniformity could be achieved among those countries which do not agree to abolish it. This card would include 'purpose of visit' on the assumption that the bulk of visitors would give the correct answer. Instead of 'permanent address', it would be advisable to ask for the country of usual residence because in the present-day world a large number of people reside in countries other than their own.

While the data on tourist expenditure would have to be obtained through the banking system or more reliably through sample surveys, it should be possible to obtain reliable information on the length of stay of each visitor if the E/D card had a carbon copy bearing the same serial number, stapled to the passport and surrendered on departure. It would also have the advantage that many countries which still insist on passengers filling out the departure card would agree to waive this formality. Since arriving passenger fill out these cards during the flight a slightly more elaborate card would not impose any hardship on them.

Customs

It is implicit in the rules of a majority of countries that the customs check a baggage of incoming passengers would be on a selective basis. But in many countries almost all baggage is opened for inspection. Several countries observe the written rule that the duty free allowance to returning residents is not allowed more than once in the same month or quarter. There are still a number of countries where the customs check on baggage is almost as severe on departure as on arrival, more as a routine that for any valid reasons. Fifteen years ago some European countries introduced the dual channel (green and red) system for incoming passengers. Those using the green channel were presumed to have no dutiable articles beyond what was normally permissible. It is a commendable system for speedy clearance of a large proportion of incoming passengers, particularly during peak periods. But the system can succeed if those selecting the green channel are challenged only in case of reasonable suspicion. According to information available it did not result in any loss of revenue; on the contrary the onus for honest declaration being thrown on passengers and the penalty for being caught being severe, the revenue yield has increased. Somehow the system has not been adopted by many countries, may be because the customs officials could not get used to the idea of letting in so many passengers without due process.

Progressive Clearance

Not all countries follow a uniform procedure in regard to clearance of flights calling at more than one international airport within the same country. The ICAO has recommended that a passenger and his baggage on an international flight making two or more stops within the same territory should be cleared through all governmental formalities at the airport of his final destination. However several countries follow the contrary practice of clearing arriving passengers at the first port of entry and departing passengers at the last port. This involves considerable delay because the entire baggage has to be off-loaded and all the passengers have to go through health, immigration and customs clearance at the first port of entry. Then the baggage of those passengers whose final destination is the next port has to be reloaded on the aircraft. Progressive clearance whereby the baggage of only those passengers alighting at each point of entry is off-loaded does present the problem of effective indentification and control of international passengers at the first point of entry, but containerisation of baggage with a little extra care of the baggage of passengers checking-in late should overcome this difficulty.

Clearance of Unaccompanied Baggage

Unaccompanied baggage may be baggage booked by a passenger on another flight coming to the same airport or it may be mislaid baggage which arrives a day or two later. It is commonsense that this should be treated as baggage and not as cargo. In the case of mislaid baggage the passenger has already been put to serious inconvenience for no fault of his, and the least he expects is that when the baggage does arrive, it should be delivered to him as speedily as possible. And yet the customs authorities in a number of countries treat it as cargo or at any rate expect the passenger to undergo a number of formalities such as filling up forms before he can recover it. In fact the problem of unaccompanied baggage has been the subject of a standing complaint against some countries but to no avail.

Health

With the progressive eradication of diseases like smallpox and cholera the health check in recent years has become a grey area. It is generally understood that one must carry a health certificate with a valid smallpox vaccination, and evidence of inoculation against cholera and yellow fever if one is coming from certain countries. A resident of a large country may not be even aware that cases of smallpox and cholera have occurred in some distant part of the country. He usually consults his carrier or his travel agent but finds that they are not in possession of up to date information on the health formalities of the countries he is likely to visit. He therefore goes through the trouble of taking a smallpox vaccination and even cholera inoculation and then on arriving at the destination finds that no one wants to look at his health certificate, or contrarily if he does not carry one he may be held up on arrival and quarantined. Interestingly enough the World Health Organisation (WHO) issued a statement in February 1980 that the entire world was free of smallpox but noted that, despite the guidelines it issued, as many as 30 to 40 countries still insisted on a valid vaccination certificate.

Under Article 8 of the International Health Regulations (Second Edition, 1974) each health administration is required to notify WHO of :

(*a*) the measures which it has decided to apply to arrivals from an infested area and the withdrawal of any such measures, indicating the date of application or withdrawal;

(*b*) any change in its requirements as to vaccination for any international voyage.

Many of the problems experienced by international travellers arise because the health administrations of the states do not always notify WHO in advance, with the result that the carrier and travel agents and other travel organisers are not able to brief the passengers sufficiently. What is worse is that the arriving passenger may get into serious trouble if the guidelines received from WHO are not conveyed promptly enough to the health staff at points of entry.

Airports

The procedure for clearance of travellers by air should be carried out if such a manner as to retain the advantage of speed inherent in air transport. But this consideration is often lost sight of when specific procedures for the clearance of passengers and baggage are established at most of the airports, particularly in some of the developing countries which have not really become attuned to the needs of air traffic. The situation becomes unsatisfactory when large aircraft arrive in quick succession and passengers have to stand in long queues because the arrival rate exceeds the capacity of the control services. Many airport buildings are too small to permit installation of additional clearance channels for both arriving and departing passengers, and in many countries even if these are available there are not enough trained staff available to man them. There is also the language problem because the staff may not have the necessary facility in the more commonly used languages to be able to scan travel documents quickly. At many airports the problem, is magnified because the immigration procedure seems to require a meticulous examination of documents for comparison with the data on the passport and the E/D card or extensive oral questioning of passengers and recording this on the E/D card. The next hurdle is to pick up the baggage from the reclaim area and again to stand in a queue for customs clearance which may mean another time-consuming delay. It is not uncommon at some airports, particularly at peak hours for passengers to take two hours from the time of aircraft landings to the exit.

It is true that a large number of airports have been expanded and new terminals built, not only in the developed but also in the developing countries, which cannot generally afford the costs of highly sophisticated modern airports. Most countries are conscious of the need of improving the facilities at gateway airports and the process of expansion and renovation is going on in almost every country. But, by and large, airport facilities have not kept pace with the growth of traffic all over the world. A modern airport is no longer a staging post linking surface transport with air transport, constituting a convenient point for conducting certain essential cheeks on the movements of outgoing or incoming passengers on international flights. The present day airport is expected to provide a much wider range of ancillary facilities than a railway station or a bus terminus such as restaurants and bars, surface transport services by rail and road, communications facilities by post, telegraph and telex, banking facilities for change of money, rest rooms, a barber shop and beauty salon, and finally a variety of entertainment. In other words an international air terminal is expected to offer ancillary facilities normally available in a large first class hotel.

With the introduction of non-reservation air services such as skytrains, passengers may have to wait for long hours at the airport until a seat is confirmed. International flights are sometimes subject to long delays and passengers cannot always be informed in advance. For various reasons there is a large element of the travelling public which has to wait for long hours at airports. Hence there is an increasing shift away from the concept of an airport as a channel between two modes of transport towards that of its being an end in itself, a centre of ancillary activities.

Present day airport buildings have thus become very large and complex. The innovation of bringing the aircraft right up to the 'fingers' projecting from the building, saves passengers both from having to commute by bus and from exposure to the weather but it also entails walking with hand-baggage through long corridors to reach the aircraft or, on disembarkation, to reach the baggage claim area. The sheer size of the terminals has also created the problem of passengers having to carry heavy baggage from street level to the airline check-in counters which may be located on a different floor or, for disembarking passengers, from the reclaim area to surface transport positions. Obviously, airport authorities should ensure that passengers can obtain assistance comprising self-help baggage trolleys and/or porterage services. The general experience of international travellers is that porters are easily available in developing countries but are hard to get at airports in Europe and North America. Of course this problem is linked up with availability of manpower and wage levels obtaining in different parts of the world. But solutions to the problem have to be found by mechanised means, such as escalators and gangway slopes or human labour, particularly for elderly or disabled passengers and women accompanied by children.

Signposting

In view of the enormous size and complex structure of present day terminals it is not unusual for passengers to lose their way. It is of utmost importance that there should be proper signposting to guide departing and arriving passengers, that the timings of flights should be continuously displayed on TV screens and, if that is not possible, on large signboards in all areas of the terminal supported by frequent announcements in various commonly understood languages. It is understood that the FAL Division of ICAO has evolved as many as 40 international signs, which if standardised and introduced universally would provide enough guidance to passengers and would also obviate the language difficulty. The problem with international signs is that unless they are universally introduced and accepted they could prove a hindrance rather than a help.

Security Checks

In recent years security checks have had to be added to frontier formalities, particularly in the case of air travel, in order to minimise the risk of hijacking and other terrorist activities. As long as the world situation remains what it is, these checks cannot be wished away. However they need not present any serious inconvenience to passengers provided they are carried out with the aid of electronic equipment and trained staff is available to examine the hand baggage quickly enough. The problem arises at many airports which are not equipped with even ordinary mechanised devices and passengers have to be 'frisked' or body-searched. Because if inadequate space and staff many airports do not have separate exists and gate-rooms for individual flights and the security check may take as much as an hour to clear the passengers of one wide bodied aircraft. So it has become customary at some airports to call passengers 90 minutes to two hours ahead of the flight to be able to complete immigration, customs and security checks. It is literally true that in the case of short-haul flights of one to two hours the passenger spends far more time on the ground than in the aircraft.

Other Modes of Transport

Because the element of speed is not inherent in other modes of transport by rail, road and sea, facilitation has not been given the same prominence. But because of the phenomenal growth of travel by road, by automobile or bus, it is just as important as in the case of air travel. Many countries have simplified the procedures of border crossing by rail or road transport and in some cases almost completely abolished them. For instance many countries in Europe have had to waive the requirements of the *carnet de passage* because the number of motor vehicles crossing the borders was too large to keep an account of and process the documentation concerning their temporary importation and re-export. A case in point is the Middle East where several countries have abolished visas among themselves and established joint inspection stations. And yet there is considerable paper work which has to be done before an automobile or bus can cross the border. The same is more or less true of a number of Southeast Asian countries which have also abolished visas by multi-lateral agreement. In some countries, crossing the border also involves transhipment because through traffic by train or bus is not allowed. Passengers are obliged to carry their baggage across the border and have to get into another vehicles which carriers them to the point of destination in the other country.

The situation regarding sea traffic has eased off because except for ferries, sea transport as a means of travelling from one country to another has more or less disappeared. Sea travel is now almost entirely by cruise ships which call at various ports in transit. In the Caribbean, since it is almost entirely holiday traffic, sensibly enough Island Governments impose minimal formalities on passengers making on-shore excursions.

Taxes on Tourists

A majority of governments have decided to levy all manner of taxes on tourists. One of the accepted principles was that a Government should not consider the passport and visa fees a source of revenue but only as a means of defraying the cost of administration. The passport issued to its own citizens should be regarded in any event as a service that a Government renders to the community. There is also no uniformity in the amount of visa fees charged by various Governments. At present they range from US $ 5 to 20. As the costs of building and maintenance of modern airports rose most Governments started charging a departure tax which has progressively increased. At some airports it is as much as $ 10 to 20. But this is hardly a desirable method and adds one extra formality at the time of departure. If a departure tax is levied, it should not be exorbitant, and it should be added to the cost of the air ticket, as has been done in Europe and in some other areas, so that the formality of having to pay it is avoided. Finally, there are many countries which try to recover the cost of tourist promotion by a tax from foreign visitors staying in hotels. It is not realised that such a heavy tax would make the hotel prices uncompetitive and would prove to be an anti-promotion measure.

Need for Co-ordination

In the matter of Facilitation the world scene, thus presents an unequal situation, ranging from highly satisfactory to appallingly bad. There are many airports and border crossings which at rush hours present scenes of utter confusion. Aside from the fact that many countries for lack of resources, have not been able to provide adequate facilities to meet the needs of the rapidly increasing traffic, one of the main reasons of the extremely unsatisfactory situation obtaining at many airports, and frontier-crossings, is that the authorities responsible for clearance of passengers and their baggage have to introduced rational procedures. Speedy clearance is a combined operation which can only be carried out smoothly and expeditiously, if the needs of passengers are given the same, if not more importance as is usually accorded to the viewpoint of official agencies, and if, following on from this, a well-designed drill is evolved which the staff handling the passengers and the baggage must observe.

This pre-supposes a single authority governing the combined operation. But in reality at most of the ports of entry the staff belonging to different departments function independently of each other and observe their own priorities. For instance, it is well-known that the immigration and customs authorities maintain a list of suspected persons. This indexed list is generally available at each immigration desk at an airport. But there are several countries where the staff at immigration desks are not trusted with it. Each passport has to be passed on to another room to be checked by a senior officer in possession of the book. In one important country the immigration and customs maintain separate books (presumably they do not trust each other); hence the passport is checked both by immigration and customs and in each case by an officer sitting somewhere else.

Another problem is that the staff at many airports is neither sufficiently trained not qualified to deal with sophisticated operations that modern tourism demands. In many countries the staff at ports of entry belongs to the cadres of parent departments—police, customs and excise, health, civil aviation and so on. They are not specially trained to deal with foreign visitors and are not sometimes fully conversant with international procedures and formalities. Furthermore, they are liable to be transferred to other duties in their departments. Good management demands professionalism, which is largely the product of training, continuity and experience and under the present system it is generally lacking.

Conclusion

While taking an overall global view of the aims concerning Facilitation in the next two decades the Conference may take into account two considerations. First, that an unequal situation does not exist in the matter of facilitating travel alone; it obtains in other areas too : agriculture, industry, education, health-care and more so in human resources. After all, many countries have been exposed to modern tourism in recent years only. Transfer of technology is neither an easy not an inexpensive process. New techniques cannot be superimposed, they have to be matched with human resources which take time to develop. Secondly, while there have been relaxations of travel barriers and considerable improvements in air and sea ports and in check-posts at land frontiers, they have been overtaken by the on-rush of visitors. It is of course necessary to go on expanding the facilities at points of entry and departure to meet the needs of increasing numbers of travellers, but there is a limit to expansion of buildings and facilities. Hence the long term solution does not lie in this direction. By the end of this century the world population is likely to touch the seven billion mark. Even if half the population remains below the poverty line relative to the per capita income of the poor countries, and consequently not able to travel, the number of people with discretionary incomes enabling them to travel will be so large that even if all the recommendations of various organisations are accepted by all countries (which is not the case at the moment), the present-day methods of keeping a head count of all visitors and checking credentials or of exercising immigration and customs controls will become obsolete. Just as the pressure of numbers has forced some governments to give up the system of the *carnet de passage* in regard to motor vehicles, the sheer volume of tourism by the year 2000 will demand new methods of handling passengers and baggage. Past experience has shown that the fear that abolition of visas and immigration, customs and other controls will endanger security has proved to be unfounded. Similarly, many of the present-day formalities will have to be abandoned and replaced by simpler methods supported by an increasing use of mechanised methods and computers. The future calls for new initiatives and ways of thinking on the part of governments.

II

What is more fundamental to freedom of movement is not facilitation of movement of travellers at points of entry and departure, but the relaxation of restrictions imposed on travel by Governments for various reasons. Whenever a country suffers a heavy trade deficit and the balance of payments situation deteriorates, travel abroad becomes of the first casualities. In the past, even highly industrialised countries at one time or another made drastic cuts in the travel allowances for foreign travel, though fortunately for short periods.

On the other hand, in many developing countries currency controls on travel have been a more or less permanent feature for a long time even though some of them have had periods of trade surpluses. In the ultimate analysis it has been proved time and again that the right approach is to promote one's own country as a tourist destination rather than to impose restrictions on one's citizens travelling abroad.

What has come to be known as the North-South dialogue, between the industrial countries which happen to be in the northern hemisphere and the developing,countries mostly in the southern hemisphere, is basically about the transfer of resources, both material and technological, from the richer to the comparatively poorer countries. It is significant that not a word about tourism as a means of transfer of funds to the Third World has ever been mentioned in all the conferences. And yet tourism is basically a method of transfer of wealth from tourist generating countries to the receiving countries, which generally means from countries with higher per capita incomes to poorer countries. Tourism has the additional advantages that (a) it does not deplete the resources of the receiving countries while the export of raw materials does. After all, the tourism product generally consists of natural, historical and cultural attractions and the friendliness of the people. Mass tourism can damage these attractions but this can be easily controlled by sound management of the growth of tourism; (b) tourism is not subject to protectionist measures that industrial countries are now progressively adopting against imports of manufactured goods produced by the newly industrialised countries.

It has been argued that since the tourist flow is mainly from 15 to 20 highly developed countries to the rest of the world, and these countries impose no financial controls on freedom of movement, it hardly matters if the developing countries do not allow their citizens to travel abroad. Admittedly the developing countries are at present running a balance of payments deficit of nearly US $ 50 billion and removal of restrictions on foreign travel would only add to the deficit. They have got used to looking upon the tourist movement as a one-way traffic. It is not realised that in the long run tourism like trade has to be a two-way movement.

The effective way of reducing the trade gap is not the curtailment of outbound travel but the build up of exports as has been done by a number of newly industrialising countries. In any case, no country can afford to shut out all imports, because some imports are necessary even to promote exports. Third World countries today have only a ten per cent share in the World trade but their long range objective is to raise this share to 25 per cent by the year 2000.

There has been a remarkable consistency in the regional distribution of tourism over the last ten years. The region-by-region analysis of international tourism shows that from 1974 to 1979 the regional share of the world market, both in terms of arrivals and receipts, has remained almost the same. If anything, Europe's share of arrivals increased from 71.0 to 72.6 per cent and of receipts from 63.8 to 66.7 per cent, while the percentage share of Africa, America and the Middle East in receipts declined somewhat. The present share of the entire Third World in the world tourism market is still only 16 to 17 per cent. It should be the aim of the developing countries to double that share by 1990. This cannot be achieved by merely promoting more one-way traffic from the same 15 countries to the rest of the world. More than 60 per cent of the world travel movement takes place within Europe. Besides, the tourist movement between Canada, the USA and Mexico amounts to nearly 30 million visits annually. It is obvious that other regions can also increase their share of the market if regional travel is actively promoted. If the present currency controls on foreign travel are relaxed both intra- and inter-regional travel will almost inevitably increase as may be seen from the case-histories of the ASIAN Group and the Middle East.

The remarkable increase of visitor movement between Sri Lanka and India in the last two years offers a most instructive example of how even a partial relaxation of currency controls can help regional tourism. Towards the end of 1977 these two countries granted a $ 500 foreign exchange allowance for travel abroad, though once in two years. The Sri Lanka Government took another imaginative step in granting a separate allowance of $ 250 for travel to India. The number of visitors to India from Sri Lanka in 1978 increased by 102 per cent. It is suggested that if certain Governments are reluctant to permit unlimited travel to their citizens, they should at least permit travel to neighbouring countries provided the foreign exchange allowance for short-haul travel is not counted against the allowance for long-haul travel. A few years experience would verify the hypothesis often advanced by economists that over a period the expenditure on travel account among neighbouring countries tends to even out. They will also realise that while tourist traffic from the industrial and developed countries to the less developed countries can continue as a one-way movement over a long period, as indeed it has done for the last 25 years, from Europe and North America to the rest of the world, tourism among the developing countries, particularly within the same region, has to be a two-way movement. They are more conscious of reciprocity in their cultural and commercial relations than countries belonging to different geographical regions and with different economic structures. International tourism has often been blamed for disrupting the cultural and social traditions of host societies. Regional travel has the advantage of creating better understanding among peoples of neighbouring countries without bringing in any alien influences.

It needs to be stressed that in the present day world there is no fool-proof method of stopping people from travelling to other countries. Most of the controls are circumvented by all manner of barter arrangements. In the ultimate analysis, practical wisdom lies in allowing at least reasonable freedom of movement. The cost of administering strict control is not worth the net saving in foreign exchange on travel account. These controls are mainly based on bureaucratic inertia, because those developing countries which have relaxed them have generally round by experience that expenditure on foreign travel has not proved to be a major factor in the balance or payments situation.

However, the appeal to Governments to allow far greater freedom of movement than has been the case so far is not mainly based on the economic justification that freedom to travel will not hurt their economies; on the other hand it will, in the long run, strengthen them, as stated by the United Nations Conference of 1963. In the past, tourism's performance has been judged by the amount of foreign exchange receipts it brings into a country, as against expenditure by citizens of the country on travel abroad, or by plus/minus figures on the travel account. Governments and the tourist industry have been playing the numbers game. Tourism's value has been judged only in economic terms in comparison with other industries.

This is a narrow sectoral interpretation of the tourism phenomenon. Part of the blame lies with the industry which inevitably views tourism in terms of commercial advantage. There has been too much preoccupation with evaluating demand and supply and devising marketing strategies. The appeal of this Conference to governments is primarily based on policy grounds. The growth of population, the increase in income levels, the rise in educational standards and the fast development of mass media to radio, television, films and the press have created a new generation which has more intellectual curiosity and zest for life than the generation that is passing away. The new generation wants to travel because tourism satisfies a deep-felt human need. It offers an experience towards the enrichment of the quality of life. It is an on-going process and the generation yet to be born will demand ever greater freedom of movement. Tourism growth, thus, is an irreversible process. There may be occasional ups and downs because of political instability in some areas or economic recession in others but the long-term growth curve is not likely to flatten out as forecast by some Jeremiahs.

Modern tourism has often been blamed for the vulagarisation of the travel experience, for causing environmental pollution and disrupting indigenous cultures and traditions. In the first place, far more damage to the environment has been done by the uncontrolled growth of industries than by tourism. The rivers, lakes and sea beaches of the world have been polluted by the effluents from factories and industrial installations by the waste thrown into them from urban centres; forests have been denuded to meet the needs of industries and a growing population. Tourism has been apply described as an industry without chimneys. Moreover, wherever tourism has caused pollution, it is because of unplanned growth. In fact tourism has often been responsible for creating the awareness of the value of their cultural heritage among the local people. It has generally heightened the interest in indigenous arts and crafts.

Despite the environmental damage caused by industries, the process of industrial growth has not been retarded. What has been suggested is that preventive measures should be taken to reduce the industrial pollution, which is precisely what IUOTO, WTO and many regional and national tourist organisations have always advocated in regard to tourism: planned development as the basis of managing future tourism growth. The World Tourism Conference calls for a positive forward-looking standpoint on tourism for the awareness of the world at large it brings to the individual, for its educational role in breaking down barriers of ignorance and prejudice, for adding new dimensions to the life of the community and for its part in creating international goodwill. Tourism deserves political backing from leaders of opinion so that it is given by states the same status as other socio-economic sectors.

8

Tourism Development : Cost-Benefit Approach

Though it is easy enough to show how irrational the quantitative concept of growth is, and though, the more and more voices have been raised in recent years in favour of a more qualified approach to the development of tourism, the fetish of growth is still widespread in the tourist industry. Nor will the industry change its outlook until the bankruptcy of a great many tourist enterprises gives concrete proof of the meaninglessness of blind growth and also until the theory of tourist economics makes it possible to pass more qualified judgments on tourism policy measures.

Three Phases for a More Differentiated Attitude Towards Tourism

All over the world discussion has begun about the costs and benefits of tourism for the economy, the environment and society, whereas before the talk was only of benefits and the economy. The same is true of the theme of the capacity of the holiday region. And it is not only some representatives of the "green mafia" (ecologists), or other contemporaries classified as extremists, who are taking part in these discussions. These questions have become a controversial topic for international organizations, countless congresses and specialist conferences, interdisciplinary research teams and the mass media.

Most importantly, these discussions are now being held in many tourist resorts, and a change of attitude towards tourism is becoming noticeable in many areas. Since I regard this new attitude as one of the key factors in the future development of tourism, and as it could be the inspiration for a fundamental change in tourism policies, I propose to explore it in more detail. I should like to distinguish three approaches.

Phase 1 : The Economic Approach

At the beginning of tourism development, and surprisingly right up to this current age of modern mass tourism (that is until about ten years ago) all the participants — the tourists themselves, the people who received the tourists, and the travel companies — seemed fairly unconcerned about the tourism concept itself. In so far as the effects of tourism were analysed at all in the holiday countries, these investigations were limited to economic aspects.

Although critical voices have multiplies, the overwhelming majority is of the opinion that tourism can make a positive contribution to the economic development of a region. It also is believed unanimously that the economic effect is variable, all depending on the stage of development and the structure of the respective national economy as well as the growth rate (harmonic or hasty growth) and the type and form of tourism, etc. The most important economic effects are :

(a) Foreign currency effect

Most important is the net foreign currency effect : from a country's gross receipts from foreign tourism one has to deduct the imports of investment and consumer goods required by tourists, the capital exports to compensate foreign investors as well as the interest and amortization on foreign capital, profit exports and so forth.

The net foreign currency effect in developing countries can vary quite a bit, all depending on the needs for imports and the form of tourism : in Kenya and Tunisia where the imports consist mainly of luxury goods, it can reach 70-90 per cent; other countries with a high import ratio (*e.g.*, some islands in the Caribbean and South Pacific) only reach a net foreign currency effect of 10-20 per cent.

(b) Income effect

By income effect we mean on the one hand direct income, resulting from expenditure by tourists and on the other hand indirect income, resulting from the, in tourism discussions, often abused multiplier effect : the first recipient spends part of his income again — *e.g.* the hotel owner spends it to buy food — and hence another income results from that. Theoretically, the so-called multiplier effect is indeed indisputable. However, it is quite difficult to comprehend it in practice as it fluctuates from country to country between 1, 2 and 4, 0[1].

Depending on the import ratio and the consumers' preferences, each country shows a different result. We do not want to bother with statistics for the developing countries at this point, as there has been little research in that field and the formula for calculation varies from country to country anyway.

(c) Employment effect

Tourism is a very labour intensive part of the service sector and creates jobs (either direct or indirect employment); *e.g.*, jobs in hotels are direct employment, suppliers of food, beverages, etc., or provides of other services are indirect employment. In order to have a better estimate of how the employment effect function, let us state some statistical facts :

1000 beds in hotels, motels, etc., create 460 additional jobs, 2/3 in the hotel business and 1/3 in other areas of the service sector. On the other hand, 1000 beds in the second home business create only 40-50 additional jobs (% figures for Switzerland)[2].

From experience, the employment effect in developing countries is usually much higher. It often is the case that merely in the hotel business, there are one or more employees per bed.

(d) Regional equalization effect

Tourism often established itself in economically poor regions which, with the exception of agriculture, do not have other possibilities for economic development. Tourism, therefore, can make a positive contribution to the development of a region and hence has an equalization effect.

However, there are consequences : although tourism brings more income and more employment, it changes the economy and society from an agricultural society into a tourism society. But one can ask whether the loss of cultural identity as a consequence of tourism is not compensated by the maintaining of the local economy and society, even though altered.

In developing countries, the regional equalization effect does not that much apply to the regions of the respective country, but much more to the reduction of the existing gap between developing and industrial countries.

Opinions regarding these effects are, as I have said, very diverse. The most important socio-economic risks of tourism are the fact that it is seasonal, its relative susceptibility to crisis, and the social inferiority of tourism occupation. In general the positive economic effects should outweigh the negative ones.

Phase 2 : The Environmental Approach

The scenic attractions of the holiday destination stand at the central focus of tourist needs and are in fact the most important tourist motivation. The structure, beauty and mood of the landscape — its whole "experience value" — are absolutely crucial. Travel companies often overestimate themselves. As far as the tourist is concerned, they are merely the means to an end : he makes use of the services they offer so that he is better able to "consume" the landscape and countryside.

The needs of the tourist are characterized by the often quoted escapism — the flight from the boredom of everyday life, the need of a change of environment, the search for something different, the concept of the holiday as a "contrast-experience."

However, the mass phenomena of modern tourism have initiated the paradoxial process "Tourism destroys tourism". The landscape loses its tourist value through its use, or rather over-use, by the tourist. Tourism has certainly contributed to mass awareness of the importance and difficulties of nature conservation, but only in the sense of therapeutic reparation. If there were no tourism, more cultural and natural scenery would be preserved. But on the other hand, more areas would become spoiled and unproductive, quite apart from the increasing depopulation of such areas (rural exodus). The landscape is the real raw material of tourism. It is the reason for the existence of tourism as well as its economic driving force. From the tourist's point of view the attraction of rural areas lies in the dissimilarity and contrast which they offer to his everyday world. So long as this contrast remains, the countryside will continue to attract him.

Just as the effects of tourism became tangible and the far-reaching changes became universally recognizable a few years ago, people began to try to come to terms with the effects of tourism on the environment. Particularly in the larger tourist areas the overwhelmingly negative effects of tourism on the environment had just become visible. To restate the key concepts:

automation; haphazard and unplanned building and settlement; architectural destruction of the landscape; disturbance of the balance of nature.

People began to recognize that they were dealing with irreversible processes, and that tourism growth tends to seize the countryside, its own reason for existing (hence the notion of the destruction of tourism by tourism itself). It damages the environment of the native inhabitants and thus reduces their quality of life. It was in tourism circles themselves that scepticism first took hold, although certainly late enough. Demands are increasingly heard for an integrated cost-benefit approach to tourism, which emphasizes all the economic, social and environmental costs (disadvantages) and benefits (advantages).

Let us again specify the importance of the environment for the concept of tourism. In any other branch of the economy — as Werner Kaempfen once succinctly pointed out — capital can be lost and multiplied again. However, once the basic raw material of tourism–the land itself–is lost, it can never be reclaimed. It is unfortunately all too easy to conclude that the tourist industry does not and will not recognize what is in fact the most important of its tasks namely the preservation of the environment.

Whether the tourist has visited just a few holiday resorts or has travelled the world over, he will not be able to escape this depressing conclusion : development and exploitation have triumphed over the care and protection of the environment almost everywhere, and without a struggle. And this pressure on the environment is increasing exponentially...........

Phase 3 : Socio-Cultural Approach

Social scientific tourism researchers have been demanding for years some discussion of the socio-cultural effects of tourism, in particular the social effects on the population which receives tourists. This discussion has only recently found its way into practical tourism policymaking. Even though one must guard against generalizations and bear in mind the need to consider different countries separately, it is nevertheless clear that the basic effects must overwhelmingly be classified as negative :

> The effect of increasing understanding between nations is, when one looks closely, almost non-existent, and it is

possible that tourism in fact has just the opposite effect.

Tourists demonstrate behaviour and attitudes which can evoke mistrust, resignation and aggressive dissatisfaction in the native population.

The effect on native customs is often that of acculturation, cultural levelling and adaptation under the influence of commercialization.

Tourism planning is usually in the hand of outside promoters–the local population is regarded merely as landowners or as a reserve of labour, not as people entitled to participate in decision-making.

Basic Perspectives for the Future Tourist Development

After having given a short description of the more differentiated attitude towards tourism, we want to give thoughts to the future development of tourism.

I thick that there are three main development perspectives in tourism :

1. Increase of the number of tourists/trips

Many studies confirm this assumption. In the year 2000, according to Herman Kahn and others, the leisure industry will be the world's largest. According to the latest Delphi-study[3] concerning the future development of tourism until the year 2010, the number of international tourists should double by the year 2000. This represents an annual growth rate of 3.5 prer cent. The World Tourism Organisation (WTO) estimates an even higher figure of 4.5–5.5 per cent and also predicts that inland tourism (four times greater than international tourism) will experience the same growth rate. Various studies have indicated that day and weekend trips will be affected by the same trends as holiday travel.

2. The movement from a sellers-market to a buyers-market

Quantitative : The tourism supplies increase faster than the demand, resulting in a supply surplus. The fight for market shares and for the consumer's goodwill will become tougher and tougher.

Qualitative : The tourist's needs and behaviour patterns become more and more differentiated. This means that we will have to deal more and more with an emancipated, experienced and critical tourist who does not want to be manipulated.

3. Increasing awareness of the local population in the tourist areas, linked among other things to the desire for more autonomy

Only the statement about a new, autonomous and individual travel culture, thus the thesis of the emancipated tourist, is controversial in literature. According to Joerges and Karsten for instance, forecasts are mainly sad[4] : "The circumstances under which tourism proceeds and the personal situation of the 'normal tourist' are responsible that the active, 'searching' and autonomous travelling—be it a trip to the past, to nature or to foreign culture—will less and less be possible. Even where it would still be possible, the growing tourist avalanche is destroying the basis for such travelling. Tourism development itself can be made responsible for the destruction of historical sites, the damage to nature and the commercialization of native customs and hospitality."

Personally, I believe that the era of the stubborn tourist has begun and that the new travel culture, the human oriented tourism makes fast progress.

Regarding the other propositions on the subject, literature is mostly unanimous. For those responsible in tourism it means that they can count on an increasing number of tourists in future, but that they will have to adjust their services and their entire policies to the needs of the tourist and the receiving population. They will loose the ruling on the market.

The Pressure for a Long Term "Operating Account"

"The size of the streams of tourists and all the concomitant occurrences must be examined scientifically, as must the anxious question of the host countries whether this phenomenon, which exerts a growing influence on human activity, has not become a burden to them which is hardly compensated for.

Indeed, demand and supply in tourism have reached new dimensions worldwide. Moreover, the quantitative elements endanger the qualitative ones. The development of transport technology has created a situation in which all regions with natural and cultural attraction are accessible to tourism." [5]

The statistics usually quoted to illustrate the growth of tourism are, in fact, mere turnover figures, collating the data of the increase in supply and demand but giving no information at all on profitability.

What we are most interested in is the operating surplus. In other words, you cannot really begin to talk about economic growth unless the operating surplus, for example the real per capita income, tax revenue or the gross national product have actually increased in economic terms.

What is in fact the "operating surplus" of tourism? Is every quantitative increase in tourism necessarily of economic value ? The answer must be no. Not every tourism development is equivalent to economic growth, that is to say, in the last analysis that it does not necessarily lead to an improvement in the standard of living of the population, especially when certain long term measures are borne in mind. Tourism is not necessarily better fitted to stimulate the economy than other economic sectors (industry, handicrafts, agriculture).

It is thus clear to see why all tourism policy decision-makers must be required, before making for permitting new tourist investments, to draw up a long term "operating account" showing the necessary expenditure and concessions and the profits which may eventually be made. This calculation should be based not only on economic factors, but also non-economic factors, (*e.g.*, ecological). What is wanted is a kind of general account showing the probable favourable and unfavourable economic and non-economic effects of a particular measure of tourism policy. It seems quite natural to call far a general account of advantages and disadvantages of tourism policy measures but there are serious difficulties of method in putting it into practice, which are however not insurmountable.

"Whereas formerly the economic aspect of this development of human behaviour was predominant, it is now the social and ecological aspects which determine assessments in the field of tourism. This makes the authorities take the negative effects of tourism seriously. But touristic circles also plead for a qualitative—as opposed to a quantitative development of tourism". [6]

This recommendation nevertheless remains a pious hope with no practical consequence because the theorists cannot provide methods which are easy to apply even if they are scientifically less precise. According to the statement that theory is no more than the advance consideration of practice, a theory can only be described as useful if it can be put into practice and thus make an effective contribution towards better, that is to say more rational, decision-making. Since it cannot be hopped that a sufficient number of those responsible for decision-making in tourism will be capable of applying the complicated methods and adapt them to practical possibilities if we really wish to bring about a substantial change in their thinking and behaviour—a change which everyone agrees is urgently necessary.....

The Cost-Benefit Approach

We start with the postulate that in all countries, and especially those which have individualistic economic systems and federal state structures, important tourism decisions have to be taken at various levels, and that the know-how and material and financial resources at the disposal of the large number of persons required to take decisions are extremely diverse. It is the public authorities at local, regional and national levels, and tourist organisations mainly in the private sector, again at all levels, not to mention certain enterprises (for examples state enterprises), which are called upon day by day to take decisions of general interest. The idea is therefore to provide them with a method they can use to rationalise their decisions and tourist policy measures such as investments, legislative enactments, publicity campaigns, etc. It should also be remembered that the people responsible for decision-making are usually neither academics nor highly-trained specialists, and that they are often unable to apply complicated decision techniques. The method of decision-making we are proposing makes use of the practical conclusions which can be drawn from the theoretical discussion of the cost-benefit approach, but does not constitute cost-benefit analysis in the strict academic sense of the term. It is more in the nature of a cost-benefit attitude of mind which should serve as the basis for future tourism policy decisions.

Two Fundamental Rules of the Cost-Benefit Philosophy

(a) The need for clearly defined, feasible goals

To be able to calculate costs and benefits, the ultimate goals that are desired to be achieved through economic development in general and tourism development in particular should be clearly defined. It is these goals which provide the criteria for evaluating the costs and benefits of a particular action.

Goals and principles of behaviour can only provide the basis for really effective and consistent assessment criteria if they are not too general and vaguely formulated, but contain clear instructions as to the action required to achieve them. The main problem in defining concrete objectives is to avoid generalisations of an "academic" nature and to concentrate as far as possible on their operational aspects expressed in the form of quantified statements.

We are all aware that such objectives are very often vague or non-existent in practice. This is precisely why, in considering tourism policy, there is very often a tendency to discuss the desirability of certain measures without first having a clear idea of what the ultimate goals are. What exactly are our aims in developing our economy? What exactly are we trying to achieve in developing tourism?

In chart 1 we have tried to tabulate possible goals towards which public authorities, actions may be directed. The tabulation is of course not intended to be exhaustive.

- *The ultimate goal is welfare.* By this, we mean the highest possible degree of individual well-being or, to put it another way, the best possible quality of life for each individual. Welfare is intrinsically a highly abstract concept and only takes concrete shape if it is broken down into subsidiary goals. From the point of view of the ultimate goals (welfare), the subsidiary goals are instruments or measures whereby the ultimate goal can be attained.
- *Subordinate goals forming part of the broader qualitative and quantitative goals.* The breakdown of the qualitative and quantitative goals into subordinate goals provides the basic features, once the subordinate goals have been given precise content and assigned priority, of the future development it is desired to achieve in a given community (local, regional, national). Giving precise definitions to these subordinate

Chart 1

POSSIBLE GOALS FOR PUBLIC AUTHORITIES

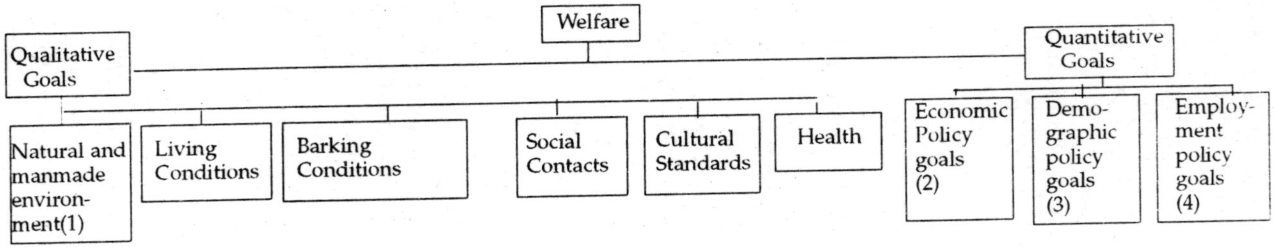

Some concrete examples

1. Air, water, fauna, flora, recreation, town and country planning, etc.
2. *e.g.* : income per capita, taxable capacity per capita.
3. *e.g.* : total number of inhabitants, age structure.
4. *e.g.* : distribution of employed persons by economic sector, distribution within each sector.

goals amounts to the formulation of principles of overriding rules of behaviour—a sort of businessman's guide to policy, a Magna Carta providing the basis and criteria for activities of all kinds.

- *Each person responsible for decision-making in tourism must initiate discussions at his particular level on the goals to be achieved.* It is mainly at the political level that the question of which goals have priority over the others must be decided. It will have to be made clear that certain goals conflict with others, and that they cannot all be achieved at once. For instance, in the case of tourism it is hardly possible to aim at a continuously increasing income per capita, *i.e.*, a constantly expanding industry, without at some stage adversely affecting the natural environment. The cost-benefit assessments of certain decisions will be strongly influenced by the setting of such priorities.
- *It will have been noted that there is no reference at all to tourism in our chart.* This is intended to bring home the point that the development of tourism can never be an end in itself but must always be a means of attaining a higher goal. It is also obvious that tourism is only one of many possible alternative kinds of activity, and that measures taken for instance in the industrial or agricultural sectors may in certain circumstances achieve the same results as tourism policy measures. There is no a priori justification for thinking that tourism will be more successful than other activities, although this often seems to be the assumption in practice. Thus, before entering into a detailed discussion as to the form tourism policy measures should take, a clear answer must be obtained to the question whether tourism measures will contribute more effectively towards the attainment of a given end than action in other possible alternative fields (agriculture, industry and handicrafts, etc.) or even than doing nothing at all. This prerequisite decision may also be taken on the basis of a comparison of costs and benefits by the method outlined below.

(b) The need to consider alternative courses of action

It is not possible to take a rational decision unless a choice exists between alternative courses of action, that is to say, unless the costs and benefits of the various alternatives can be compared and the one offering on balance the bestcost–benefit relationship selected. Once the general decision has been taken in favour of tourism (see above), it will also be necessary to examine various alternative way if implementing the tourism policy decision which follow.

The purpose of decision-making theory is to prevent the decision-maker from adopting forthwith the first measure which appeals to him, without considering other possibilities which may offer greater chances of success. Irrational, spontaneous or intuitive action is still very widespread in tourism, however, and yet this is a field in which it is urgently necessary that decision-making should be put on a rational basis.

CALCULATING THE EFFECTS ALTERNATIVE TOURISM POLICY MEASURES

This is the central problem in rational decision-making. The most important practical lesson to be drawn from cost-benefit theories in this connection is that it is essential to make a comprehensive study of all the effects a tourism policy measure may have on any of the social welfare goals (see above). This global approach must replace the blinkered, sectoral, piecemeal approach which is still the rule today, particularly in dealing with tourism policy questions.

To facilitate a global approach of this kind, we suggest that as detailed as possible a check list should be drawn up to cover all the fields which could possibly be affected by tourism policy measure. In Annexure I we give our own attempt at such a list. In line with the discussions held in the OFCD, three different categories of effects are shown, as follows :

– economic effects.

– social effects.

– environmental effects.

Other methods of classification could of course be devised[7]. The various fields which might be significantly affected have been listed under the three category headings. A much more detailed breakdown of some items might be necessary to provide as realistic a picture as possible.

The check list illustrates another essential feature of the cost-benefit approach, namely the attempt to "quantify" (that is to say, to express in terms of figures) the effects of a particular measure. When this is not possible, the effect must be described in words. Another feature taken from the cost-benefit approach is the breakdown into direct, indirect, short-term and long-term effects.

With the aid of the check list, the tourism decision-makers can then make an item-by-item assessment of the advantages and disadvantages, the benefits and costs of each of the alternative courses of action. It will of course be necessary to extend the list considerably so that it can be used for all tourism policy measures and, in particular, for long term investment decisions. What we have produced here is the rough outline of a preliminary proposal.

The final stage of the assessment process is to draw up a balance sheet of the costs and benefits on each of the alternative courses of action considered and to select the one showing the greatest net benefit. Doing nothing is also a possible alternative. As stated above, this last phase of the process presupposes that a set of clearly defined higher goals has already been chosen.

We agree with Kaspar[8] that the cost-benefit concept is of great importance today, but that one should not fail to recognize the accompanying problems as well :

"The question concerning cost and benefit of tourism must also be asked because the costs do not completely enter into the price of touristic services. Additionally, we have noticed that the costs rise disproportionally in the face of the tourist's intensive utilization of natural and human resources. In the light of the fact that so far investigations into tourism have mainly been conducted from the point of view of the economy and with the aid of purely economic methods, it is necessary to make use of examination techniques from other disciplines. The cost-benefit analysis, for instance, has the great advantage of comparing quantifiable costs and benefits with each other. Its disadvantages is that it is rather difficult to consider nonquantifiable costs and benefits, and that it may therefore present a distorted picture of the interdependencies between tourism and both economy and society. It appears necessary to redefine the terms cost and benefit of touristic resources. Important non-economic elements along the lines of the market economy, such as social advantages and costs as well as advantages and costs in the framework of the natural environment, must be included in this definition."

Our proposal is intended to provide tourism decision-makers

with a new method for considering and solving the problems they encounter. Of course, as Rentsch[9] says, the rationality of a decision suffers whenever gaps in theory have to be bridged by value judgments. But even the more rigourously defined elements of cost-benefit analysis which have not been applied to practice undoubtedly contain a number of such gaps. The fact that its rationality is defective is not sufficient justification for condemning our proposal as unusable. Compared with previous practice, as Rentsch also says[9], it will be a considerable advance if the cost-benefit approach has no more than the negative effect of preventing the misallocation of resources. Our proposal ought at the very least to achieve that.

We are fully aware that the method of rational tourist policy decision-making which we propose still leaves room for a wide range of value judgments and involves many uncertain factors and other defects which may academic purist would consider inadmissible. We would however reject – for the time being at any rate—the criticism that we have "grossly over-simplified" the problem.

Conclusion

Our proposal is that the instrument in question should be based on a cost-benefit approach which would ensure that decision-makers clearly understand that every tourism policy measure.

- gives rise to costs (disadvantages) and benefits (advantages)
- which may be direct and/or indirect
- which may take effect in the short and/or long term
- and which may affect several fields. (economic, social, environmental)
- and that, to arrive at any decision on the basis of rational criteria it is necessary
- to draw up a list of possible effects of all kinds
- to quantify them if possible and if not, to describe them verbally
- to draw up a final balance sheet and so calculate whether a particular possible action would produce a net surplus or a net deficit, and which alternative is, from that point of view, likely to have the greatest chance of success. The criteria used to make the assessment would be the general goals which the decision-makers had previously set themselves.

Balance of Advantages (Benefits) and Disadvantages (Costs)

The overwhelmingly negative effects of tourism on society and the environment are the price paid for the economic benefits derived. However, people are beginning to ask how high this price must be, and are beginning to reflect on the more or less limitless development of tourism. There is a real danger that indiscriminate tourism development could cause the fundamentally positive economic effects to be outweighed by the disadvantageous social and ecological implications, and could even change the economic advantages into disadvantages. A growing consciousness and sensitivity to these negative effects is becoming noticeable in the tourist areas. This is not only a consequence of tourism development itself but is also the results of a general trend, and is mirror-mage of changes in consciousness and in social structure throughout society.

This is all evidence of the development in many cases of a new "differentiating" tourism policy. However, in other areas, the ruthless changing of countryside into tourist area, and of farmers into tourist-servants goes on in the same old, familiar way, and still as yet unpunished by market forces. The same mistakes are made again out of sheer ignorance or against people's better judgment. There is clearly little willingness to learn from the countless frightening examples to be found all over the world, partly because such policies are still relatively successful in the market-place, and partly because until now there have been no spectacular collapses which have brought about any inter- national awareness.

Each new supplier of tourism, whether politician or state, planner or business, seems to want to rediscover tourism. Everyone imagines himself to be a tourism expert. Ignorance and arrogance may be attributed in part to the vast range of bodies responsible for tourism, and also to the fact that almost everything seemed possible with the trend of tourism growth. Further factors include the lack of information, and, not insignificantly, the language problem. Hardly anybody gets to know the tourism policies and experiences of a country where another language is spoken. Even in regions where the same language is spoken however, the level of ignorance is often frightening. Parish-pump politics still reign supreme.

Consequence : New Strategies in Tourist Zones

"It remains, therefore, to search for a still wider platform, such that would enable the association of all interested as well as obliged parties to maintain the ecological balance, and thus to preserve the tourist resources. However, such platform should contain exact and objective definitions of interests and obligations, based—in the case of tourism—on the relations between realized social values and the costs of maintenance of the quality of tourist resources.

It is also true that this fundamental aspect of the future development of tourism in the world will have to be tackled in connection with other expected quantitative and qualitative changes in tourism, since it is apparent that tourism seeks new paths to follow as well as a new sense of its existence, so that it could adapt to other changes in the developmental tendencies experienced by the humanity at large. In this process, it will be necessary to harmonize mutually the tourist policies of those countries which are predominantly receptive and which still belong to the less developed group, so that these policies may then be made responsive to the needs and capabilities of the countries which are mainly generating and which today from the group of more developed and even most developed countries."[10]

What are the consequences to be expected of this more differentiated and critical approach to tourism ? The basic tendencies in brief are as follows :

1. Tourism regions are tending to shake off outside influence, to take matters into their own hands, to determine developments themselves and to participate in them. This means that they will increasingly regard their region first and foremost as the home of its native population. Lower priority is given to the role of providing recreation for others. Tourism is losing some of its importance.
2. Efforts are being made to win back the decision-making power in essential matters rather than leaving it to outside people, companies and institutions which are mostly in the cities of the industrialized nations (transfer back of decision-making processes). The will of the local population to participate will not only manifest itself in the tourist areas, but also find its way back to the countries of origin of the tourist (marketing channels).

3. The readiness to replan overambitious targets and to submit to limitations will increase, to give protection against the unwanted effects of tourism. New policies of land and environmental use will develop in the tourism regions, with consideration of limits to capacity. People will increasingly try to define the economic, environmental and social-psychological limits to the capacity of a region, and adopt appropriate political measures to secure development within this framework. Does not one sometimes get the impression that the native population in the tourist areas is tired and exhausted, as in the contradiction formulated by Jeanne Hersch : "They do everything to make the tourists come but would do anything to stop them coming". Have the social-psychological limits already been reached ? However that may be, the range of planning, defensive and protective measures to secure the desired conditions will become more comprehensive and incisive, and the circumstances to be taken account of in the development process will become more numerous, more differentiated and more restrictive. We are particularly thinking of:

   — Zone planning in local, regional and national planning to restrict tourism (*e.g.*, opposition to tourism on a national scale). Tourism will be allowed in certain zones, and other zones will be protected from it. There will be an increasing tendency for tourism in ghettos (or reserves) as a "hygienic solution." There will be protection from encroaching ecological, and above all intellectual and cultural "infection" ("culture-conservation"). This would secure economic advantages for the area concerned, but restrict contact with the tourist to a small geographical area and restrict number of people.

   — The increased and thorough application of the "polluter-pays principle"—*i.e.*, the responsibility for all infra-structure costs should be shifted to private investors (the state no longer assumes pre-investments in this area).

   — Stipulations regarding size and style of tourism constructions.

   — Stipulations regarding the better use of existing capacity, including second homes, private boats, etc.

4. The appropriation of new areas in the industrialized nations for tourism development is meeting with growing opposition.
5. One must assume that in the future even more countries, especially developing countries will deny access to tourists following political upheaval, as has been the case in Cuba, China, Vietnam, Ethiopia or Burma.[11]
6. Developmental alternatives to tourism are being studied with a new intensity – for example within the framework of a comprehensive national research programme in Switzerland.
7. Alternatives in tourism itself are being discussed more and more; for example the recent experiment in Austria regarding a "soft" non-technical tourism (in Virgental).

All the changes described above make a new conception of tourism policy absolutely necessary. All suppliers of tourism will have to work according to a new scale of values. It is clear to me that two new forces will regulate the market : (a) the growing role of the consumer's value-judgment as against that of the producer–this means that the producer will be forced to consider consumer needs within tourism policies; and (b) the increasing assertiveness of the native population in the tourist region and more restrictive attitudes towards tourism.

The first priority of a new human and environmentally oriented tourism policy would read something like this :

Guaranteed optimal satisfaction of the different kinds of tourism demand for people of all classes within the framework of efficient tourist facilities and in an unspoiled environment, consideration being given to the interests of the local population.[12]

Joerges and Karsten express the same opinion :

"Tourism policy should above all be a consumer-oriented policy whereas both, the travellers and the hosts should be consumers. If the policy fails to do that and remains fixed on its growth and advantages of the tourist industry, it will sooner or later be confronted with a 'rebellion of the tourists' as well as a 'rebellion of the local population against the tourists".

This aim implies that new tourism policies will no longer concentrate on economic and technical necessities alone, but will emphasize the demand for an unspoiled environment and consideration of the needs of the people affected, *i.e.*, the tourists and the local population. I would call a kind of tourism which fulfils these demands "soft tourism", and that which obeys purely economic and technical forces, "hard tourism". Long before Robert Jungk published his list, "Hard travel–soft travel"[13] there were other lists of demands for the realization of soft tourism.

We have tried to restructure the propositions which we put forward in our book "Die Landschaftsfresser"[14]. We have juxtaposed this with Jungk's list, although it should not be taken without reservations (see Annexure II). The "Ten propositions for defensive tourism" which Zolles and Dignoes recently compiled are along the same lines (see Annexure III). The propositions which I formulated at that time are still topical, as the countryside—devourers are still at work—in many places more so than ever before. (see Annexure IV).

The Annexure II-IV give an extensive general view on how to improve the cost-benefit balance in tourism (not only for developing countries). But beyond that, let us make some propositions with regard to developing countries. Here are some results of an international seminary on "The costs and benefits of tourism in developing countries," held at the University of Berne in 1980 :[15]

1. In general

— no one-sided (sectorial) view of tourism; tourism has to be considered in relation to the general situation of developing countries (North-South dialogue and East-West contrast).
— the population of developing countries should demonstrate more self-consciousness.

2. Planning (product policy)

— limit and control growth (against "giantism").
— control speed of development.
— planning should not be left to financial experts and architects only, but should include psychologists, tourism experts and tourists.
— architecture should be accordance with the culture of the host country, traditional architecture, forms of accommodation in local style.
— include local products; no tourism facilities to be

concentrated in areas with insufficient food production.

— decentralization: no longer large scale tourist centres but promotion of small projects (also in underdeveloped tourist regions).
— reduction of investment needs for large-scale projects and hence less dependence on foreign capital.
— the luxury image of tourism in Developing Countries has to be removed encourage simpler forms of tourism (camping, bungalows, etc.), include and develop public transportation and also include the already existing hotel facilities into the international tourism movement by improving hygienic conditions.
— tourism should make use of and reinforce the existing infrastructure which serves the general public, making it accessible to both foreigners and autochhones; development of infrastructure according to the local needs, *e.g.*, domestic tourism, local economy, etc.
— avoid one-sided orientation of tourism on climate and water (monoculture of the sun)—diversification—promote other travel forms (*e.g.*, travelling on one's own responsibility, camping, bungalow-holidays, homestay).
— qualified planning (learn from mistakes; accept planning-aid; not take over western modes of thinking).
— constancy in tourism policy (goals of development).
— participation of the local population (democratic planning; local population has to have a say in the matter; feasible planning; partnership in decision-making.

3. *Information/Education*

Traveller

— no over-emphasis on the pedagogical approach with respect to travel; no forced learning during the holidays.
— geography lessons at school as preparatory for "correct" travelling.
— improved travel preparations.
— education for more autonomy and hence reduce the importance of the tourist-guide.
— remove existing barriers; confrontation instead of gaping; furtherance of the contact with the local

population.

— serious and regular on-the-job-training for the tourist-guides and animators.

— information advertising policy.

Host

— prepare/inform the host population.

— mass-media should inform the population about the tourists.

— train specialists in the receiving countries itself rather than abroad.

Final Remarks

Robert Jungk states, "Just as the change from hard centralized technology will not happen as quickly or as completely as many proponents of a softer technology hope, tourism will only gradually and in certain areas develop in new less destructive directions. A change of course will definitely occur. But how decisive it will be depends on human, political and social necessities and developments which no one would risk specifying exactly, unless they believed, like an arrogant technocratic planner, that history is a machine whose behaviour can be determined and controlled".[19]

As we have seen, there are many indications of changes of direction in tourism policies. The most important thing is to speed up the process, and encourage the development of soft tourism as we have described it. We must find new horizons within the available time and in the necessary areas. But for this we do not need yet more scientific reports—e.g., on capacity problems—but politicians and people at all levels who possess the courage to make subjective and qualitative observations, and who have the courage to support measures which are unpopular, since they will be perceived as being against the short-term interests of many people.

It is a question of treading a path to the bastion of greatest resistance. We will not make it without skid-marks. There are enough arguments in favour of soft tourism. We do not need any more theory, but practical politics.

A "careful" tourism policy has become necessary for the following reasons :

— the special vulnerability of the rural environment;
— the irreversibility of certain processes;
— the special importance of the environment as the raw-material, the basis of tourism and its economic driving force;
— the lack of evidence and the uncertainty we experience (measurement of damage to environment, see-saw effects, when they appear, etc.);
— the sensibilities of the local population and its claims to independence.

Where we have doubts about the wisdom of particular developments, we must tread carefully. In uncertain decisions the "smaller" solution (the less damaging) is always the better solution, since then future generations will have a greater degree of freedom and better possibilities for adaptation to changing environmental conditions. Let us now stop pretending that we can decide in the space of one or two generations what will be important in the future. We ourselves are unsure of the long-term consequences of our actions, and we could be depriving those who will come after us of much of their room to manoeuvre and the opportunity to develop themselves as we have done. Tourism policy should concentrate more on the understanding that our descendants will most probably not thank us for what we actually have built, but for what we have not built any more.

Notes and References

1. See *e.g.*, Schawinski, R., Die sozio-oekonomischen Faktoren des Fremdenverkehrs in Entwicklungslaendern : Der Fall Guatemala; St. Galler Beitraege zum Fremdenverkehr und zur Verkehrswirtschaft; Reihe Fremdenverkehr, Vol. 5, Bern 1973, page 130 f.

   and Hunziker, W., Wachstumsprobleme des Fremdenverkehrs; Sonderdruck aus "Zukunftsufgaben in Wirtschaft und Gesellschaft". St. Gallen 1963, page 180.

2. Guhmidhauser, H.P., Der Beschaftigungseffekt des Fremdenverkehrs im tertiaeren Sektor, dargestellt am Beispiel der Schweiz; in : Festschrift zur Vollendung des 70. Lebensjahres von Prof. P. Bernecker; Hrsg : W. Ender, Wien 1978, page 56.

   and Bezzola, A., Probleme der Eignung und Aufnahmekapazitaet touristischer Bergregionen der Schweiz, Bern und Stuttgart 1975, pages 111 ff.

3. Krippendorf, J., Tourismus in Jahre 2010 : eine Delphi Umfrage ueber die zukuenftige Entwicklung des Tourismus in der Schweiz; Interpretation und Schlussfolgerungen, Bern 1980 (3. Aufl.) pages 6-7.
4. Joerges, B., Karsten, D., Tourismus und Kulturwandel : in : Zeitschrift fuer Kulturaustauch, Stuttgart 1978, page 8.
5. Kaspar, C., Interrelation between benefits and costs of tourist resources in : Publications de I 'AIEST', Vol. 23, St-Gall 1982 page 13.
6. Kaspar, C., Interrelation ..., *Ibid*, page 13.
7. Especially a classification on the lines of the chart of goals given above might be useful.
8. Kaspar, C., Interrelation..., *op. cit.*, pages 13/14.
9. Siehe Rentsch, H., Kosten-Nutzen-Analyse im Tourismus; Rueschlikon Lecture "Fremdenverkehr im Wandel" in : Monatszeitschrift des Gottlieb Duttweiler-Instituts", No. 6, Zurich 1972 und Reritsch, H., Die volks-und Fremdenverkehrswirtschaftlichen Auswirkungen einer Autostrasse Lauterbrunnnen-Wengen; ein Beitrag zur Problematik der Anwendung der Kosten-Nutzen-Analyse fuer Infrastrucktur-projekte in Fremdenverkehrs-gebieten ; University Thesis, Berne 1973.
10. Team of Yugoslav Experts; Social value and economic pricing of spatial tourist resources; in : Publications de I 'AIEST, Vol. 23, St-Gall 1982, pages 26/27.
11. Joerges, B., Karsten, D., *op. cit.*, page 7.
12. Beratende Kommission fuer Fremdenverkehr des Bundesrates *op. cit.*, page 58.
13. GEO-Magazin vom 10. Oktober 1980, pages 154 ff.
14. Krippendorf, J., Die Landschaftsfresser; Tourismus und Erholungslandschaft–Verderben oder Segen ? Bern 1981 (3. Aufl.), pages 84 ff.
15. Forschungsinstitut fuer Fremdenverkehr an der Universitaet Bern; Von den Kosten und Nutzen des Fremdenverkehrs nach Entwicklungslaendern, Berm 1981, pages 41 ff. (Dokumentation zum Fremdenverkehrsstudium, Heft 3).
16. GEO–Magazin vom 10, Oktober 1980, page 156.

Annexure I

CHECK LIST FOR CALCULATING THE COSTS AND BENEFITS OF TOURIST POLICY MEASURES

Repercussions (effects) of tourism policy measures	*Benefits (advantages) direct and indirect short-term and long-term*		*Costs (disadvantages) direct and indirect short-term and long-term*	
	in quantitative terms	*verbal description*	*in quantitative terms*	*verbal description*
A. Economic effects				
1. Income per capita				
2. Income distribution				
3. Tax revenue per capita				
4. Balance of payments of tourism (foreign exchange)				
5. Capacity utilisation (supply)				
5.1. Tourism services (*e.g.* percentage of hotel beds occupied, capacity utilisation of transport, etc.)				
5.2. Other services (*e.g.* building industry, handicrafts, etc.)				
6. Quality of Supply				
7. Willingness of the public and private sectors to invest and take risks				

(*Contd.*)

Annexure I (Contd.)

Repercussions (effects) of tourism policy measures	*Benefits (advantages) direct and indirect short-term and long-term*		*Costs (disadvantages) direct and indirect short-term and long-term*	
	in quantitative terms	*verbal description*	*in quantitative terms*	*verbal description*
8. Capital expenditure (1) on general infrastructure				
8.1 Traffic and transport				
8.2 Watter supply				
8.3 Energy supply				
8.4 Sewage removal				
8.5 Refuse removal				
8.6 Telecommunications				
9. Capital expenditure (1) on tourism infrastructure (tourism facilities)				
9.1 Transport				
9.2 Accommodation				
9.3 Catering facilities				
9.4 Entertainment				
9.5 Physical activities (sports)				
9.6 Para-medical treatment and convalescence				
9.7 Tourist information				

10. Capital expenditure (1) on advertising to promote tourism
11. Capital expenditure (1) in sectors complementary to the supply of tourist facilities

B. Social effects

1. Size of population
2. Distribution of population
3. Age structure of population
4. Sectoral distribution of working population
5. Distribution of working population with sectors I, II, III
6. Public health
7. Cultural level of population (religion, art, science)
8. Education
9. Popular Customs, folklore, mental attitudes, hospitality

---

(1) In this connection there are three main types of direct costs: planning costs, investment costs, and maintenance and operating costs.

(*Contd.*)

Anexture I (Contd.)

Repercussions (effects) of tourism policy measures	*Benefits (advantages) direct and indirect short-term and long-term*		*Costs (disadvantages) direct and indirect short-term and long-term*	
	in-quantitative terms	*verbal description*	*in quantitative terms*	*verbal description*
C. Environmental effects				
1. Countryside				
2. Plant life				
3. Animal life				
4. Climate				
5. Water				

Annexure-II

HARD TOURISM VERSUS SOFT TOURISM

Hard tourism	Soft tourism
A. General concepts	
Inconsiderate	Considerate
Offensive	Defensive
Aggressive	Cautious
Fast impetuous	Slow / thoughtful
Long strides	Short steps
Unchecked	Controlled
Unregulated	Regulated
Maximal	Optimal
Excessive	Moderate
Short term	Long term
Particular interest	General interest
Outside control	Self determination
Least resistance	Greatest resistance
Sector based	Entirety based
Price conscious	Value-conscious
Quantitative	Qualitative
Growth	Development
B. Tourism development strategies	
1. Development without planning	Planning before development
2. Project-thinking	Concept-thinking
3. Each community plans for itself	Centralized planning for larger areas.
4. Indiscriminate development	Concentrate development on particular areas
5. Haphazard and scattered building	Conserve land, build in concentration, keep open spaces
6. Exploit especially valuable landscapes particularly intensively	Conserve especially valuable landscape (reserves)
7. Create new building-stock. Build new bedspaces	Improve use of existing building-stock Exploit existing bedspaces

8.	Build for indefinite demand.	Fix limits on expansion
9.	Develop tourism in all areas	Develop tourism only in suitable areas and where local population available
10.	Tourism development left to outside concerns	Opportunity for decision-making and participation by local population
11.	Utilize all available labour [also outsiders]	Development planned according to indigenous labour potential
12.	Consider only economic advantages	Weigh up all economic, ecological and social advantages and disadvantages [costs benefits]
13.	Regard farming population only as landowners and tourist labour	Preserve and encourage agriculture
14.	Leave social costs to be said by society	Leave costs to be paid by perpetrators
15.	Favour private transport	Encourage transport
16.	Provide facilities for maximum demand	Provide facilities for average demand
17.	Remove natural obstacles	Preserve natural obstacles
18.	Urban architecture	Local architecture [building design and materials]
19.	General automation of tourist resorts	Selective technical development, encouragement of non-technical tourism forms

C. Policy frameworks

Retain concentration of holiday departures	Stagger holidays
Admit tourism personnel without certificate of ability	Improve education of those responsible in tourism
Spread 'stereotype' holidays on offer	Prepare travellers
Hard selling	'Heart selling'
Regard tourism as economic panacea	Seek new options within, and alternatives to tourism

Hard travel	**Sofe travel**
D. Tourist attitudes [Source : R. Jungk]	
Mass tourism	Travel alone, with friends or family
Little time	Plenty of time
Rapid means of transport	Approprite [or even slow] means of transport
Fixed itinerary	Spontaneous decisions
Outside-inspired	Self-inspired
Imported lifestyle	Native lifestyle
'Sights'	Experiences
Comfortable and passive	Strenuous and active
Little or no intellectual preparation	Previous research on destination country
Unable to speak the language	Learning to speak the language
Feeling of superiority	Willingness to learn
Shopping	Bringing presents
Souvenirs	Memories, disaries, new perspectives
Snaps and postcards	Photography, drawing painting
Curiosity	Tact
Loud	Quiet

Annexure III

TEN PROPOSITIONS FOR DEFENSIVE TOURISM

A defensive tourism policy will be necessary in future both for the wellbeing of the tourist and for the needs of the native population, according to the administrative director of Austrian Tourist Advertising. Dr. Helmut Zolles, and the OFVW-Latin American Co-ordinator, Oskar Dignoes, who delivered a lecture at the COTAL Congress in Torremolinos. They presented ten propositions which they felt would achieve great success in the long term, but in the short term would bring little rejoicing.

The propositions are :

1. An inventory of unused stretches of land suitable for recreation-tourism, flora and fauna in "non-nature conservation areas", as well as of original architectural units both urban and rural, and those established by immigration before 1900, a local, regional, national and continental level.

2. Declaration of areas with specific stipulations as "tourist reserves".

3. Passing of special laws against urban disfigurement, architectural ruin and damage to the environment.

4. Provision of unlimited plans for the designation of special areas—particularly natural landscape [partial use for tourism], urban areas [including tourist settlements] and industrial areas.

5. The devising of plans for the reacquisition, restoration and preservation of old city-centres, to make them habitable and useful for tourist purposes.

6. Examination of the effects of the investment of foreign capital in tourism projects and of the social and economic changes in the affected region.

7. Protective measures to combat irresponsible and purely profit-motivated exploitation of natural resources for tourist purposes.

8. Avoidance of superlatives and eulogies in statistics and advertising.

9. Education of the population to regard tourism as a duty and irreversible right.
10. To weigh up possibly devastating consequences or possible profits, before areas are developed for tourism and streams of tourists are enticed into the country.

Annexure IV

STRATEGIES FOR A HUMAN ENVIRONMENT ORIENTED TOURISM POLICY

23 Theses for a Desirable Future

I have drawn up 23 requirements for a human and environment oriented tourism policy. The fundamentals are often inextricably associated with each other and form an integrated system. They can only bring about the intended correction of the circumstances if they are followed not individually, but as a whole. Let it be understood : the theses are not fixed and unalterable dogma, but are in need to some extent of consolidation and more intensive clarification. They should be flexible, handled, completed where necessary and properly adapted.

Thesis 1 : Reconsider the main aims of the tourist policy.

Thesis 2 : First plan, then develop — withold building permit as stop-gap.

Thesis 3 : Think in large areas.

Thesis 4 : Concentrate on main points—discard the "watering-can" principle.

Thesis 5 : Fix the carrying capacity of the landscape.

Thesis 6 : Give the local population power of decision and participation.

Thesis 7 : Weigh costs against benefits.

Thesis 8 : Conserve land, concentrate building operations.

Thesis 9 : Conserve and strengthen agriculture.

Thesis 10 : Keep particularly valuable landscape free : scenery for all.

Thesis 11 : Cultivate forestland.

Thesis 12 : Protect sea, lakes and rivers.

Thesis 13 : Give priority to public transport.

Thesis 14 : Create conditions for gracious living in towns.

Thesis 15 : Solve economic problems associated with and use planning.

Thesis 16 : Present those responsible with the bill.

Thesis 17 : Stagger the holiday periods.

Thesis 18 : Utilize more effectively existing bed capacity—curtail expansion.

Thesis 19 : Encourage non-technical tourism.

Thesis 20 : Improve the architecture of holiday and leisure.

Thesis 21 : Intensity tourism research.

Thesis 22 : Raise the standard of training of those responsible for tourism.

Thesis 23 : Inform and interest the public.

9

Development and Marketing Strategies

Facts, Figures and Expectations

The Government plans to spend Rs. 39,100 crores over the next three years to draw five million tourists but a leading trade body has suggested the formation of a tourism venture fund and an investment of Rs. 40,000 crores to attract six-to-seven million travellers by 2000 AD. The fund, proposed by the Federation of Indian Chambers of Commerce and Industry (FICCI), will help involve people in far-flug areas and small businessmen develop infrastructural facilities. S.N. Yadav, FICCI Secretary (Development), who has made a study of the tourism sector, says Rs. 40,000 crores would have to be pumped in the sector over the next few years to meet the target by the turn of the century. The State Governments and private sector participation will have to be sought in a big way to create and improve existing infrastructural facilities so that the sector can emerge as the single largest foreign exchange earner and employment generator, he adds.

Foreign investment to the tune of Rs. 1,715 crores in hotel and restaurants and Rs. 1.92 crores in tourism had already been approved by the Government up to April, 1995. The Government's action plan aiming to draw five million tourists, says the state will bear one-third (Rs. 13,640 crores) of the costs while the rest is expected to be covered through public expenditure (Rs. 11,600 crores) and private investment (Rs. 13,860 crores).

Tourism at present is the third largest export industry in the world after transport equipment and petroleum products. India remains at the periphery of the international tourist map with less than 0.5 per cent of tourist arrivals which is over 500 million, world-wide. Foreign exchange earnings through 1.88 million tourists last year were about $ 1.4 million (Rs. 4,340 crores). The figure does not take into account the money spent by domestic travellers who must be anywhere between 10 and 15 million. says Mr. Yadav, revealing that official count of in-house tourists has not been maintained. He suggests that maximum stress must be laid towards developing good accommodation facilities and communication links to main centres of attraction. For a tourist who, on an average, spends 30 per cent of his expenditure on lodging, the country would have to spend about Rs. 4,000 crores to increase its hotel-room capacity to 1,25,000 rooms from the present 50,000.

State Governments should help the hotel industry achieve the target by amending building laws like allowing it to construct 25 per cent additional rooms and exempting it from the land ceiling act. As tourism development has a multiplier effect on economy, State Governments, will have to take a lot of interest in building good road and communication networks as also improve upon provision of hygienic facilities. Development along these lines alone has the potential of generating about 10 million additional jobs, says the expert, adding that the sector at present employs 6.39 million directly and 8.68 million people indirectly. The Government has proposed to involve private sector in the construction and management of some toll highways.

FICCI recently organised a conference to evolve a strategy to boost tourism where one of the suggestions was to involve the private sector in maintenance of monuments and developing facilities near them. Establishment of restaurants with proper resting facilities after every two-to-three km along main tourist circuits and setting up a "tourist police" for special help to travellers were among other ideas suggested. The Indian Tourism Development Corporation (ITDC) has proposed to rebuild the Lodhi, Janpath and Ranjit hotels here under a Rs. 250 crores project, a senior ITDC official has said. ITDC has also decided to convert the entire sixth floor of the Ashok Hotel to into an executive floor to cash-in on the boom in overseas corporate tourism.

Of the 1.88 million foreign arrivals last year two lakhs or nine per cent were business travellers and actual leisure tourist arrival was about eight lakh or 44 per cent. Others were people from Pakistan and Bangladesh, who mainly come to meet relatives. ITDC, which earned a record profit of Rs. 42.25 crores in 1994-95, is also taking up a Rs. 18 crores projects this year to refurbish some Ashok group of hotels in the country.

Government Initiatives

The Ministry of Tourism and Civil Aviation is evolving a package of programmes for boosting the tourism sector in India and to upgrade its rank as a foreign exchange earner. This was indicated recently by no less than the earstwhile Union Minister for Civil Aviation and Tourism, while inaugurating the national conference on tourism organised by •Federation of Indian Chambers of Commerce and Industry (FICCI). More chartered flights would be brought to India shortly. The experience of the Government with the chartered flights was extremely encouraging. In four years' time from a meagre number of 36, the chartered flights had increased to 1000. With the modernisation of the airports in different parts of the country, many other destinations in India, especially in the North-East, would have the facilities for landing the chartered flights. This would give a boost to the tourism industry in the country.

The State Governments have been asked to draw up comprehensive tourist development programmes. In this regard, two communications had been sent to the Chief Ministers to give an account of the problems being faced by them so as to draw up a uniform programme for the entire country. In this regard, it must be conceded that tourism has received only scant attention by the State Governments and the budgetary allocation for both aviation and tourism are very insignificant to take up any massive modernisation programmes. An advice has also called upon the State Governments to declare tourism as an industry. Most of the State Governments had agreed to principle to declare tourism as an industry. A group has been set up involving the Chief Ministers, Finance Ministers and Tourism and Culture Ministers of the Southern Region to look into the passenger tax which had adversely affected the movement of tourists between the states. In respect of the need for higher foreign investment in the tourism sector, a cell was set up in the Ministry to oversee the flow of investment in the tourism-related areas. A massive propaganda also would be taken to impress upon the foreign investors the return on investment in the tourism sector in India.

The number of tourists coming from abroad today is 1.9 million. This just reflects the phenomenal rise since 1950, when the number was a paltry, 17,000. This is evidence enough that we are certainly not underselling India to the foreign tourist. It has to be conceded that we have left no stone unturned to woo foreign tourists. Among the methods used have been innovative schemes and routes that have made India a tourist's delight. The minus point has been the problems regarding the infrastructure, but that is being taken care of. Very soon, this will cease to be a stumbling block. But there still is a lot to be done. For instance, if the number of flights to India were to increase tomorrow, there would be a quantum jump in the number of tourist visitors. Already, flights coming to India are generally booked to capacity. In fact, in the peak season the companies which operate tours have to turn away many a potential tourist. But the potential is so great. The need of the hour is new strategies to sell India as a destination.

To cite an example, the Buddhist circuit has evoked keen interest amongst people of Eastern countries. That was encouragement enough for us to explore the possibility of wooing more tourists from that area. And it is in this context that it had been suggested to Minister for Tourism that we devise an Islamic circuit on the same lines. He was very enthusiastic and wanted the idea implemented right away. The route would include Nizamuddin, Chisti's Dargah at Ajmer. Sarhind is a historical shrine and can also be included in this circuit. Similarly, Christianity in India is quite old, dating back to the first century A.D. Besides, there are wonderful churches in the country. We would thus do well to devise a tourist circuit, in this case to be financed by an affluent western government. So the authorities are working out viable, revenue-generating projects that will greatly enhance our image abroad and encourage many more people to visit the country.

Selling and Marketing : Problems of "Packaging"

If these ideas work, we should be able to get financial aid amounting to hundreds of crores of rupees to fund these projects, and also a sizeable increase in the number of tourists. Our plan is to devise circuits, which can be tunded by that section of people who are interested to visit places of religious and cultural interest to them, and with a heritage as rich as ours, that is not a problem. It is imperative to understand that selling India is an ongoing business. To say that we are underselling India is a comparative statement, and comparisons, as it is always believed, are odious. The foreign tourist traffic to the country has touched an all-time high record of 18.86 lakhs during the year ended 1994 registering a growth rate of 6.9 per cent over the corresponding period of last year when only 17.65 lakhs such tourists had arrived. The highest ever tourist arrival of 2,20,000 was registered during December, 1994 breaking the earlier records. The significant upsurge is due to the incidence of plague and its adverse publicity abroad resulting in serious setback of arrival of tourists during September, October and November last year. Foreign exchange earnings from tourism touched Rs. 4,848 crores in 1994 registering an increase of 11.6 per cent compared to the figure of Rs. 4,251 crores earned during the previous year. In dollar terms it was 14 per cent more at $ 1.56 billion in 1994 compared to $ 1.40 billion during the corresponding period of 1993.

The increase in tourist arrivals is mainly due to the concerted efforts made by the Department of Tourism, State Governments, Travel Trade and Hotel industry. Following adverse plague publicity abroad, the Government of India initiated several steps to counteract it, dispelling the fears from the minds of the tourists. The other reasons attributable for the increased tourist arrivals are liberalised charter policy of the Government.

The Rs. 188 crores India Tourism Development Corporation (ITDC) has evolved a strategy to combat the negative publicity the country has earned by way of the plague scare and which in turn had dealt a blow to the tourism industry here. It not only includes schemes to motivate the corporation's staff here to better their performance but also involves sending delegations abroad to dispel the fear among foreigners. The Corporation had lost business worth Rs. 3 crores in the month of October, 1994 alone, but it hoped to achieve its sales and net profit target set for 1994-95. The occupancy levels in ITDC hotels outside Delhi were very low (around 35 per cent as against the usual level of 80 per cent during this season) while the rate in Delhi was 80 per cent. While ITDC's net profit for the seven-month period in 1994-95 has gone up to Rs. 11.93 crores from the last year's level of Rs. 1.43

crores for the same period, a jump of 737 per cent its turnover too has increased from Rs. 92.78 crores to Rs. 113.96 crores. In 1993-94 for the months April to October, the hotel division made a loss of Rs. 4.82 crores, but in 1994-95 seven months period it made a net profit of Rs. 91 lakhs. The duty-free shops of ITDC increased its net profit from Rs. 5.94 crores to Rs. 10.66 crores.

The Corporation has introduced in its organisation a motivation scheme to improve its performance. Though the scheme has yet to be implemented, and is under discussion with the ITDC union, it envisages sharing a part of its increase in gross profits with its employees, the ultimate aim being to motivate the staff. The incentive scheme, which once implemented would come into effect from 1994-95, is expected to benefit not just the officer staff but also the workers of the corporation. The incentive will be given to all, from the vice-president level right down to the lowest level in the office, the ITDC board has already cleared the incentive scheme and it now with the union for further discussions. It was expected that everything will be settled in a month's time. The scheme would envisage that with every unit of increase in gross operating profit, a fixed amount would be given as percentage.

Another step which has already been implemented by ITDC to motivate its staff is the review of the cadre. "For long there had been stagnation of posts and no new post had been created. But with the cadre review scheme, we changed all that. The unions have already signed the scheme and it is under implementation," the ITDC Chairman has reportedly said. ITDC, which consists of hotels, duty-free shops. Ashok Travels & Tours, will be spending Rs. 10.70 crores during the 1994-95 and Rs. 18 crores during 1995-96 from its own internal resources so as to keep the properties modern and contemporary. The Ashok Hotel in the Capital here will have a new look by the end of 1994-95 with the addition of a new coffee shop, an Indian restaurant, executive lounge, and party rooms. A convention hall with a seating capacity of 500 seats and 72 guest rooms have been added at Kovalam Ashok Beach Resort, and 12 new cottages have also been added at Temple Bay Ashok Beach Resort, Mahaballipuram.

The ITDC Chairman had disclosed that the emphasis on human resource development has resulted in improving quality of service. The Manpower Development Centre conducted 357 in-house training programmes and trained 651 executives and

3,463 non-executives during 1993-94. The corporation already has a customer satisfaction scheme, under which all the suggestions received from the customers are analysed and acted upon. Six elite hotels of ITDC will be entering into a management and marketing tie-up with a reputed international chain of hotels in three to four months time. The Ashok Tour & Travel would be tying up with an Indian transport company to operate the transport business of the corporation.

Tourist Traffic

The international tourist traffic in India, which accounted for barely 0.72 per cent of the total traffic in 1988, has further slumped to 0.46 per cent, even as tourism managers predict a rosy immediate future. According to officials in the Department of Tourism, even the regional tourism receipts have declined from 74.0 per cent to 70.0 per cent in the same period. Apart from citing problems of law and order, which may have hampered tourist movement in the aftermath of the Ayodhya riots, the officials admit that poor communications and bad management may have also hit tourist movement in the country.

While ministry officials say that an action plan including reassurance campaigns in the overseas market, visit of promotional delegations to tourist-generating countries and invitation to media and trade representatives to India are on the anvil to boost tourism, Government figures themselves remain highly skeptical of what our offices abroad are doing. Take, for instance, tourist statistics of 1993 released by the Department of Tourism. The percentage distribution of travel agents to tourism was 14.6 per cent; Government of India offices 12 per cent ; international carriers 7.4 per cent; Air India and Indian Airlines 7.1 per cent; Indian missions abroad 7.1 per cent and hotel chains 4.7 per cent.

Added to this are the internal discrepancies in the department itself. An internal audit report for the department highlights certain typical nuggets. It sanctioned Rs. 4.91 lakhs as Central Government assistance for the construction of a tourist lodge at Bhanghonem on the Tripura Hills on the promise that it will be constructed within a period of six months. Much after the date had elapsed and an advance given to the State Government, the internal audit noted that "the estimates given by the State

Government were incorrect and the estimates were now prepared much earlier than the sanction of the project." And even after the release of the third instalment of money, it turned out, that the transfer of land in favour of the Ministry of Tourism had not even taken place. Then again, the Department invited quotations from various agencies for the production of 50,000 copies of a folder. Twenty-seven agencies submitted their quotations. A committee was formed to consider the quotations and it promptly recommended the job to an agency which was quoting Rs. 2,14,000 as its total cost. In addition, the department would also pay for sales tax and freight extra. The lowest tender, the audit noted, was Rs. 1,95,000 which was rejected out of hand, thus rejecting the time-honoured practice of awarding the contract to the agency which was quoting the lowest.

The audit also pointed out mass bunglings in placement of colour advertisements. An order was placed with ITDC for two full-page colour advertisements for a total cost of Rs. 1.20 lakhs. According to the sanction the department was to be supplied 1500 copies in English and 500 copies in Hindi on a complimentary basis. Later, when the audit investigated, it turned out that the ITDC had supplied 1500 copies in English while the copies, in Hindi has been left out. When ITDC submitted the bill, it was found that Rs. 7,000 had been paid to them for the work they had not undertaken. Observes the audit : "It has been observed that 10,000 copies of Rs. 20 each of *Discover India* were purchased for supply and sale during 1990-91. But out of the above-mentioned copies, nothing has been supplied and all copies are now lying in stock. All the copies of *Discover India* have now become outdated and nothing can be supplied at this stage. The whole expenditure of Rs. 200,000 has thus become wasteful"

Economic Force

Tourism is one of the greatest employment generators universally but even more so in India. It is estimated that even in a lean year like 1994-95 when plague struck and there was a sharp drop a visitor arrivals, there were more than million persons in India owing their employment to tourism. The perception in the common man's mind is that tourism is an elitist activity confined to five-star hotels and, therefore, does not affect him. In fact, nothing could be further from the truth. Every rupee invested in tourism creates more employment and economic activity than any other industry. It has much lesser ecological impact compared to other industries. It has the potential to create more goodwill in the international sense and generates more feeling of national integration for domestic tourists. it is the largest earner of foreign exchange (with the least outflow).

The liberalisation of the Indian economy has encouraged a much larger number of business visitors to India than ever before. This has led to a great shortage of hotel accommodation in the gateway cities for both business persons and leisure travellers. Accommodation which is available in places of tourist interest is not being utilised at the same rate as in the metro cities. The Department of Tourism and the travel trade have been seized of the matter but, unfortunately, not much has been achieved to overcome this problem. It takes years for hotels to come up and unless something is done quickly, the problem will become even more acute in time to come. The Associated Chambers of Commerce (ASSOCHAM) has set up an expert committee headed by a leading expert in the private sector hospitality industry, to look into problems facing the tourism industry and it has come up with a very comprehensive report and plan of action. The Committee has studied the world tourism scenario, as also the situation in India as compared to other Asian countries. India's 2-million-plus arrivals sharply contrast with China (23 million arrivals), Singapore and Thailand both exceeding six million.

The ASSOCHAM expert committee has coined an acronym, 'AIM' to highlight its strategy for increasing tourism. "A in AIM is for Awareness, I is for improvement in the infrastructure and M is to market India's multifaced attractions abroad. To achieve these objectives ASSOCHAM has formed three sub-committees. It also proposes to create similar structures in the North, South, East and West. The expert committee has decided that the 'Golden Triangle'—Delhi-Agra-Jaipur—which is visited by 60 per cent of the foreign tourists, be used as a model circuit for development purposes. The expert committee has already persuaded the Ministry of Railways to run a new train, the 'Golden Triangle Express' between Delhi, Agra and Jaipur.

The committee has also recommended the speeding up of construction of a four-lane express highway between Delhi and

Agra and then extending it to Jaipur. The highway should be fenced to prevent accidents due to cattle and other animals straying into it.

With regard to infrastructure, the ASSOCHAM Committee feels that to achieve a target of 5 million arrivals by the turn of the century the country needs another 70,000 rooms out of which 30,000 would be required in the next three years (at present there are 58,000 rooms). The current regulations for building of hotels on Government land need to be rationalised. The building of new airports and upgradation of existing ones is also a priority areas. We spend years in debating instead of acting immediately. Years ago many people were bitterly opposing introduction of colour television in India as it was felt it was a non-priority areas. Not only did its introduction revolutionise the industry (which was further augmented by satellite television) but even an export industry has been established. The Banglore airport is an example of our indecisiveness. The present airport operated by HAL is woefully inadequate. After long deliberations a new airport has been recommended. Now HAL has again asked the Government not to proceed with the projects. Goa also needs another airport as the current one run by the Navy cannot accommodate even two airbuses at the same time. Contrast this attitude to that of Hong Kong where a quick decision has been taken for a new airport. Airports take even longer than hotels to build, so we should take early action. Even though Khajuraho is a major tourist destination, yet no attempt (or even plan) has been made to link it by rail.

Marketing India should of course not be taken for granted. The ASSOCHAM Committee is very keen on inviting high spenders to India as it feels a large majority are low budget tourists at the moment. However, one has not to forget that people like Steve Jobs, founder of Apple Computers spent one year in India virtually as a back packer. Of course, earnings from tourism should be maximised and the domestic tourist's requirements should also be taken into consideration. For marketing India, Navin Berry of Cross Section Publications has been holding travel marts. The South Asia Travel and Tourism Exchange, SATTE was held in the Capital early in 1996. This showcasing of the Indian travel industry by inviting buyers from overseas and their meeting sellers is a step in the right direction. The Department of Tourism along with the travel industry has been spending a lot of money in publicising India at various international for a like ASTA World Congress, ITB-Berlin, World Travel Market, London, etc. Its policy of inviting travel writers in collaboration with Air-India gets a lot of mileage for India. These travel writers go back and write about India. The articles by them have far more credibility than advertising (which in any case is limited due to budgetary constraints).

Other Chambers of Commerce, industry associations and travel trade organisations should join hands with ASSOCHAM in changing the mindset of the bureaucracy to set tourism on an established path. The enthusiasm of the current Director-General Tourism to create new infrastructure unfortunately does not filter down to the *babus* and engineers of local municipalities, city administrations and State Governments. No hotel or road can be built without their participation, sanction or approval. What is most unfortunate is that in many cases even funds from foreign organisations like DECD (for example) for construction of roads by Bihar Government for the Buddhist Sector) lapse because they are not utilised in time.

As mentioned earlier the awareness of the benefits of tourism is very low in India. The Department of Tourism had at one time launched a campaign to educate the different segments of people who come in contact with the tourists. These include officials from customs and immigration, taxi drivers, guides, etc. The approach was by seminars and spots on television. The immigration department is managed by State Police Officials who consider this as a "punishment posting". The Home Ministry has at one time visualised integrating all of them under one cadre but several years have passed without any action.

Tourism Lobby

The need to create a tourism lobby in the country is imperative. The ball seems to have been set rolling by the Rehman Committee of Associated Chambers of Commerce but much more needs to be done by the travel trade, city, State and Central Governments to reap much larger economic benefits for the country.

Spokespersons for the various departments of tourism both at the state and Union Ministry levels, are not unlike a ventriloquist with his dummy, no one is really sure who is doing what, where or why. They all have the same tune to sing and mostly of the broken record variety. Just as they keep on saying, India really does have a lot to offer, but what are they doing it besides standing at the airport exist gate and counting heads! Not very much and generally even that little is too late. What is the point, for instance, of issuing a brochure on Himachal Pradesh winter holidays in February when the season is past its peak ? People in the trade have been forced to take their own initiatives and advertise abroad. Sikkim, India's smallest state, has been gone so far as to create a CD-ROM package, a sort of encyclopaedia on the areas that comes complete with history, pictures maps, local music, and a video presentation. At present this is mostly for the Swiss market, but, as a result it hopes to increase its tourism turnover. By itself, however, it is just a bagatelle, for without the Ministry's help in expanding the infrastructure and providing more hotels it can only generate a small amount of extra business. Too much expansion is impossible because there is just nowhere to put up tourists. This is the story nationwide.

Delhi is the starting point for most holidaymakers, but it is also the nerve centre of the liberalisation policy, so the many five-star hotels in the Capital are already booked as office space, etc., for multi-national companies trying to get their foot in the door. The common or garden tourist therefore is asked to form a queue somewhere else and maybe they will get a room, but then again, may be not. The Department of Tourism produces statistics about heads through the door, these are naive jottings which suggest that anyone with a foreign passport is a tourist, not a businessman or a courier or an NRI with family connections. A few inflated figures makes it look good ? So what price Indian tourism?

What is India to an outsider ? Or to another Indian for that matter. It is a combination of the staggering old world mixed with the brave new world interlaced with a vibrant other worldliness, both in and out of the urban setting. India has a great appeal for a certain type of traveller, the sort who are looking for an experience. But for the great majority of would be tourists in this ever diminishing world of ours, it is a complete nonstarter.

The PHD Chamber of Commerce and Industry (PHDCCI) has mooted a proposal for constituting a national tourism authority to formulate programme for overall development of tourism industry to earn over Rs. 15,000 crores worth of foreign exchange by the year 2000. This suggestion has been incorporated in the 'Strategy Integrated Action Plan' drafted by the Chamber for discussion with Minister of State for Tourism. It suggested the formulation of a common strategy by various segments of tourism industry to market the select tourists destinations. A marketing campaign should thereafter be launched in the tourist originating markets of the United States and Europe.

Special attention should also be focussed to tap emerging new markets in Japan, South Korea, Singapore and Malaysia. The Department of Tourism has been suggested to prepare contingency plan of action for dealing with crises such as riots and natural calamities.

Aviation Saga

With one Puss Moth, one Leopard Moth, one palm-thatched shed, one full-time pilot and two apprentice mechnica to the repealing of Air Corporation Act 1953, the civil aviation industry in India has come a long way. Gone are the days of long queues, stranded passengers and non-courteous staff. The ending of state monopoly in the aviation sector has already resulted in more air-carriers, better services and of course, fare wars. Undoubtedly, privatization has opened up new avenues in terms of services and facilitations, for an air traveller. But even as we head for an entirely new era of development, the question is have we really achieved our objectives ? "No", said erstwhile Civil Aviation Minister. "The very purpose of the open skies policy was to augment the existing network of air routes by offering services to places previously unconnected by air. Instead, it has only succeeded in adding more flights to the major trunk routes." The gainer of course is the consumer who is no longer at the sole mercy of the national carrier. Today, he can pick and choose among an entire host of ATOs offering him a variety of services from ground facilities to in-flight comforts.

While the travelling public, the media and the industry have all welcomed the repeal ordinance that made such expansion possible, caution has been urged on all sides. For one thing, some regulation of routes and control over fare levels is essential. There is also the possibility that India could became a dumping ground for obsolete aircraft from the west. Moreover, it would require sound financial management for the industry to generate the required funds—estimated at Rs. 37,000 crores spread over 15 years and sustain its growth level. On this latter aspect of sustainability, it is strongly felt that there should be a specific set of criteria and basic requirements to regulate entry into the field; it should not be possible for just about anyone to pay the government a certain amount of money and claim a licence to fly. The new guidelines to the Act would seem to satisfy this demand echoed by several ATOs, for big private operators must now have a minimum equity of Rs. 15 crores and small operators Rs. 5 crores. The chairman of a leading cargo airliner, agreed that Government vigilance is necessary, especially in the matter of "fly by night" operators who spoil the reputation of non-scheduled airlines. A direct offshoot of this policy has been the shake-up in the national carrier that no longer has a monopoly of the Indian skies. Indian Airlines says that IA has launched new training programme to ensure that its staff keeps pace with the changing scenario, especially where passenger handling is concerned. Inflight services have been overhauled and fresh marketing strategies have also been initiated. But the fear that ATOs may throw IA out of business is not really warranted. It is true that a large number of travellers have begun to patronise private airlines but IA still captured 77 per cent of the domestic air traffic last year.

"Private operators are treated like unwanted, children" is the feeling voiced by the chairman of a hill-routes air charter company. The main grouse is against fuel surcharge and the inland Travel Tax (ITT), both of which are unanimously termed "unjustified". At present, domestic operators have to cough up nearly twice the ITT prices prevailing in the international market. Further, the ATOs complain of unnecessary delay on the part of the OGCA when it comes to giving approvals. To top it all, aircraft maintenance facilities are virtually nil. Recently, the APAI-formed by 5 major ATOs-called for a code of conduct for fixing shares, as well as sharing counters and ground equipment. The Association also urged greater mutual co-operation, saying that passengers should be able to fly on alternate airlines in case of any disruption of services. The government countries these charge of discrimination with its own tale of woe. While most ATOs restrict their operations to the major (urban) routes, India

Airlines is forced to fly the non-economical sectors too. "So who is being given the stepmotherly treatment—the ATOs or Indian Airlines?" asks the civil aviation minister.

Notwithstanding these problems, the prospects for the industry are bright. "The picture is certainly very rosy", said the chairman, India International Airlines. Until December 1, 1993, no less than 17 operators held permits for operating air taxis. Another 20 companies had obtained no objection certificates for preparatory arrangements. Interestingly, among those entering the fray is a consortium of seven Gujarat companies that proposes to start a new airline operating on network, linking Bombay, Broach, Bhavangar and Surat.

Apart from increased airlinks, particularly on feeder routes, companies are coming up with innovative promotional drives to corner more space in the market. Cuts in fares and various other concessions have become the norm. IA and others like East West and Modi Luft have also tied up with hotel chains to provide different kinds of passenger discounts, thus facilitating travel as well as stay. East West, in fact, is now setting its eyes on the regional market, hoping to extend operations outside the country to important regional centres like Hong Kong. If the Government accepts this proposal it could mean the opening up of a whole new vista of challenge and excitement. Another airline that is unswervingly optimistic about the future is Sahara India whose Chief Controller avers that his company is "here to stay".

The Government for its part, is busy setting its own house in order. A standing committee has been set up to look into the major problems of the domestic airlines, including fuel surcharge and ITT. In a welcome gesture of co-operation, the maintenance facilities of IA have also been opened up for the use of private operators. At the same time, the civil aviation ministry has announced that all major ATOs must now compulsorily take on non-economical routes as well, starting with the North-East Sector. This particular move has of course come in for a fair degree of criticism from the private sector. The Chairman, Jet Airways and President, APAI, has said that private airlines would operate on feeder routes only if they were provided engineering and allied facilities. However, the Chairman, Archana Airways, throws his weight behind the Government decision. The whole point of the open sky policy, he affirmed, is to provide additional services to neglected sectors. The major trunk routes are already adequately serviced and the cut-throat competition created by a further onslaught on these routes will only end up harming the customer. The solution is to create new routes and to convince customers that in the final analysis, air-travel in both time-saving and economical. The industry then is at the crossroads. And though the cynics are only too ready to predict a short-lived boom, things seem to be going well, with active interest being taken by both the Government and the private air taxi operators to ensure consolidation and enhancement of present gains. As for the rest, only time will tell.

Meanwhile, Chairman, Jet Airways, said that the air taxi operators face on uphill task in securing allocation of space and equipment from the airport authorities on an equitable basis. Also, the airport and air traffic control timings across the nation need to be reviewed and revised, for they are at present tailored to meet the requirements of Indian Airlines alone. He called for a clear-cut and consistent government policy which would facilitate long-term investment, enabling the ATOs to build up the required infrastructure.

Cloudy Skies

The Indian skies have turned cloudy again. The freak accident if a Sahara India plane crashlanding on a parked Russian Aeroflot resulting in the death of a number of persons early last year, and the grounding of the Damania fleet a few days later because of its failure to observe certain conditions laid down by the Directorate General of Civil Aviation, have once again raised doubts about the safety factor of the private air taxi companies.

By repealing the Air Corporation Act of 1953 the Government has converted the two national air carriers—Air Indian and Indian Airlines—into companies and regularised the entry of private air taxi companies, (ATCs) into the Indian skies. The main objection raised by aviation experts is that the government, in a hurry to repeal the Act, has ignored the safety factor completely. From day-to-day maintenance of aircraft, training of pilots and cabin crew, to refresher courses keeping them abreast of the latest technology and especially safety regulations of the Directorate General of Civil Aviation are usually acknowledged only to be ignored by these private taxi operators. Much of the reason for the present woeful state is because the ATCs have been granted licenses to operate in the Indian skies with gay abandon. It is no secret that several operators fall short of safety standard stipulation by the DGCA because they lack adequately trained engineering personnel for the very purpose. At present this lacuna goes unnotices because the ATCs have a fairly good safety record.

Again, it is a well-known fact that the DGCA is not geared to face the additional responsibility in the light of the entry of ATCs, no step has been taken to strengthen it—But then the formation of the National Airports Authority has reduced the DGCA to a mere regulatory body, with responsibility only to oversee the working of the national carriers. Thus with several ATCs entering the arena, the DGCA quite naturally, finds itself helpless and redundant.

Initially, of course the private air taxi operators began by poaching on both the pilots and engineers of the domestic carriers. And today there are more than 110 pilots of Indian Airlines who have joined the private airlines. Moreover the aircraft brought from the foreign airlines either on dry or wet lease were in good flying condition after carrying out major and minor overhauls. However, the day is not for off when the problems start cropping up and the DGCA better be prepared for it. But then even the training facilities in the country are hopelessly inadequate. With not many airlines keen to incur the heavy costs is sending crews and engineer abroad for training, unless maintenance and training facilities are made available to the ATCs, the whole purpose of the open policy will be defeated. There is also the danger of ATCs compromising on safety norms if the DGCA's hands are not strengthened. With Indian airports becoming increasingly congested as ground handling equipment belonging to various airlines is scattered all over the tarmac, the likelihood of mishaps on the tarmac has risen considerably.

However, the advent of the private airlines has been welcomed by the public at large because it has provided some respite from the Indian Airlines' casual attitude towards passengers. And already the ATOs have made their presence felt. Particularly in the wake of the cripping pilots strike that rocked the already beleaguered Indian Airlines during 1992-93. The private operator, East West Airline, a leader among the ATOs at least in terms of fleet strength, made the most out of the strike. For the weary air traveller the goodies provided by the ATOs has literally come as a manna from heaven. Instead of being forced to accept what is available, he now has a wide choice with the ATOs vying for his attention. In their scramble for business the big guns have literally gone overboard to induce the travellers. Good food, on-time flights and a ready smile from the airhostesses are something that promises the air-traveller more than a mirage in the desert of Indian skies.

New Era Begins : Welcoming the 2 Millionth Tourist

When Mr. John Stewart Hillman and Ms. Shenkman Dasch landed at the City's International Airport one night not long ago, a big surprise awaited them. No, there were no hassless with the security or immigration or customs. On the contrary, they were to be received by none other than the Union Civil Aviation and Tourism Minister. It took them only a few moments to discover why they were chosen for a big traditional welcome—they were the last of the two million tourists arriving in India.

So, India that night crossed the two-million line in international tourist arrivals with the arrival of the two British Nationals. The country had crossed the one million international tourists arrivals mark in 1986. Both John and Shenkman were garlanded as they emerged out of the Air India New York-London Delhi flight. Mr. Hillman had the privilege of becoming the two millionth tourist. They were also presented gifts. The Minister of State for Tourism, the Director General of Tourism, the India Tourism Development Corporation (ITDC) Chairman-cum-Managing Director, Air India's Regional Director, and senior officials of the national airline and tourism departments were also present on the occasion. Both Mr. Hillman and Ms. Dascha would be the ITDC's guests for three nights. They were lodged at the ITDC's flagship Hotel Ashok early this morning. They would be leaving for Udaipur and stay at the ITDC's Lakshmi Vilas Place Hotel. Their stay would be complimentary.

In the area of promotion of international tourism arrivals, it was a matter of pride for the country that it had crossed the two million arrivals of tourists. The arrivals continue to rise and authorities are confident that in the near future people from Europe, America and South East Asian nations would be looking forward to visit to this beautiful and ancient country. A boom in arrivals became visible since September and the arrivals during the month recorded a growth of 12.1 per cent over the corresponding month of the previous year. The month of October, registered the highest growth of 82.8 per cent followed by an increase of 39.6 per cent in November. On the basis of current rate of arrival per day it became definite that the Department of Tourism would achieve the two million mark on this day.

The South Asia region had exhibited the second fastest growth in tourism arrivals after East Asia and Pacific. The World Tourism Organisation had stated that this would continue into the 21st century. As India got 51 per cent of the tourists in South Asia, it could expect a boom in arrivals in the coming years. The tourist arrival during the year was likely to be about 2.1 million, contributing foreign exchange worth Rs. 8400 crores.

The Department of Tourism is focusing its attention on the improvement of infrastructural facilities through private investment. About 6000 enquiries from the private sector had come to the department for investing funds in building up infrastructural facilities.

With cancellation levels in various hotels reaching as high as 35 to 40 per cent, travel institutions are gearing up to offer major sops to tourists in the aftermatch of the plague threat. The Indo-American Chamber of Commerce has planned a major media campaign in addition to offering free visits to foreign trade and travel organisations. The visits are expected to be underwritten in consultation and assistance with prominent hotel and tourism organisations. The Department of Tourism has reportedly offered all help in organising the trips so that an on-the-spot assessment is made possible by interested parties.

So far, Air India's offer for free passages to foreign media groups and travel institutions has not met with the kind of success that the Ministry of Civil Aviation had hoped for. A couple of American and Dutch television companies had shown interest, but they too have backed out at the last minute. Invitations haye also been extended to international exporters to come down and meet their counterparts and discuss the modalities of increasing business. In the connection, prominent travel house SITA Travels is said to have proposed to some of the Capital's top hotels that it should seriously consider the Government offer of a 50 per cent discount to international travellers. In a letter to some of the prominent hotels, SITA has asked them if they were considering offering discounts until at least the middle of December when the situation is expected to ease quite a bit and some of the travel groups have actually managed to cancel their reservations and go ahead with the Indian trip.

They have also proposed that in case a blanket policy is not acceptable, there could be a case-to-case decision on the subject. According to industry leaders, the plague threat had come at such a time when tourism could have been really pushed up. For effect, they quote a study conducted by the World Tourism Organisation (WTO) which has suggested steps to promote tourism to South Asian destinations. India is regarded as a major tourist destination in this region. According to the WTO, India has been largely responsible for the region's 3.4 million tourist arrivals with about 1.8 million coming to the country in 1993 alone.

Training Personnel for Tourism

One out of nine work opportunities in the world are in the travel and tourism industry. According to the World Travel and Tourism Council, the total number of jobs this year is 212 million and by the year 2005, this would be 338 million. With renewed interest in India, both by tourists as well as the business traveller, the travel and tourism industry is on the move here too. The development, promotion, management and administration of tourism in all its aspects—specifically travel and communication, hoteliering, public relations, holidays resorts—offers varied opportunities for employment. Job opening exist in both the private and public sectors.

Being a service industry, travel and tourism requires professionals who are enthusiastic and hard working, have communication ability, liking for people, irrespective of colour race, creed, religion or nationality, interest in travelling, ability for organisation knack for handling tough situations and knowledge of Indian culture and heritage. At the government level, the Department of Tourism at the Centre and States formulates policies for the development and promotion of tourism, selects and develops centres to attract foreign and domestic tourists provides travel arrangements to and from tourists sites, catering to international and national travellers; publicises the sights, sounds and experiences unique to India and provides detailed tourist information. This department is aided by the transport and cummunications industry—in effect by the road, rail, water and sea transport systems and the various systems of communication. The department functions through its many offices at home and abroad. Tourism Development Corporation in the different states and at the Centre offer a range of services such as hotels, tours and publicity programmes, for domestic and international tourists.

Work opportunities in these areas have varies openings for those who have a general degree as well as for those with professional qualifications. Information Assistants at the office counters of the tourism departments/ directorates/development corporations deal with queries of tourists and help them to plan their itinerary. They may also be at the "Welcome to India" desks of the Government of India tourist information offices at the international and domestic airports, greeting tourists on arrival, helping them to sort out their arrangements for stay and travel, guiding them on different sightseeing trips with details of various tours and packages on offer. The work requires a good knowledge and information base which has to be constantly updated and refurbished, patience with repetitive and trite questions, and the capacity to help people make up their minds.

A general or professional degree may be acceptable but with vocational study of tourism available at the degree level, those with interest in this industry should opt for this particular course. Not every aspect of job can be handled on the basis of academic knowledge. A person's initiative and tact in dealing with clients goes a longway towards making a success of the job.

Ticketing and reservation is usually a short-term course provided by vocational training institutes and polytechnics in cities as well as Indian Institute of Tourism & Travel Management (Delhi, Gwalior). Some travel agencies also conduct this course. Eligibility is Plus-Two or its equivalent.

Tourist Guide

Graduates with a background Art/ Archaeology/History can join the short-term courses organised by the government tourist offices, IITTM (Delhi, Gwalior), Kurukshetra University, etc.

A comprehensive course in Tourism may be taken up after successful completion of Plus-Two at the College of Vocational

Studies, New Delhi; Davar's College of Commerce, Bombay; Garware Institute of Career Education & Development, Kalina, Santa Cruz, Bombay-400 098, to name the prominent ones. IGNOU offers a certificate programme (six months) in Tourism Studies. There are also one-year diploma programme in travel and tourism and two-year post-graduation courses in tourism administration at several universities.

Promotion to the officers' cadre may take time. The administrative and policy-making responsibilities are handled by officers usually drawn from the administrative cadre of the Central and States' civil services.

The Indian Tourism Development Corporation (ITDC) usually handles the bulk of foreign tourists while the state tourism development corporations find themselves catering to a mix of foreign and domestic tourists. Naturally, the approach and environment differ.

One can also take on the responsibility of escorting tourist groups around a tourist destination or across the country. This work in a government tourism development corporation is assigned to candidates who have a professional/vocational background in tourism administration. Selection is based on the basis of the written paper dealing with questions on Indian culture and heritage and a review of the industry while the interview assesses personality and drive for the responsibilities.

Tourist guides are also employed by the tourism department on the basis of a written exam conducted by the department in association with the Archaeological Survey of India. Questions focus on your knowledge of India's heritage as well as general awareness. However, persons trained in tourism and travel management at the post-graduate level do not get the opportunity to join the government in the officer cadre. Such an opportunity may arise once a specialist tourism cadre is created.

Openings in the private sector exist in travel agencies, hotels, transport services, resort hotels, etc. This sector offers far greater scope for professionalism in entrepreneurship, expansion and specialisation than the Government sector. The variety of openings in travel and tourism call for various levels of training.

10

Aviation and Airports in Tourism Development

Air Transport

It is the invention of the jet propulsion engine which has revolutionised travel in this century and led to the international travel explosion of the post-war era. In 1951 there were 25 million tourist movements across the frontiers; in 1980 there were 279 million. The world figure of total number of air passengers, both international and domestic, was estimated at 745 million, of which the scheduled air services in the same year carried 594 million. In India 5.5 million people travel by rail and eight to nine million by bus every day excluding commuters. As against this the air traffic within India is about 6.5 million passengers a year, of which foreign tourists constitute less than five per cent though their revenue yield is presumably much higher.

A significant change in the mode of travel of the last 50 years is that passenger transportation by sea has virtually disappeared from the world scene. What has replaced it is cruise holiday traffic, which is currently running at four million people a year. The cruise business has continued to record a higher rate of growth than air traffic, both in numbers and in revenue yields. The Caribbean and the Behamas and Bermuda far and away constitute the main cruise circuit, accounting for nearly 90 per cent of the world cruise market. For instance, while stop-over visitors by air in the Bahamas in 1981 were 1,030, 640 showing a decline of 12.8 per cent, cruise traffic amounted to 596,870 recording an increase of 3.3 per cent.

Air transport has now become the dominant means of long-haul travel. For domestic and even short distance international travel among countries with contiguous land frontiers surface transport, if it is reasonably well organised, still claims a major share of travel. According to the OECD report on International Tourism (1981), among the industrial and relatively affluent countries "the private car still ranks high among the modes of transport used by tourists for personal travel whenever the geographical characteristics of the route permit, notwithstanding the substantial increase in the price of fuel over the past few years. For instance, there is as yet no significant switch to collective transport where this category of travellers is concerned in Western Europe or between the USA and Canada". But this is not quite true of developing countries.

Evolution of Airports

All travellers need halting stations for embarkation and disembarkation. But there is a qualitative difference in the modes of travel which has necessitated the construction of far more sophisticated and expensive airports than seaports and railway and bus stations. A modern airport is no longer a staging post linking surface transport with air transport, constituting a convenient point for conducting certain essential checks on the movements of outgoing or incoming passengers on international flights. The present day airport is expected to provide a much wider range of ancillary facilities because air passengers are often obliged to wait for long hours for connecting or delayed fights. Compare JFK airport with Grand Central station or New York seaport. A modern airport has become a symbol of a country's commitment of tourism. It is expected to provide restaurants and bars, facilities for communications by post, telegraph, telex, change of currency, well-stocked duty free and other stores, rest rooms, a barber shop and beauty salon, and opportunities for a variety of entertainment. At one of the important international airports in Europe there is even a prominently located sex shop. The airport at Dhaka has a Prayer Room for devout Muslims who offer five to seven prayers a day.

Despite the enormously high cost involved, the developing countries have effected considerable expansion and improvements in their international and even domestic airports. Many of them have also relaxed some of the frontier formalities and simplified the procedures for clearance of passengers and baggage. Nevertheless, generally speaking neither the improvements in the airport and ancillary facilities nor the streamlining of procedures in the Third World countries have kept pace with the growth of air traffic and its present day requirements. Among the Asian and African countries the outstanding examples of new or renovated international airports offering sophisticated passenger facilities are those of Singapore, Hong Kong, Bangkok and Nairobi. The airports at Manila, Colombo, Dhaka and Bombay are good examples of improvements effected in the last few years.

The investment in the first phase of Changi Airport of Singapore has been over S $ 1500 million and it can be handle ten million passengers a year and 5000 passengers per hour at peak hours. At present of provides 42 parking positions for aircraft including four in the cargo complex. It has also perhaps the largest columnless hangar where there wide body aircraft can be parked side by side. About half of the positions are designed for the future aircraft versions. In the passenger terminal building there is a centralised passenger handling system at two levels for arriving and departing passeners respectively. The two finger piers and more than half a kilometre long fitted with passenger loading bridges for aircraft to 'nose-in'. To reduce the walking distance in these piers moving sidewalks have been installed.

The cost of the recent development programme of Hong Kong airport completed in 1981 has been HK $ 600 million. Like Changi airport it can handle about ten million passengers a year and during peak hours can meet the demand of 5000 passengers per hour. Further expansion costing HK $ 270 million would be undertaken and completed in the late 1980s. At the same time a replacement airport to be commissioned in early 1990s is being planned at an estimated cost of more than HK $ 9.6 billion. This is still a far cry from the cost of Jeddah airport on which US $ 4.5 billion were spent several years ago and Riyadh airport nearing completion at a cost of US $ 3.5 billion. But then Saudi Arabia can afford it.

The international airport in Bangkok has also undergone a sea change from what it was only some years ago. Its maximum capacity per hour at present is 3250 passengers. But this is inadequate for the growing traffic. Hence a new expansion programme is also underway with a new runway, a cargo terminal and separate terminals for international and domestic flights. The project estimated to cost US $ 250 to $ 300 million will meet the projected demand until the year 2000.

Of the four international airports in India, Bombay and Delhi between them handle nearly 80 per cent of air traffic to India. A year ago the movement of international embarking/disembarking passengers through Bombay airport was 2.6 million and through Delhi airport was 1.65 million. The projected demand for Bombay for 1985-86 is 6.3 million and for 1990-91 it is 10.1 million. In the case of Delhi it is 3.05 million and 4.98 million respectively. As against this the present capacity of the new international terminal in Bombay is 2.5 million and the second phase will raise it to five million per year. In the case of Delhi the present peak hour demand for arrivals and departures is 1280 passengers while the existing capacity is for 500 arrivals and 350 departures per hour. The first phase of the new terminal in Delhi is expected to be ready by the end of 1985. The situation at Delhi airport has been extremely unsatisfactory for the last few years and will continue to remain so far another few years. At present even if there are passengers departing by flights of several carriers at quick intervals there is only one exist from the departure hall which has been aptly described as 'strait is the gate'.

The overall development programme of the four international airports of India is a story of too little too late. Even when the planned construction of expanded or new terminals is completed it will barely meet the projected demand and not keep ahead of it. At the present cost of construction plus normal escalations a new terminal with a capacity to handle four million passengers, embarking, disembarking and transiting, would cost US $ 250 to $ 300 million in an average-priced Asian or African country. The amounts earmarked in India for future expansion, and for that matter in most of the South Asian and African countries, are too small to provide the necessary facilities for quick movement of passengers and baggage.

Role of Airports in Trade

I have so far discussed air travel and the evolution of modern international airports. What still needs to be established is the relationship between international airports and the development of a region. Besides providing employment to a large number of local people, airports in recent years have come to play an indirect role in promoting trade. A great deal of cargo is being shipped by air transport, particularly since the large scale introduction of wide body aircraft. The supersonic passenger aircraft, Concorde, introduced by the joint British-French venture has not been a commercial success, may be because of its design or extraneous factors. Anyhow, the future technological innovation does not seem to lie in that direction, despite the innate predilection of the modern man for greater speed. Because of high-priced fuel and other sources of energy which are providing to be even more expensive, the future lies in fuel-saving aircraft designs which, according to some aviation experts, are likely to revert to narrow body or at any rate less wide body aircraft with a passenger capacity of 150 for short-haul traffic and 250 to 300 for long-haul travel. Nonetheless, cargo trade by air is likely to increase, may be by new aircraft designed for this purpose.

The compulsions of present day commerce demand speedy transportation of certain types of goods. Currently, one of the favourable factors is the persistent high rates of interest which make air transportation of a large variety of goods competitive, if not cheaper, than transportation by sea. The four international airports of India handled 156,054 metric tonnes of cargo in 1981-82 as against 84,450 metric tonnes in 1976-77. Even in the case of domestic airports in India the increase was quite substantial. Collectively the cargo which has loaded or unloaded at international and domestic airports of India increased by 82.3 per cent in the last five years. I do not havē global statistics but I would not be surprised if the cargo shipments by air have shown a higher rate of increase in the world trade than in the case of India. It seems reasonable to suggest that air transport is going to play an increasing role in world trade and the international airports world have to be equipped for large scale cargo handling.

Role of Airports in Regional Development

But in the case of developing countries much the most important aspect of the developmental role of airports is to open up new growth areas. An adequate rail and road network supported by telecommunications is undoubtedly a *sine qua non* for the overall development of a country. However, it is not easy to build railway and roads over mountainous terrain or through dense forests. For instance, it is easier to make certain parts of Nepal accessible by air than by rail or road transport. A countryside broken up by large rivers swelling up with seasonal floods, as in India and China, presents enormous difficulties in bridge construction. It has been a most difficult task to build any bridge over the Brahmaputra river in northeast India. Its span in the rainy season could be as wide as three miles and it changes its course frequently.

Yet another set of problems exists in countries which consist of a group of islands. The Bahamans are a typical example of this. It consists of 700 islands spread over an area of 75,000 square miles of sea with a total population of 200,000 and nearly 1.5 million visitors a year plus about half a million visitors by cruise ships. Besides the two main population centres, Nassau and Freeport, there are about 30 other sparsely populated islands with flat soft-sand beaches. Air transport is the obvious answer. Not surprisingly, there are 52 airports and only two seaports. Four of these airports can take jet aircraft. In this rather unique situation the airports have been the main factor in the growth of Freeport in Grand Bahama, Rock Sound on Eleuthera and a large number of other resorts in the Out Islands.

Airports and Tourism

In the whole range of developmental aspects of a region what makes accessibility by air a decisive factor is that it promotes tourism, provided that a specific region has certain outstanding tourist resources. In a sense every town or area is promotable but obviously not in the same measure. Tourism then becomes a catalyst for stimulating other activities, economic, social and cultural, a tool for overall development. The great advantage that air transport enjoys is in the saving of time, which is particularly important from the standpoint of foreign visitors. For instance, the flight from Delhi to Srinagar in Kashmir takes an hour and by rail-cum-road transport it takes 30 hours, sometimes 48 hours. One could cite many similar situations that exist in Asian and African countries. There is a highway linking Lusaka with Harare but the sheer distance makes it much easier to fly from these cities to Victoria Falls on the border between Zambia and

Zimbabwe and then cruise on the Zambesi. Some of the great wildlife parks in Zambia, and in Tanzania, up in the mountains, can best be reached by air, which underlines the need of an airport close to the park. Thailand has also discovered over the years that a jet airport was a necessary part of Chiang Mai's infrastructure despite reasonably fast rail and road services from Bangkok.

Case History of Khajuraho

Khajuraho, in Central India, 365 miles south of Delhi, is a classic case of the role that an airport has played in the development of an area that not many people had heard of 30 years ago. The nearest railhead is 60 miles away. The journey from Delhi to Khajuraho takes 18 hours. I first came to realise its tourist potential when I came across a book called 'Sacre Inde' by a Swiss photographer in 1954. Khajuraho was the centre of a medieval kingdom ruled by a Hindu dynasty of Chandela Rajputs who built a large number of maginificent stone temples in the 10th and 11th centuries A.D. Thousands of exquisite statues and carved bas-reliefs, some of them erotic, adorn the exteriors of the temples which are among the best examples of Northern India temple architecture.

Twenty five years ago Khajuraho was a small village with just a few shops selling food in an arid wilderness, because for lack of water there was no landscaping. The cattle and pariah gods who roamed freely around the temples outnumbered the visitors. What Khajuraho needed was, first water supply; second, a small hotel, and third, an airport. The first two attempts to dig tube wells were a failure. Even the Geological Survey of India failed to identify spots likely to yield underground water. Out of sheer desperation I hired a water diviner and unbelievably succeeded where engineers and scientists had failed. We installed not one but two tubewells. But as recently as 1965 Horace Sutton, Travel Editor of Saturday Review (New York) who visited Khajuraho reported, "We searched the poor village for a bottle of cold water and found none. By purest chance we met an Indian friend who, as far-sighted as a computer-minded westerner, is planning to put up a hotel. He and a small staff were living in tents, and if tigers or robbers did not get them they soon expected to start work on the hotel to be called Chandela".

Meanwhile I had an abandoned airstrip 30 miles from the temples repaired and persuaded Indian Airlines to start a subsidised twice weekly DC-3 service from Delhi. The passengers landed at the airstrip in the morning, travelled by a ramshackle bus on a bumpy road to the temples and returned to the airstrip before dusk in order to take off for Delhi. Traffic started flowing to Khajuraho and its popularity snowballed. It was soon realised that a jet airport had to be built to place Khajuraho on the tourist map. The airport three miles from the temples was opened eight years ago. Now Khajuraho is a thriving township with shops, banks, post and telegraph office, tourist information offices and guides, a museum and half a dozen hotels providing employment, direct and indirect, to several thousand people. There is a daily Boeing 737 air service. Bus-loads of middle class Indian tourists also arrive from far and near.

The one unquestioned economic benefit of tourism is that it creates employment among relatively unskilled and semi-literate workers in developing countries which usually suffer from chronic unemployment or underemployment. Besides Khajuraho I would like to quantify the employment generated by resorts on the west coast of Sri Lanka, namely, Negombo, 29 miles north of Colombo and a 20 mile sea belt from Beruwala, Bentota to Hikkaduwa, 60 miles south of Colombo. Fifteen years ago there was not a single hotel in this belt. Now it is lined with a large number of small and medium size modest priced hotels and ancillary facilities for shopping and recreation. It has been a reasonably well-planned development which has not ruined the environment. No building has been allowed to rise above the height of the coconut trees on the roadside. Large groups of tourists landing at Katunayake airport at Colombo generally drive straight to these four beach resorts for a week to two weeks holiday. The hotels and other facilities have created 5000 to 6000 jobs and indirect employment for another 8000 to 9000 persons. According to the Ceylon Tourist Board's estimates of 1979 the investment cost per job in the tourist industry was Rs. 59,283 (US $ 3200 approximately) and in the hotel sector Rs. 69,455 (US $ 3700 approximately) which placed tourism half-way in the cost : job ratios of ten other industries in Sri Lanka.

Tourism and Leisure

The two most important factors which have made world tourism the fastest growing industry of the world in the post-war era are the increase in leisure time and the rise in discretionary family incomes in real terms. Paid holidays which were first introduced as a social welfare measure 50 years ago have now become an accepted feature, not only in industrialised countries but also in many developing countries. The working week has come down to 40 hours or even less and in some countries public holiday are so arranged that long weekends of three or four days have become a routine feature. Other factors which have helped travel are improved educational standards and better health care which has made it possible for senior citizens to undertake travel for pleasure. Taking a vacation, generally twice a year, has become a way of life of industrial societies. It is a sign of the times that tourism which formed part of the Ministry of Transport in France for a long time has now been re-designated as the Ministry of Leisure and Recreation. Three years ago I also came across a professor of Leisure Time at the University of Brussels who was then investigating the relationship between leisure and tourism.

Several research surveys* have revealed that despite the escalation in prices less than ten per cent persons are willing to forego their annual vacation as against a much larger number willing to defer the purchase of a new automobile, household gadgets or furnishings. One per cent increase in the income level in real terms generally results in 1.5 per cent increase in propensity for travel**. In the reverse, a fall in the income levels that has taken place in the last two years in the OECD countries has resulted in near stagnation in global tourism. The world economy was able to bounce back after the 1973-74 crisis resulting from an unprecedented escalation in fuel prices, but the economic recession from similar escalations which started three years ago in still continuing. The economic experts have been prophesying that recovery was just around the corner but that tempting corner has been slipping out of reach. While the growth rate of tourism in the eighties is likely to be considerably less than it was in the seventies, there are still several reasons for taking a long-term optimistic view. Tourism is basically an irreversible phenomenon.

* WTO Survey in 1978.

** The Economist Intelligence Unit—Special Report No : 62 on International Tourism 1979.

For all these reasons the holiday segment of travel has grown proportionately at a faster rate than other segments. In this context it needs to be explained that the UN-WTO definition of a 'Tourist' is based on an economic concept and not on motivation. In summary, "a tourist is a visitor to a country other than the one in which he usually resides, stops over for 24 hours, and is not remunerated from within the country visited". If he is a day visitor or a cruise passenger (even if staying overnight on the ship) he is defined as an Excursionist. The upper limit has not been defined but most developing countries limit it from three to six months. The European countries generally fix the maximum limit at one year and the USA has left it undefined. Thus all visitors, say to the UK up to one year, for reasons of business, conference, health, studies, meeting with friends and relatives, but spending their own money are 'tourists.'

The pleasure periphery of European and American tourists which ended at the Mediterranean and the Caribbean now extends to the beaches of Asia, Latin America and the Pacific islands. Winter sports have also, had a phenomenal growth, but because it is a much more expensive and specialised activity and because of geographical reasons it is still mainly confined to Europe and North America. There is a great deal of trekking and mountaineering going on in the Himalayas but not winter sports.

To meet the demand for warm water beaches major sea resorts have come up in the last 15 years at Pattaya (Thailand) and Penang (Malaysia), in Bali and Sri Lanka, and more recently in the Maldives and other Indian Ocean islands such as Seychelles, Mauritius etc. Mexico has developed two great resorts. Acapulco and Cancun, and so have Venezuela and Brazil. Among the African countries Kenya has taken the lead in developing Mombasa. Egypt had the historic resort in Alexandria and has now developed Aswan Dam on the Nile.

Gateway Airports

It is still a moot point whether in the long term it is more economical to develop the existing international airports or to build new gateways close to the resorts. It has been argued that most airports such as Frankfurt, Zurich or Paris are not saturated and it is better to centralise traffic. But this pre-supposes a good network of surface transportation and spare capacity on domestic air carriers. Unfortunately neither premise is true in developing countries. India has the third largest network of railways and road transportation in the world and Indian Airlines ranks 13th among the domestic air carriers. Group traffic in India accounts for only ten per cent of the total visitors, but if it were to increase to 30 to 40 per cent, as is the case in several Asian countries or to 60 per cent as in Sri Lanka, neither surface transportation nor Indian Airlines would have sufficient capacity to carry to from the four international airports to tourist destinations. This observations is as applicable to a majority of developing countries as to India.

Consequently, whenever a major resort is not within easy motorable distance of an international airport is has been found necessary to build a gateway airport close to it *e.g.*, Penang and Denpasar (in Bali). Jamaica did the same in the case of Montego Bay. When the Indonesian Government insisted on routing international traffic to Bali through Jakarta there was a sharp decline in tourism. Malaysia and Sri Lanka have found by experience that for the development of their entire east coast regions a gateway airport is a necessary. India has a coastline of 5000 kilometres but has so far developed only two sea resorts on the west coast, Goa and Kovalam, near Trivandrum the capital of the southern state of Kerala. There has been some argument whether Goa and Trivandrum airports should be upgraded to gateway airports with all the concomitant facilities and immigration and customs services. But if package tours, mainly from Europe to these resorts or a similar resort on the east coast of India have to be competitive with similar 'packages' for Maldives, Sri Lanka, Thailand etc., then they will have to be equipped for point-to-point long-haul flights with full all-up weight of wide body aircraft, body for landing and take-off.

Dispersal Versus Centralisation of Airports

We recognise that there are several arguments against the building of new gateways mainly to serve the needs of resorts. For one thing a modern airport equipped with all the necessary navigational aids and even basic passenger facilities is a highly expensive proposition. For another, trained staff for immigration, customs and security arrangements is in short supply in developing countries. Besides the volume of traffic may not justify the engagement of fulltime staff. But as already explained dispersal of tourist traffic to different regions of a large country cannot be achieved by centralising traffic in a few, however well-developed, international airports. A more important argument is that many developing countries are going through a process of rapid industrialisation. New gateway airports, therefore, are needed for overall regional development and not merely for promoting tourism. This has been experience of even medium and small-size developed countries which have, besides one great central airport, several other airports where international flights can land and take-off, and passengers can go through the usual immigration, customs and security formalities. The newly industrialised countries (NICs) in Asia, Latin America and the Middle East are now going through the same process, of dispersal for reasons of economic, if not tourist, development.

The problem is of scale. Singapore, Hong Kong and Sri Lanka can do with one major international airport, may be even Thailand, but not larger countries of the size of Malaysia and Indonesia; nor can Mexico, Brazil and Argentina. The size of population would also be another determining factor. India now has about a dozen cities with a population of over one million and many others with a population of more than half a million which have become important industrial centres. They attract a great deal of business traffic which prefers fast transport services, not only within the country but also overseas.

Another argument against centralisation is that, despite all the mechanical aids for the ease and comfort of passengers and signposting for their guidance, the sheer size of great airports like London, JF Kennedy, Orly, Frankfurt, can be self-defeating. Passengers feel harassed, walking long distances with hand baggage and moving up and down from one floor level to another to catch connecting flights without the help of porters. In my personal experience of travelling through a hundred countries over the last 30 years, I have often come across nerve-racked passengers, losing their way at very large sprawling airports. The language problem adds to their bewilderment.

Facilitation

Before closing I would like to comment on facilitation at airports, a subject in which I have had an abiding interest for a long time.

That the first and last experience of a visitor to any country has a lasting impression may have become a trite saying, but is nevertheless a valid consideration in evaluating the impact of an international airport on the image of a country. I have some across hundreds of travellers associating their impression of a country with how they were treated on arrival and departure.

There are three aspects of the problem of passenger handling at international airports. First, the physical facilities; second, the procedures for clearance of passengers and baggage; third, the calibre and attitude of the health, immigration, customs and other staff dealing with passengers.

The first aspect has already been described in considerable detail in the case of number of Asian airport and I have noted the all-round improvements that have taken place or are in the process of being effected. But it is in regard to the second and third aspects that the situation in a majority of developing countries is highly unsatisfactory, in some of them to the extent of being a strong disincentive for tourism growth.

The procedures for clearance of air travellers should be carried out in such a manner as to retain the advantage of speed inherent in air transport. But this consideration is often lost sight of when specific procedures for the clearance of passengers and baggage are established at most the airports in developing countries which have not really become attuned to the needs of air traffic. It is highly gratifying that despite such heavy traffic, passengers are cleared through Singapore, Hong Kong, Bangkok and a few other airports in 30 to 40 minutes. But there are many airports in Asia, Africa, Latin America and the Middle East where it takes as much as two hours or more during peak time to reach the kerb outside and look for a coach or a taxi. There are also many countries where the departure formalities are still as cumbersome as those on arrival.

Aside from formalities the more important problem in most developing countries is that the staff working at the airport has not been specifically trained to handle international travellers. Often the immigration staff is drawn from the usual police cadre whose normal duties are to deal with law and order problems of the country. In many cases they are not conversant with the internationally accepted procedures, nor have they been briefed on international conventions on health, immigration and customs to which their governments may be signatories. They often betray a lack of courtesy arising from inherent suspicion. This of course is also applicable to some of the developed countries which have a tradition of brusqueness to the point of rudeness.

Finally, there is lack of co-ordination because the staff belongs to different departments of the Government and are governed by their own priorities. They are liable to frequent transfers to other jobs in their respective departments. But good management demands professionalism which is largely the product of training, continuity and experience. If a large international airport is to function as a well-organised entity there has to be some measure of control vested in the airport authority. At present the one thing an Airport Authority in most countries lacks is 'authority'. A travel journal described them as 'toothless organisations'. In the absence of juridical authority which presumably most governments would be relunctant to grant them I would strongly urge that the Airport Controller should be empowered to hold co-ordination meetings at which attendance by heads of other official and private agencies working at the airport should be considered essential. This presupposes that the Airport Controller should enjoy a sufficiently senior status, which is not the case in many developing countries.

11

Ecological Dimensions of Tourism

Ecology being an interdisciplinary science has remained very much an understudied area of study, 'Ecology of Tourism', its latest offshoot, is yet to be clearly defined. With the growth of world tourism as an all-embracing phenomena, its many-sided effects, nagative and positive, have been recently pronounced, distinctly. Multidisciplinary impact-studies, carried out in developing and developed societies support the hypothesis that unplanned and unguarded tourism growth leads to 'erosion-syndrome' which has often been metaphorically pronounced '*creative destruction*'. The economists award it a positive side, sociologists and anthropologists point towards many adverse consequences (xenophobia and acculturation) and ecologists declaim it a hazard to *environment* — 'Using it, to the extent of 'using it up.' In many cases tourism seems to be sinned against its sinning as the reports lack convincing empirical field data. Many biocentric organizations have invented shibboleth against tourism.

We have to accept that Tourism is an industry and it has its economic, its social, cultural and environmental aspects. In the world scene, in 1971 there were 180 million tourists. In 1980, the figure was 286 million—an increase of 100 million in one decade. In 1993 it is well over 1.5 million, a virtual explosion of travel for business, trade and pleasure. Now while Tourism has brought in a lot of foreign exchange, helped us in the balance of payments in the developing world as a whole, it has also created problems, is as much as we have to spend a lot of money on creating facilities. Similarly, while it has undoubtedly helped us to create jobs for local employees it has also cost a lot of money in creating jobs. For instance for each job which has been created in the area of Tourism, Tunisia has had to spend something like $ 13,300 !

Equally mixed are the social effects of Tourism. Sometimes Tourism has resulted in the dislocation of local people and damaged their economic interest, caused inflation, changed their life-style, challenged their cultural and even their other beliefs.

It has good and bad effects on our arts. On the one hand there is mass production of articles with no artistic value: only to walk down Janpath is evidence of that. But on the other hand, as Dr. Karan Singh very aptly said, dying arts and crafts of India have been revived. This must be very pointedly emphasised. Equally mixed are the effects on Environment—and that is the point with which we would like to deal in greater depth. On the one hand it has led to protection of physical environment—historic sites, monuments, and also of wild life. On the other hand, it has caused irreversible damage to some of these. Many a coast-line has been altered. Tourists themselves have choked the narrow streets of historic cities and over-crowded the picturesque countryside. The fragile eco-system, particularly of the islands, as also of the Himalayas, has been affected. There has been cost-pollution. And they have been left behind irreversible damage. And this has to be looked into properly.

Now with reference to vegetation, it is one of the important allurements with a large number of tourists. Particularly when people come from abroad they straightaway make a beeline for the alpine-like meadows in the Himalayas. Now what follows is : collection of flowers, an indiscriminate collection of flowers. Similarly with pilgrims going to Badri, Kedar: the bigger a person is the larger the number of Brahma Kamals that he must offer to the Lord Shiva. So what is happening is that in this way a species which is our cultural, religious, social heritage starts getting wiped out. These are some of the reasons that are behind certain endangered species.

Then, there are possibilities of forest fires due to carelessness, chopping of trees for tent-poles and firewood; high in the alpine areas we have a juniper and when yatris go to Amarnath they collect firewood, because it has the resin, it can burn when it is wet, and in the wake of that, that particular juniper is getting extinct.

Dumping a garbage attracts a lot of weeds. Weeds have always followed Man wherever he has gone—and a new element is introduced in these fragile eco-systems.

Traffic due to pedestrians and also vehicles alters the composition of vegetation. And the road systems that we build create disturbance in these Himalayan systems. Actually, if I have to go from Batot to Kud, or Kud to Batot, I never follow the road that they have constructed. As a highlander I will go my own way. Or if I have to go from Kazikund to Banihal, I will never follow the road, I'll go my own way. Of course, roads are important. But they have to be constructed in consonance with the terrain , with the eco-system and so on. Camping also brings in its wake certain ill-effects. All these factors, then, affect the eco-system.

Then come water bodies, like lakes, rivers and coastal areas. There is a lot of biological pollution. One mentioned the Dal Lake, he feels sore about it and so assure you do we. The amounts of boats there today result in the Dal Lake being little else but faecal matter and pathogens, and it poses a big health hazard. And this also adds a lot of nutrients, which result in profilic weed growth, choking the lake. The result is that Dal is now almost a dying lake— unless we do something very radical about it. You see, as a child, one used to go to Tulamala at Khir Bhamani via Anchal lake. There is no Anchal lake today. Perhaps one is rather primitive but we really pine for that trip in the little boat we used to take, winding through these little water channels to Tulamala.

Then come recreational vehicles. Every one must insist on surf-riding, petrol-driven vehicles, with the result that gradually, the water becomes polluted. This is another aspect which has to be looked into. Then, detergents. Trace elements from tins and bottles and so on. Now there is so much fluctuation in bio-chemical oxygen demand of the river systems as also of the lakes that the whole topography of the lake biologically changes and the whole water quality is thrown out of gear. Let us not forget certain other situations, like the Kumbh Mela. At one given point of time lakhs of people must congregate at one place and bathe. Well, we cannot change this fact. But what we can do is to bring Science to bear on the situation, to prevent the increase in colliform. Before Kumbh Mela, Colliform is normally around 300. Soon after Kumbh Mela, it jumps to 65,000. Now Science and Technology has to come in and solve this problem.

To touch briefly on air quality : the exhaust emissions of vehicles has an indirect effect on air quality. Although we are assured that the jet-run sports vehicles are supposed to be non-polluting, no studies have been made on the subjects as yet. And in any case, where jet-run vehicles are concerned, noise pollution has also to be taken into account.

Finally, the wild life. Wild life has been affected by hunting, by invading their natural habitat, photographing and so on. While the impact on larger mammals and birds is apparent, nothing has so far been reported on the reptile and the insect life, both of which are equally important. If tourism is to be handled on a *sustainable* basis we must remember that what is important is not the *number* of animals, but the *quality* of animals. In East Africa in one of these National Park, the Masai herdsmen told us that when their buffalos stop grazing and all look in one direction, that indicated the presence of a lion in the vicinity. Today, the presence of a lion is announced by a number of jeeps and Landrovers at a given point. The Masai herdsman, of course, is not happy about this. So the first result of indiscriminate tourism is that ferocious animals have lost their ferocity. Some time back, travelling from Bombay to Delhi, we had a look at the 'Swagat' magazine. (This is not a criticism of anyone). I found a series of photographs of lions in India. There is one photograph which shows a lion, a full-grown lion, skulking—and there are two people with rifles and a little buffalo tied to a tree. We felt very sad, seeing this. We thought "if this is the quality of our lion—well, we have numbers, but we do not have quality."

We have to think about this. These lion-shows and so on : well, we are destroying our wild life, in the name of tourism. This is not tourism. This is not sport. We have made beggars out of the lion. This is hardly a thing that we should be doing. Tourism has also affected feeding and breeding habits. Everyone insists on shaking hands with the lion, everyone insists on going to bird sanctuaries. This is not correct. The animals have to have their own privacy, and we must respect that. Their breeding methods : if we breed in privacy, they have an equal right to breed in privacy, and we have to respect that. Take the Great Indian Bustard. Everyone insists on going and seeing its nest and so on. So it do not breed. Now these may be the laments of a student of Biology, but you would not like to take them into account to the extent it is possible to do so.

Then, the killing of smaller animals through vehicular traffic is another very important factor to contend with in the ruining of our wild life, and it must be taken care of.

We are now going to have bio-sphasters and we would like to take some of these into consideration. Attending a meeting of bio-sphasters in Russia, who have done commendably well, they have created a small zoo right in the forests. Within six months, there were big, burly, brown bear. But any time anyone would pass, the bear would open his mouth. I could not understand this at first, so I asked my host, "Why is he opening his mouth?" He said, "He wants chocolates!" Now if this is the sort of tourism we have to develop, I am not very happy about it. There were a pair of wolves just sulking; whenever anyone would pass, they would whack their tail and would ask for some thing. So we need to look at these animals, but not in a manner whereby they would lose their ferocity. If we do this, we are in danger of disrupting the natural balance, the relationship between predator and prey. Man can have his tourism, humankind can have its tourism—but not at the cost of destroying this delicate balance, a balance about which we are not really clear. We should not do anything by which we might destroy these subtle relationship which are extremely important. Disruption by imposition of human interference is not correct.

Equally important is the disruption of the whole eco-system. Many African parks have been protected and the elephant population has increased. Elephants have an uncanny habit of uprooting trees. So what is happening in Africa is that forested areas are getting converted into grasslands. Then, share tourism : because they have been brought together, lots of people visiting, these are certain important changes that are taking place which are to the detriment of the eco-system. Litter and garbage piles : these attract rodents, they attract bear, they attract birds : and the whole habitat is altered.

There is an increasing demand for wildlife souvenirs. Furs, skins, ivory, ornaments, horns, tails, key-rings from hooves, so on and so forth. The result is that the curio trade has increased and we all know that animals are slaughtered for this purpose, that elephants are slaughtered for the ivory trade, and so on. In Manila, there are shops upon shops where stuffed animals are sold. One was appalled. We took some pictures and asked them about it. They said, "Look you're a foreigner. You cannot buy them." But it is appalling to see the number of stuffed animals there : crocodiles, turtles, bear, everything. We do not think that is implicit in the sort of tourism we want to foster. Even in

Eastern India we have butterflies slaughtered for this very purpose. So we have now started butterfly-farming, since we feel that for souvenirs it is preferable that we farm the butterflies rather than allow them to be collected from Nature. We could carry on telling more and more about the specific effects on eco-systems and so on; suffice it to say that during the 1970s, the upper limit of tourists was reached in several sides, and there were several indications which showed how poor the planning was, because it was apparent that tourist traffic itself had become counter-productive to the tourist industry. Two things need to be done.

First of all, research needs to be taken up, working out in depth the effect of tourism on different eco-systems, terrestrial and aquatic: the terrestrial to include mountains, sub-mountains and several other eco-systems that we have; as also effect on air, water, flora and fauna. We must know for certain in concrete terms what is the extent and nature of the effect, so that we can chalk out the mitigative measures. Secondly, we need to look once again at the worth of the Manila Declaration of 1980. To quote this Declaration: "Tourism development at both the national and international levels can make a positive contribution to the life of a nation provided the supply is well-planned and of high standard and protects, respects, the cultural heritage and values and the natural, social and human development."

Thus, in effect, what does it come to ? It indicates the *carrying* capacity of a particular site. Tourism has to be related to the carrying capacity; not that we should indiscriminately inject tourists into a particular site when the carrying capacity is not there. Tourism must be related to the resources that are available, and this needs to be looked into carefully. Because tourism has now become an international and even regional or sub-regional issue, co-operation is called for in this particular area. Because we know that Environment does not recognise Politics, it recognises Geography. And it is high time that we look at tourism from a regional, sub-regional or even an international level.

Lastly, we have to recognise one difference : the difference between the human socio-economic system and the natural eco-system. Now when we talk of an eco-system is an undisturbed state, it's a living, dynamic, continuing state, where plants animals and micro-organisms bloom together, and in a self-supporting, continuing manner. There is no waste in an eco-system. If an animal dies it becomes food for several other kinds of animals, micro-organisms, bacteria and so on and is forth : it is ultimately resolved back into the earth : "*Yatraya patragatha*." A natural eco-system is never hitched to any one, two, three or four species. It is a system. On the other hand, when you talk of the human system it is hitched to only one species and that is the human species, with the result that there is waste. After all, what is the major component to human socio-economic system which spoils the environment ? It is waste. And the waste gets piled and piled and piled and it is totally bio-degradable because it is not injected with the system which normally would have degraded it.

So the lesson is that the two things have to go together and have to be a symbiotic relationship. This is borne out even by our ancient Vedic perceptions in this regard: *prakriti* and *purush*. *Prakriti* is Nature, *purush* is Human kind. They are two inseparable things, and we have to take our lesson from them. Take our spirituality and philosophy. (Dr. Karan Singh is much more well-versed in this area). Where was it built ? It was not built in air-conditioned rooms. It was built under the trees, in *tapovans*, by our rishis, munis, and seers : this is a great lesson that we have to draw from there. And that lesson must be then applied to environment.

Take our non-violence : "*ahimsa per modharaman*". Now this does not mean non-violence between human species. The concept is wider. It implies non-violence against plants and animals. If we respect Nature—and then foster tourism, there will be no problems. You see, unfortunately Modern Man thinks that he is a co-creator, with Nature. That is the greatest fallacy, and that is the reason why he is going to destroy himself in this game. Whereas the Primitive Man (we do not know whether he *was* primitive) he had respect for Nature. He would bow down before the trees, he would bow down before the sun. Not that it is necessary, it is his attitude one is talking about. He would take from Nature only whatever he required, to the extent that he required it—not plunder it greedily.

All said and done, we have tourism, because tourism is essential. But tourism, economic development and environment have to go hand in hand, *have* to have a symbiotic relation. And it should be such that it should not affect our eco-systems, for whatever they are worth. They are already under strain and if you strain them further by adding another element it would be the same thing as the story of the golden goose.

Ecology and Conservation

Ecology is another name for conservation. The concept of 'environmental limits', 'thresholds' 'carrying capacity' are pointers to the health and wholesomeness of the 'ecosystem'. Any development process, to be called benign or benevolent must respect resilliency of ecosystems which have varying degree of tolerance for man-created problems of waste. Some of them may be more fragile for tourism uses that their cybernatics would be irreversibly damaged for any redress. It is here that the developer must be careful in harnessing them. Incidentally, such sensitive resources, physical and cultural, are often demanded for tourism promotion (*viz.*, virgin meadows, silent river valleys, white waters, cultural mores and tribal life) and paradoxically, the third world countries have then in abundance. Tourism for all its economic premises comes to the fore. (Singh 1983). And this is also true that in most cases tourism enters with little planning preparedness which helplessly contributes to environmental destruction. Cohen (1978) in his most informative paper 'The impact of tourism on the physical Environment' expresses concern that developing countries with no tradition of conservation and awareness of the need for environmental protection must be very cautious in promoting tourism. Cohen sees tourism possessing peculiar environmental dynamics of its own, amenable to management regulation and control. He tends to view the option in terms of opposing alternatives—protecting the environment for tourism and protecting the environment *from* tourism. Sadly, in the third world countries economic goals supercede ecological sanctity. More often than not eco-cries are heard when the resources has suffered irreparable damage. Some of the studies conducted in the third world countries have attempted to prove that ecological consequences were the direct result of sheer ignorance and non-challance or the decision-makers and developers where tourism entrepreneur was unable to grasp the implication of his profit-making operation on the overall environment—the transformation character of tourist development. Houts (1979) comments that big cities seem to able to withstand tourist invasion better than the open countryside and other delicate environments.

Some of the negative ecological effects spelt out in the 'Konfrez Himalaya 1983'; (Singh, 1983) German Alpine Club, Munich were, pollution, destruction of forests (firewood) concentration, noise and overcrowding, damage to nutrient—water energy system, encroachment upon flora & fauna, destruction of grazing lands by campgrounds, garbage trails and soil erosion; overburdening the population in tourist areas and promotion of a 'throw away mentality'. But at the same time positive effects of tourism were also highlighted. One of the brighter side of tourism was creation of parks, wilderness areas preservation of Nature monuments, ecological awareness and better understanding of tourism as partner and preserver of regional ecology associated with religious and nature myths and geopiety. Mass tourism and Environment can hardly reconcile, the obvious result is pollution; physiological, (air-water and thermic) physical (soil erosion, destruchorin of landscape); biological (damage to plant and animal life). Sciological and psychological side effects were other impacts. While these impacts may be general statements, location specific studies have succinctly proved that only 'soft' and dispersed tourism activity can help maintain the health of eco-system. Burmeister (1977) ably sums up various short term/long term impacts of tourism by taking six variables. He found that effect was more conspicuously negative and direct in developing societies.

Tourist attraction, is a unique blend of resource and infrastructure. A tourism resource of average quality may fuel to the fire. Right from Ladakh to Gangtok the Himalaya burgeon with touristic activity which has damaged the resource not so much by human visitations as by inadequate infrastructure, lack of planning strategies & clear policy goals. In Garhwal Himalaya the two recently created National Parks; the Valley Flowers and the Nanda Devi had to be banned for visitors. Many an area of Himalayan wilderness, silence and beauty are being opened for wanderlust tourism with little sense of ecological propriety—the result would be eco-disaster, and tourism shall be blamed. The purpose of this discussion is not to discard tourism but to pinpoint the policy and typology of development which should benefit the local people and upkeep the environment. Unique creations of Nature, like the Himalaya, should be open to

TOURISM DEVELOPMENT AND ENVIRONMENT QUALITY

ALTERNATIVE FORMS

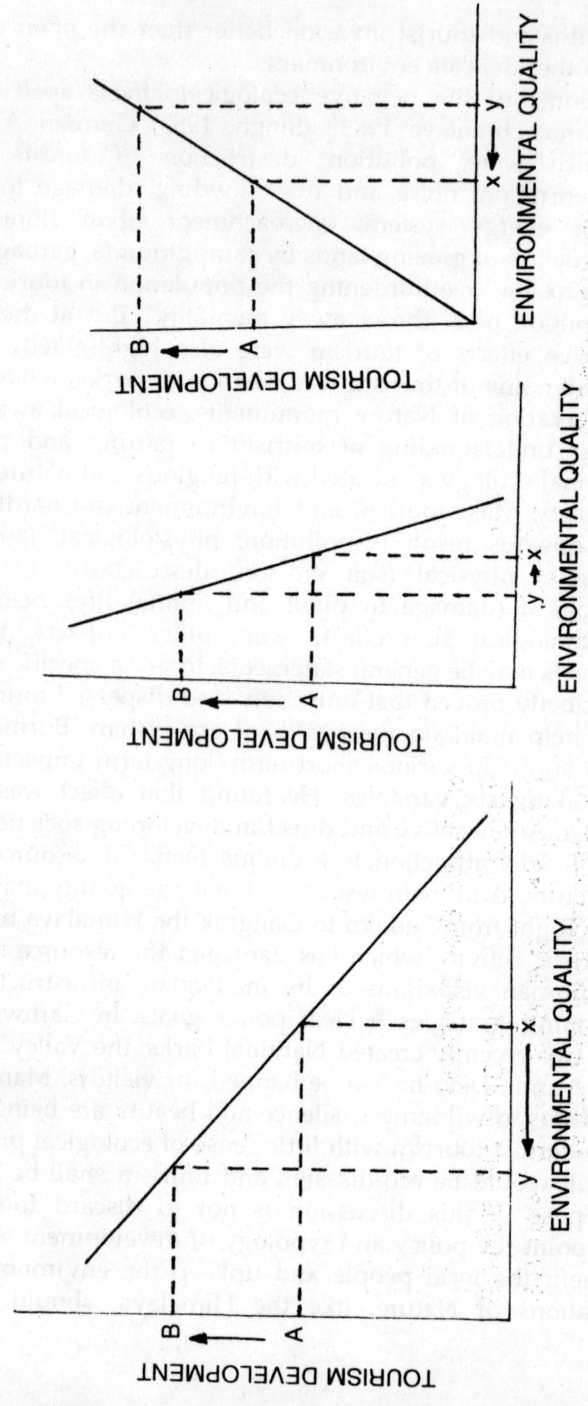

Fig. 11.1 Environmental Quality

enjoyment in a manner that posterity is not deprived of these nature monuments. Tourism and Environment can be equal partners in the development process if they mutually agree and not come in conflict (see Fig. 11.1). Burmeister identifies some specific tasks for the survival of tourism which may be cited here for the guidance, particularly for the policy makers of the third world countries :-

— How to create agglomeration without creating cities in the bad sense ?

— How to create possibilities for solitude without creating loneliness ?

— How to create possibilities of relaxation without excluding stimuli that are desirable ?

— How to create a new architecture that is part of the landscape and not vice-versa ?

— How to avoid the absorption of free space by tourism, even more difficult if we try to avoid urbanised centre ?

— How to avoid a decrease in beauty when in reality for most people an empty beach is more beautiful than a full one : a primitive winding street with trees more beautiful than a highway and gas station ?

— How to avoid the noise that goes with any concentration of people, when some concentration is unavoidable and even desirable ?

— How to avoid pollution that the sectors of industry catering to tourism cause directly or indirectly for tourists?

Some of the answers to such penetrating questions can be give when tourism problems are tackled by interdisciplinary approach, for ecology is a science in which everything is related to everything else—and so is tourism.

Appendix - 1

A FRAMEWORK FOR THE STUDY OF TOURISM AND ENVIRONMENTAL STRESS (AFTER OCED)

Stressor Activities	*Stress*	*Primary Responses Environmental*	*Secondary Response (Reaction) Human*
1. Permanent environmental restructuring.	Restructuring of local environments expansion of built environments land taken out of primary production.	Change in habitat, Change in population of biological species.	**Individual**—impact on aesthetic values collective measures.
(a) Major construction activity expansion transport network, tourist facilities, marinas, ski-lifts; sea walls. (b) Generation of waste residuals Urbanization/ transport.		Change in health & welfare of man. Change in visual quality.	Expenditure on environmental improvements; Expenditure on management of conservation; designation of wildlife conservation, and parks. Controls on access to recreational lands.

2.	Generation of waste residulas. Urbanization Transportation.	Pollution reading emissions, effluent discharges solid waste disposal, noise (traffic, aircraft).	Change in quality of environmental media, air/water soil. Health of biological organism Health of humans.	**Individual defensive measures.** locals/air conditioning recycling of waste materials protest and attitude change tourists/change of attitude towards the environment/decline in tourists revenue collective/ defensive measures. Expenditure of pollution abatement by tourist related industries cleanup of rivers & beaches.
3.	Tourist activities skiing, hunting train biriding colecting.	Trampling of vegetation and soils. Destruction of species.	Change in habitat, Change in population, of biological species.	**Collective, defensive measures.** Expenditure on management of conservation designation wildlife conservation and national parks. Controls on access to recreational lands.
4.	Effect on population dynamics. Population growth.	Population density (seasonal).	Congestion Demand for natural resources, land & water energy.	**Individual**—Attitudes to overcrowding and the environment, Collective growth in support services, e.g. water, supply, electricity.

12

Travel Formalities and Procedures

ARRIVAL FORMALITIES

Visa

Of the 150 member states barring 44 members of Commonwealth countries all foreign visitors to India have to obtain a visa. It is understood there are 170 Indian missions overseas of which presumably one-third are in Commonwealth countries. It is estimated that 46 per cent visitors come from Commonwealth countries and of the remaining 54 per cent, the bulk of them come from about 15 countries, namely ten countries of Western Europe, USA, Japan, Pakistan, Indonesia and Mexico. The number of Indian missions in these countries is inadequate : four in the USA, two each in Germany and Pakistan and one each in the rest. A large number of visitors are residents of towns far away from the nearest Indian mission. According to the Indian procedure three copies of the visa application form have to be furnished with the passport and, because of the formalities involved, the visa is not issued the same day. At best it may take two days but usually several days. The visa is for triple entry; for tourist the validity is three months and for others shorter periods according to the applicant's intended duration of stay. It is not known if, as a result of the re-imposition of the visa, any extra staff has been appointed in these missions. An applicant living far away from the nearest mission has the option to send his passport by mail but most people are reluctant to do so for fear of the passport being mislaid. Finally, group visas are not issued.

International Practice

Usually one visa application form is required, with or

without photograph, and the visa is issued within half an hour, or at any rate the same day, particularly if the applicant is not a resident of the city where the mission is located. Most European countries issue multiple entry visas valid for six months regardless of whether the applicant's intended duration of stay is only a week or more. Group visas are issued.

Arrival

Passengers deplane and are transported to the terminal by bus at Delhi, Madras and Calcutta airports. At the new terminal in Bombay two 'fingers' have been provided for aircraft to nose-in. The same arrangement will be provided at the new terminal at Delhi to be ready in 1985 or thereafter. Two 'fingers' would perhaps suffice until the total annual passengers do not exceed about two million a year. But Bombay already has about 3.2 million a year and Delhi about two million. In addition India's geographical position is such that most flights originating at convenient timings from Western Europe or Sydney and Tokyo in the east arrive at Indian airports between 10 pm and 6 am. Hence the bunching of flights at Bombay and Delhi is unavoidable. Their landing fees are already considerably high—higher than at several Asian airports with better facilities. Any further raise in landing fees during night hours in order to divert the flights to Madras or Calcutta will be counter-productive. The International Airports Authority's efforts to this effect have not been successful.

Health Check

Inside the terminal all passengers have to line up at the health counter which is usually not manned by a doctor but a Health Assistant. He only checks from the passenger's reply in the Immigration card if he has passed through an endemic yellow fever area in the previous six days. The endemic areas are only Central Africa and the Amazon region of Brazil, but the whole of Africa below the Sahara is considered a yellow fever area by Indian health authorities. Since there is only one health counter it takes considerable time, may be half an hour, to check the cards of all the passengers.

International Practice

There is no health check. With the virtual disappearance of

smallpox practically all countries including the most health conscious Western countries have abolished the health check. The WHO issues a monthly bulletin for the guidance of all member states and if a particular country, say Bangladesh, has recrudence of smallpox or cholera, a health check may be reimposed as a temporary measure against passengers coming from that particular country.

Medical Argument

Only four countries in the world, India, Pakistan, Sri Lanka (may be now also Bangladesh) and Indonesia continue to have a yellow fever check. In the Indian subcontinent this check was apparently introduced back in the twenties or thirties when it was more or less under one Administration. The argument was that these countries climatically are susceptible to the spread of yellow fever, through the mosquito which is the carrier. But in fact the whole of Southeast Asia and Burma with their hot and humid climate are equally, if not more, susceptible. They never imposed this check and yet in the last 30 years, since the growth of tourism, yellow fever has not spread there. The health ministry had no argument against this even 25 years ago except that this danger must be avoided. Some eminent medical experts I consulted at that time agreed that this point was worth investigation and suggested that a research project should be initiated by the health ministry. But the later was adamant : the check should continue. Medical science has progressed phenomenally since this check was introduced 50 years ago by some well-intentioned British Director General, Health Services. Its validity needs now to be investigated by a group of medical specialists.

Proposal

The mere fact that a passenger has passed through sub-Sahara Africa can be checked from the passport even by an Immigration Officer. A passenger who has done so can then be referred to a representative of the health department on duty at the airport. In fact the IAAI made this proposal a year ago and suggested the abolition of a separate health counter. It was, as expected, turned down by the Director General, Health Services.

Immigration

Considering the congestion of traffic at night there should be at least six Immigration counters at Delhi and eight at Bombay but the number in operation are usually half of this. How many counters should operate at peak hours and at other periods at each airports should be determined by a time-motion study by IAAI and then staff must be provided by the immigration and customs authorities.

The Immigration Officer should quickly scan the immigration card, stamp the passport and be able to clear five or six passengers per minute which is considered the normal rate internationally. In India he first compares the entries in the card with the passport, then fills out the section 'For official use' and makes notations in ink on the passport in addition to the stamp while the passenger waits. The officer is generally not well educated and unfamiliar with foreign names and places; hence he is slow and usually clears one passenger per two or three minutes. If each queue is 30 to 40 passengers long, the last passenger has to wait for one hour.

International Practice

An Immigration Officer runs his practised eye very quickly through the card and the passport, stamps the passport and keeps the card. He *never* writes anything on the card or the passport while the passenger is waiting. He is well educated and trained and may ask one or two questions: purpose of visit, how long the passenger is going to stay in the country etc. Generally he can speak one or two foreign languages and is quite familiar with foreign names and places.

Red Book (Sometimes called Black Book) : This book, with an indexed list of names of undesirable persons usually given to every Immigration Officer is kept under the desk and referred to discreetly if a passenger's name rings a bell. (The US Immigration Officers, not credited with good manners, keep it right on the desk and look into it blatantly while the passenger is looking on). In India the officer at the counter is not entrusted with it. If he feels suspicious he asks the passenger to step aside and wait while he sends his passport to the senior officer, usually a DSP, who has the Red Book. It is most embarrassing for a passenger to have to wait, if it is found, as is generally the case, that the suspicion was unjustified. Besides if the counter officer is not familiar with the list of names in the Book how would be identify an undesirable passenger ?

Baggage Clearance

The baggage starts arriving within about 20 minutes of landing. But from the trolley it is unloaded manually and placed on the conveyer belt. Generally, one or two trolleys make several round trips between the aircraft and the terminal. So the baggage comes in by instalments and generally moves around two belts and the passenger has to keep jumping from one belt to another like a cat on hot bricks. Sincc half the passengers are cleared late or quite some time after the baggage started arriving, the porters have usually taken off he unclaimed baggage and dumped it on the ground, and they have then to go round looking for their baggage, all over the place. The international arrival areas in Delhi, Bombay and Calcutta are quite large and there is no excuse not to have installed a sophisticated smooth running conveyer system which can take on the entire baggage of each wide body jet, not for lack of trolleys and the manual unloading of baggage.

Customs

The Indian immigration card was modelled in 1957 on ICAO's E/D card of 6 × 4 inches, but with nine instead of seven entries. The customs declaration in writing was abolished and substituted by oral declaration both on arrival and departure. It was a somewhat retrograde measure that around 1969-70 the present E/D card was introduced. Its virtue is that it contains a health declaration plus a separate portion for customs.

Green/Red Channel System

This was first introduced in 1962 in Sweden, in 1965 at London and is now followed by many countries including India. It is a great step forward. But passengers choosing to follow the green channel are still usually questioned if they have any articles not normally allowed, particularly electronic items such as video sets, tape recorders, cine cameras etc. If so, a re-export declaration has to be furnished and a notation is made in the passport.

But going through the red channel is a time consuming exercise. Passengers have to wait for lack of sufficient staff. The baggage is usually opened and rummaged and the passenger closely questioned. The passport has to be shown and is generally sent to the Assistant Collector sitting in an office behind the counters. The customs have apparently a separate Red Book available to the Assistant Collector only.

International Practice

There is a common Red Book shared by immigration and customs. Hence the passport having been examined by immigration is not required to the shown again to the customs. The baggage declaration is oral and examination is on a sample basis. Either none is opened or one out of two or three cases is opened. The time taken is usually a couple of minutes per passenger. (The USA is an exception with close examination and an impolite attitude).

Unaccompanied Baggage

According to Annex 9 of ICAO, entitled 'Recommended Standards and Practices For Visa, Passport and Frontier Formalities', unaccompanied baggage should be treated as baggage and not as cargo in respect of customs clearance. Annex 9, usually published every two or three years, is considered the Bible of facilitation and contains about 200 pages of recommendation. Reservations to recommendations not acceptable to a Government have to be filed within six months. In the early years India had filed more than 50 reservations, next to Australia the highest in number.

The question was first raised in India by international carriers as far back as 1953, at the newly constituted National Facilitation Committee which had been set up according to the ICAO recommendation and consisted of representatives of international carriers and of the government departments concerned. This joint committee functioned actively from 1953 for many years and its regular six monthly meetings should be revived.

However, the Indian Board of Revenue refused to accept this recommendation and treated it is cargo.

Definition of Unaccompanied Baggage

It may be of two types : (a) A passenger may book one or two heavy suitcases on a flight ahead of arrival or it may be delayed baggage because it was inadvertently off-loaded by the carrier at an intermediary point; (b) Extra baggage may be booked as unaccompanied baggage on the same flight because the freight charges are practically half. In either case it should be cleared according to rules applicable to passenger baggage. In India it was sent to the cargo division and a passenger had to fill out several forms and usually took half a day to clear it. More recently, delayed baggage is kept in the passenger terminal in the custody of customs in a separate room which operates only from 10 am to 6 pm. A passenger on arrival finds that his baggage has not arrived and waits for it anxiously. He may be leaving shortly according to his itinerary and has to go through a tiresome procedure to recover his suitcases even if they arrived within two days. Meanwhile the passenger is living on borrowed clothes or emergency purchases of essential clothing and toilet accessories. It is a most illogical and annoying practice which is not followed by any other country.

Progressive Clearance

Both ICAO and IATA have recommended that in regard to clearance of flights calling at more than one international airport within the same country the passenger and his baggage should be cleared through all governmental formalities at the airport of his final destination; in the reverse, the departing passengers should be cleared at the first port of embarkation and not the last airport of the country from which the aircraft leaves. Most countries follow this uniform practice but India follows the contrary procedure. For instance, a large number of Air India flights coming from Europe or Australia halt first as Bombay and next at Delhi. The baggage of even those passengers who are travelling to Delhi is taken off the aircraft and customs cleared at Bombay. It is then sealed and re-loaded. The passenger himself is cleared at Delhi through immigration and customs. This has quite often resulted in some baggage being left in Bombay and when it arrives by another flight it is treated as cargo and not a accompanied baggage. In the reserve direction passengers embarking at Delhi by aircraft going via Bombay to an onward destination are not cleared at Delhi but at Bombay. This causes considerable inconvenience to passengers at odd hours of the night.

Facilities After Clearance

International Practice

At most airports when a passenger comes out after customs clearance he finds a row of desks belonging to road and rail transport operators, hotel chains etc. He can book a hotel room or a seat on a coach going to the city, hire a car or make a rail connection. After a long journey he is tired and at midnight or thereafter he wants to make the arrangement in getting to a hotel in a civilised manner.

India

At none of our airports does this facility exist. He is ejected out of the terminal and then pestered by dozens of touts, taxi drivers, hotel representatives. If he has not made a prior hotel reservation he cannot make one. Even if he has one and gets into a taxi it often takes him by the longest route and charges him exorbitantly, Rs. 200 to Rs. 400. In many cases, it is also reported, the taxi driver takes him to an unknown guest house or to the wrong hotel on the plea that the hotel recommended to him was oversold. Though the Tourist Department mans a counter both in the international and domestic arrival area it is of little help to rectify the situation outside the terminal. The Hotel Associations of Delhi, Bombay and Calcutta have for 20 years been asking the DGCA and later the IAAI to provide them with counters which will be manned by the Associations and not by individual hotels. They have been denied this on the plea that there is no space. This is manifestly untrue because there is ample space available both in the domestic and international arrival areas, and secondly the ITDC which is a member of the Hotel Federation was given counters many years ago.

Departure Formalities

International Practice

In a majority of countries, and certainly in almost all countries which profess to promote tourism seriously, there are only two check-points on departure: First is Immigration where the passport is checked and stamped and second is the Security check which amounts to walking through a barrier but there is no body search or physical frisking. The embarkation card has been more or less universally abolished. The passenger checks in at the airline counter first and the baggage goes directly from there to the aircraft.

There is no direct payment of departure tax in Western European countries because it is made part of the cost of the airline ticket and is reimbursed to the Government by an accounting system between the carriers and the local Government. In many Asian countries, if it is not absorbed in the cost of the ticket, it is paid by the passenger while checking in at the airline counter.

India

(a) The departure tax has to be paid at a separate counter manned by State Bank of India. There is often a long queue and with the usual lackadaisical attitude and slow procedure of the bank clerk, it takes anything from 15 to 20 minutes to make the payment. Until about five years ago the departure tax was paid at the airline counter in India too and it is not understood why this retrograde step was introduced.

(b) Since Indian passengers are entitled to US $ 24 foreign exchange allowance, regardless of whether they have been given a separate allowance by RBI for a particular visit, most of them go to another SBI counter to pay the amount in rupees and obtain the extra US $ 24. However, this is not applicable to foreigners.

(c) The Departure Card which is more or less modelled on the ICAOE/D card has to filed out and presented at the immigration counter with the passport. The Immigration Officer checks the entries in the card against the passport and then stamps the passport but again make some notations in ink, though not as many as on arrival. There are not enough immigration counters and usually it takes 20 minutes for clearance.

(d) There is a customs check on departure for all passengers though their baggage is checked roughly on a five to ten per cent sample basis. Ninety per cent baggage is allowed to move on the conveyer belt and ten per cent is taken off and placed on the

floor. It is incumbent on the passenger to check that his suitcase has not been taken off the belt because it is duty to pick it up and take it to the customs counter for checking. This has often created problems for foreign travellers not aware of this procedure because without noticing the baggage on the floor they may walk over to the customs desk and on to the departure area. There have been cases when the passenger has boarded the aircraft but his baggage has been left behind or an announcement is made and he has to go back to identify his baggage and have it cleared through customs. The result is unnecessary delay of the aircraft on the ground.

(e) The most formidable hurdle is the security check. The present departure hall at Delhi airport which accounts for 37 per cent of total air departures has a maximum capacity of about 100 chairs or standing room for about 200 passengers. If there are two flights leaving around the same time, and sometimes there are three, passengers of all the flights have to find standing room in the departure hall. It is not airconditioned and for eight months in the year very uncomfortable, particularly as many of them going to Europe are wearing rather heavy clothing. The hall has two exist doors but only one is kept open—generally half open. It is a most confusing situation because long undulating queues of passengers of two flights which have been announced are going through the same exist simultaneously. The security check is by frisking and not mechanised. It usually takes 45 minutes or more to get out of this congested and uncomfortable hall to the final departure area.

(f) There are not many shops in the Duty Free area where passengers can spend some time buying things. The duty free shop is not well stocked and has only a few brands of whisky and cigarettes but not much else. In 1981 the total turnover of duty free shops at airports around the world was estimated at US $ 25 billion. There are seldom many passengers at Indian duty free shops and it is my guess that if they were properly stocked India could have earned may be ten times more than it does now.

STRUCTURE OF INDIAN AIRPORTS

All the four international airports in India were makeshift war-time constructions. Palam Airport (Delhi) consisted of one storey barracks and Santa Cruz (Bombay) was until 1957 in a hangar. It was in 1930 that a small specially constructed airport was opened in Delhi at Safdarjung which was in use till the fifties and is still used by the Delhi Flying Club.

It would have been on the whole cheaper and better to demolish these barracks and construct new terminals in the early fifties. This is what I had suggested to the Director General Civil Aviation and Secretary, Communications in 1953-54. It was, however, decided to build a new terminal at Santa Cruz and improve and expand the barracks at Delhi, Calcutta and Madras. Despite Mr. JRD Tata's strong bid that an experienced foreign architect should be asked to design the new terminal at Santa Cruz, a CPWD government architect who had never seen a foreign airport and was completely unfamiliar with procedures of the flow of in-coming and out-going traffic and baggage, designed it. When the building was almost ready in 1955 it was found that the customs was located in a separate hall unconnected with the immigration area, and that no transit area had been provided at all. The architect said that no one had ever told him that an international airport should have a properly equipped transit area. Many changes had to be made at that stage and hence the delay by two years. But it has remained an elongated building with much wastage of space and awkwardly located facilities. This also explains why the Madras terminal is a maze of corridors and on the whole highly unfunctional. The next new terminal was built at Calcutta but by a CPWD architect, who was sent abroad to study the structure of a few foreign airports. Nevertheless, it is not a particularly well-designed functional building.

Now that more international experience has been gained by the IAAI has built one or two airports overseas as well, it was expected that the new terminals at Delhi, Bombay and Madras and the expansion of the Calcutta terminal would be on the right lines. The new terminal at Sahar (Bombay) is reported to be not functioning well, may be due to poor maintenance.

But the chief problem is that according to traffic growth projections made by IAAI each new terminal, by the time it is ready, will barely absorb the traffic density. Of the total international passengers passing through our international airports : arrivals, departures and transients, Bombay and Delhi handle about 75 to 80 per cent. In 1982, the international passenger traffic at Bombay airport was 3.288 million and at

Delhi 1.968 million. The IAAI's projected demand for Bombay for 1985 is 6.3 million and for 1990 it is 10.1 million. In the case of Delhi it is 3.05 million and 4.98 million respectively. The present capacity of the new international terminal at Bombay is 2.5 million and the second phase to be completed by 1985-86 is expected to raise it to five million per year. At Delhi the present peak hour demand for arrivals and departures is 1280 passengers while the existing capacity per hour is for 500 arrivals and 350 departures. The first phase of the new terminal at Delhi will be ready by 1985 and its capacity will fall short of the projected demand of 3.05 million by half a million and of the Bombay terminal by 1.3 million.

A wise practice is that every new terminal should be built with extra capacity to absorb growth of traffic for five years after completion. The Changi airport at Singapore which opened 18 months ago has a capacity for ten million against the present traffic of seven million and the next phase to be completed by 1986 will have a capacity of 15 million. The same is true of Hong Kong. It is true that airports cost a lot of money. Changi airport has cost S $ 15 million (about US $ 8.5 million). India could find sufficient resources for at least two airports of Bombay and Delhi with the highest growth potential.

IATA Report

A time-motion study made five years ago by the regional IATA office (Singapore) consisting of representatives of three international carriers and one from IATA headquarters, Geneva, showed that at Indian airports the average time taken by a passenger from the point of landing to the point of exist was 90 minutes. IATA makes periodic studies and may be a more recent one of Indian airports is available. This compares most unfavourably with the smooth operation at Singapore, Bangkok, Hong Kong etc. The claim made by the Changi airport (Singapore) which is handling seven million passengers annually is that the average time from the point of landing to reaching the kerb is 30 minutes. This claim is supported by the National Association of Travel Agents of Singapore. The pity is that until 10 to 12 years ago, barring Hong Kong and Singapore, the arrival and departure procedures at other Asian airports were just about as tiresome and time consuming as at Indian airports. They have gone ahead, more purposefully than we have.

If the first impression on arrival is unpleasant, the impact of departure formalities is much worse. At Delhi a new building, spacious and well-equipped, was built as a rush job at a cost of more than Rs. 20 million, and used as an Arrival terminal for the Asian Games in 1982, then used for the Non-Aligned Conference in March 1983, and again closed down to be used as an arrival area for the Commonwealth Heads of Government Conference in December, 1983. Hopefully, after the conference it may be made available as a departure area for the use of ordinary passengers. Meanwhile about a million passengers who departed from Palam between the Asian Games and the Commonwealth Conference were denies its use. So much for Tourism !

Recommendations

From the above account it would be apparent that among several shortcomings the two that need to be urgently attended to are improvement in immigration procedures and modernisation and upgradation of the terminals at the four international airports, and in fact even some of the domestic airport terminals which, with the growth of traffic, have become quite inadequate in the peak season. Srinagar is one of the worst examples where the new terminal built only five years ago is so heavily congested in the peak season that it takes a long time to go through the security check or to clear the baggage on arrival.

Procedures

The present arrangement of appointing immigration staff on loan from state/local police forces has been an utter failure. First, the staff on loan is not fully trained in immigration procedures; second, it is not interested because immigration duties do not offer much authority, nor yield means of making 'extra income.' This may explain some of the disturbing stories that immigration staff at Bombay has been accepting large amounts from rich Arab and other visitors to let them through quickly, if not in some cases illegally; third, their assignment is often for a couple of years and in the absence of continuity they cannot achieve professionalism; fourth, the policemen by training and temperament are used to dealing with law and order problems and not with sophisticated air travellers; fifth, as ordinary police officers they are not smartly dressed and usually give the appearance of sloveliness.

The traffic has grown sufficiently at the four international airports plus subsidiary points of entry *e.g.,* Patna, Rameshwaram, Trivandrum, the Attari border and land check posts between India and Bangladesh to justify the creation of a separate Immigration cadre. In fact such proposals made in the past were turned down on the ground that the overall strength of immigration staff was so small that there would not be sufficient prospects of promotion to attract qualified personnel. This argument does not hold good any longer. In course of time there may be more gateway airports and the cadre is likely to grow in size. This would also step the present practice of immigration personnel being diverted from the airports to do emergency duties on special occasions when extra staff is needed.

If such a cadre is created it should be possible to fix higher scales of pay, attract educated personnel and ensure special training and continuity. There may be other administrative alternatives such as creating a separate cadre in the police of each state. But it seems that an all India cadre would probably be the best solution.

Terminals

As already mentioned, by the time the new terminals are ready the capacity will have been overtaken by the growth of traffic. One of the reasons is that a well-equipped air terminal to handle say four million passengers a year with peak period capacity of 1000 passengers an hour would not cost, at the current Indian prices, less than Rs. 2000 million. The amounts sanctioned to IAAI are generally less than half of what is required at each terminal. The IAAI projections of traffic growth were made three years ago. Perhaps the projections are rather optimistic and they may prove to be a saving feature. But the argument is still valid that IAAI should be given sufficient funds for building terminals which should have extra capacity to absorb traffic growth for five years after the terminal is ready. If certain types of specific equipment is not made in India there should be a provision that IAAI be allowed to import such equipment.

Other Recommendations

- The International Airports Authority lacks 'authority'. At present it cannot ensure that sufficient staff is provided by other governmental agencies *e.g.*, police, customs, health or trolleys and buses by handling agencies etc. It is true that in no country is the Airport Authority empowered to control immigration, customs and such other staff. But what is needed is that IAAI is given the 'teeth' to ensure co-ordination among various official agencies controlling staff and facilities. Secondly, it should be incumbent on other agencies to meet the demands for staff and facilities estimated by the port authority. To ensure co-ordination there should be weekly, or may be monthly, meetings of senior representatives of the port authority and other agencies concerned. This pre-supposes that the Airport Controller representing the Airports Authority should be an executive of much higher status than is the case at present, with corresponding status of representatives of other departments and agencies, not to postpone decisions on the plea that they would refer even routine matters to higher authorities of their department for decision.

- The necessity of the health check in respect of yellow fever should be examined afresh by qualified medical specialists and, if it is required, the present routine health check should be entrusted to the Immigration Officers.
- The practice of paying the departure tax at the airline counter should be revised and the separate SBI counter be abolished.
- The embarkation card should be abolished as also customs check of the baggage on a sample basis in the departure area.
- It is most important that the present practice of the Immigration Officer making notations on the disembarkation card and on the passport should be prohibited by specific orders.
- Progressive clearance of aircraft in accordance with international practice should be enforced.
- Unaccompanied baggage should be treated as baggage and not cargo.
- The disembarkation card should be redesigned to conform as closely as possible to the ICAO card. The extra portion for customs clearance should be abolished. Any extra entry such as purpose of visit, or to make a headcount of India visitors resident abroad may be introduced to serve certain specific purposes.

Special Recommendations

- Estimates made by market research companies of average length of stay have been often questioned by foreign experts. To ensure a more reliable estimate which in the ultimate analysis would determine the volume of tourism and foreign exchange earnings, the American system of a carbonised card may be introduced. The original copy is retained by immigration and the carbon copy is stapled to the passport and surrendered by the visitor on departure. Since both copies have the same serial number it should be possible by computerisation to know the exact length of stay of each visitor to the country. Such a card would also obviate the necessity of having to fill out an embarkation card on departure.
- Without waiting for the completion of new terminals, arrangements should be made as soon as possible for providing hotel reservation and car rental facilities etc., for arriving passengers through recognised agencies operating in the terminal building.
- An extra factor which currently creates problems is the blind wall behind the customs area which prevents arriving passengers from seeing if their friends or relatives or representatives of travel agencies etc., have come to receive them. It is understood that at the insistence of the customs the present system of a blind wall will be maintained even in the new terminals, thus preventing any visible contact between the passengers and those outside. There have been many cases where those having come to receive visitors have left the airport after a long wait in the belief that the passenger has not arrived.
- Many official tourist organisations (NTOs) have a special cell for facilitation. In the Indian situation it is particularly necessary. An officer of the rank not below a Director, and with some international experience in the Department of Tourism, should be assigned the responsibility of collecting and recording information on visa, passport and frontier formalities, on airports and other check posts. The officer may have to visit the entry and exit points from time to time and keep in touch with the main travel agencies and carriers and take note of their complaints regarding all such matters. The

officer concerned should also keep in touch with Annex 9 of Facilitation issued by ICAO, the list of reservations filed by the Civil Aviation Department and the justification thereof, and also with the facilitation wing of IATA (Montreal), its regional office in Singapore and the reports issued by IATA teams; also with similar agencies *e.g.*, IMCO (London), IRU (Paris), International Custom Union (Geneva), and Frontier Formalities published periodically by WTO. But WTO's book is to be used with caution because it is a compilation of rules and procedures regarding visa, passport, immigration, customs etc., as communicated by each NTO. Such a compilation does not state the real story of what actually happens on the ground. Most NTOs tend to present a somewhat rosy picture. Nevertheless it is a useful inventory.

The National Facilitation Committee under the Director General Civil Aviation, as required by the ICAO, if it has become defunct, should be revived.

Index